A Sociology of Human Systems

SOCIOLOGY SERIES

John F. Cuber, Editor
Alfred C. Clarke, Associate Editor

A Sociology of Human Systems

Joseph H. Monane

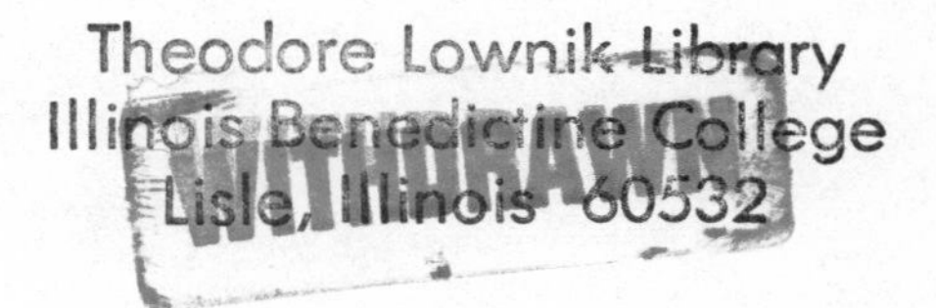

New York
APPLETON - CENTURY - CROFTS
Division of Meredith Publishing Company

For information address the publisher,
Appleton-Century-Crofts,
Division of Meredith Publishing Company,
440 Park Avenue South,
New York, New York 10016.

657-1

Library of Congress Card Number: 67-18503

PRINTED IN THE UNITED STATES OF AMERICA

E 64595

To the increased understanding of social systems

PREFACE

It frequently happens that one does not know exactly the kind of book he wants to write until he starts to write it. He has the plan firmly in mind, true enough, and he is quite sure that that is what he is going to do. But not until he actually begins chapter 1, page 1 does he face the writer's special moment of truth. Sometimes then may come the realization, as in Eliot's *The Love Song of J. Alfred Prufrock,* "That is not what I meant at all; That is not it, at all."

My original plan was to examine modern system scholars—Parsons, Merton, Homans, Sorokin, Loomis, and others—in terms of their specific contributions. Several of these may be found in the present work. But as I began to write, the scope of my plan enlarged.

What the present book actually does, accordingly, is to formulate a structural science of social system action. It provides an architecture for a sociology of human systems.

The emphasis throughout is upon tight, teachable constructs. Thus little space is given to the analysis of social institutions as such because of the difficulty of saying very much that is concrete about institutions *as* social systems. The rigorous findings of sociology concerning institutions apply almost entirely to smaller social systems within them: on-the-job patterns rather than "the economy," families rather than "the family," and organizations rather than "bureaucracy."

From the fields of general systems theory, cybernetics, and information theory I have drawn items of use for sociology and built them into the ground plan of the present structure. While my approach is different, the work of Talcott Parsons has been a major specific influence. I am indebted also to Bernard Berelson and Gary A. Steiner, who in their collection of empirical findings (*Human Behavior: An Inventory of Scientific Findings* [N.Y., Harcourt, Brace & World, 1964]) have provided an important source of useful data. Finally, the careful preparation of manuscript by Mrs. Audrey Payne is deeply appreciated.

J.H.M.

CONTENTS

A Sociology of Human Systems

CHAPTER 1

THE SCIENCE OF SOCIAL SYSTEMS

Social systems are the patterns of action of people and culture. They may involve one or many persons, together with cultural phenomena such as words, ideas, artifacts, rules, beliefs, and emotions.

Figures 1, 2, 3, 4, 5, and 6 show several social systems and some of the units involved in each. A system is as big as the actions and the things it includes. They set its boundaries. System parts move to, from, with, in, and through one another. They build crisscross networks of sending and receiving, and they spiral through cylinders of time/space.

A persistent problem confronting the social sciences is that of the interrelationship of the individual and group. Figure 1, an American family system, involves four people. Figure 2, a personal hygiene system, involves one; Figure 3 includes two; Figure 4 may have fifty; Figure 5, several hundred; Figure 6, several million. Chapters to follow suggest that a social system operates in certain basic ways regardless of the number of people and other units in it. The point of central attention in this book, therefore, is neither the individual nor the group as such. It is the social system and its action,[1] in which one or many persons—interactive with other units such as artifacts, attitudes, and emotions—may figure. It may be noted in this connection that systems involving one human component (for example, man-machine systems) have occupied the attention of researchers for some time.

The interplay of men on the job, of husband and wife, of

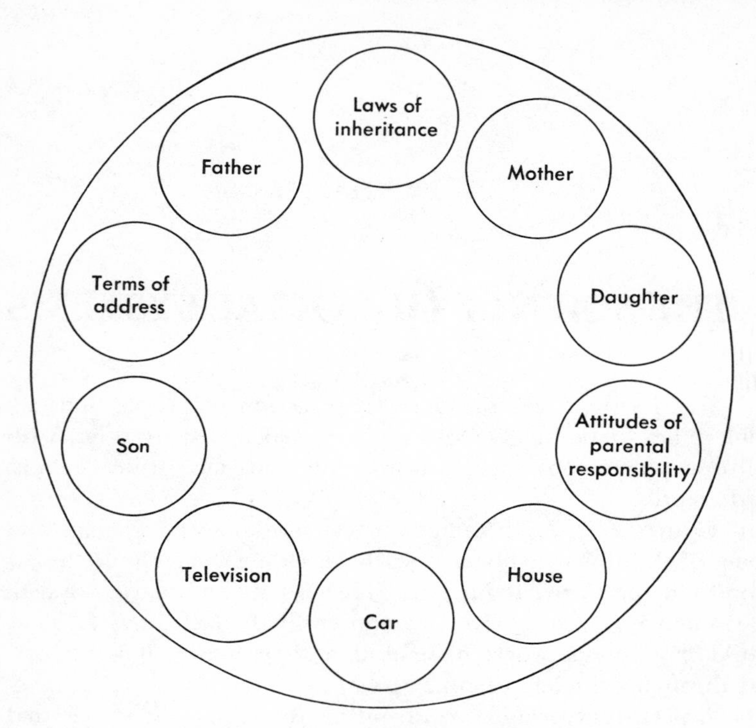

Figure 1. An American Family System.

nations at war are all social systems that involve the sending and receiving of energy/information. System action will be examined as this movement of energy/information (1) *within* a system (Figure 7) and (2) *between* a system and its environments (Figure 8).

In Figure 7, the components A_1, A_2, A_3, and A_4 act (send or receive) with one another. In Figure 8, System A operates with its environments which are here the systems B and C. The latter may include pieces of natural environment as well as other kinds; systems, it will be shown, act in certain basic ways with their environments whether the latter be natural or man made. In present usage a system's environment is anything external to it *to which* it sends or *from which* it receives. Environmental inflow and out-

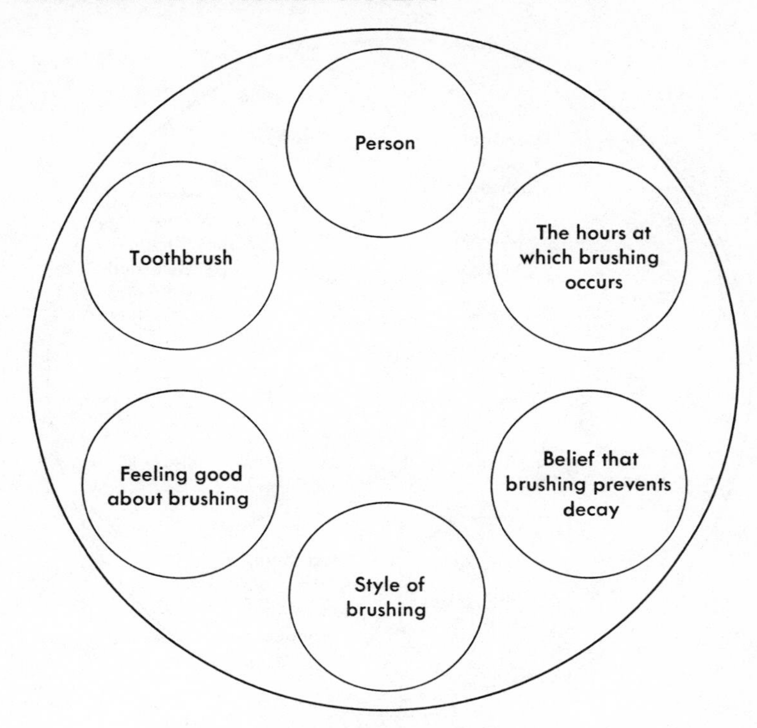

Figure 2. A Personal System of Dental Hygiene.

flow, to be looked at intensively in Chapter 3, come in and out through system components, for example, people and things, which serve as gateways. By definition, however, system components influence one another. Thus inflow and outflow through one component are *total*-systemic in their impact.

The normal social system is composed of (1) components (people, artifacts, ideas, emotions) of varying manipulative power in regular, nonrandom patterns of action with one another. This involves the (2) sending and receiving of energy/information among components of the system. The system is simultaneously involved in the (3) sending and receiving of energy/information with its (4) environments, including other systems. Its patterns

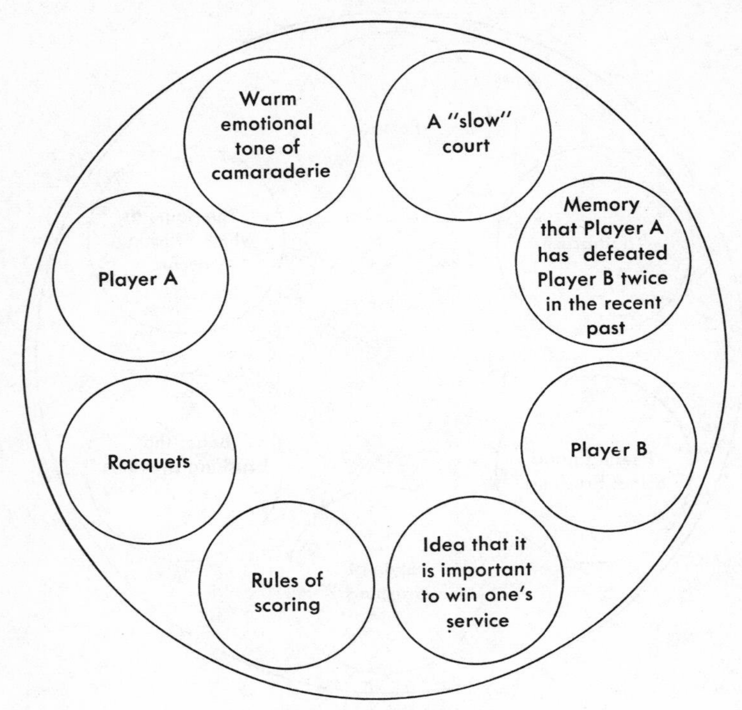

Figure 3. A Tennis System.

of action within, and with its environments, constitute (5) modal norms providing it with a distinctive identity. Its (6) power units, internally and in their action with the system's environments, seek (7) positive feedback implementing their directing of system action and resist (8) negative feedback impeding this action. (9) Change (arising within the system, or involving inflow or outflow with its environments) that is perceived by a system's power units as providing positive feedback is permitted and encouraged, while (10) change that is perceived as providing negative feedback is resisted internally through patterns of (11) expulsion, confinement, or conversion; externally, such change is resisted by withdrawal, a tightening of gateways, or

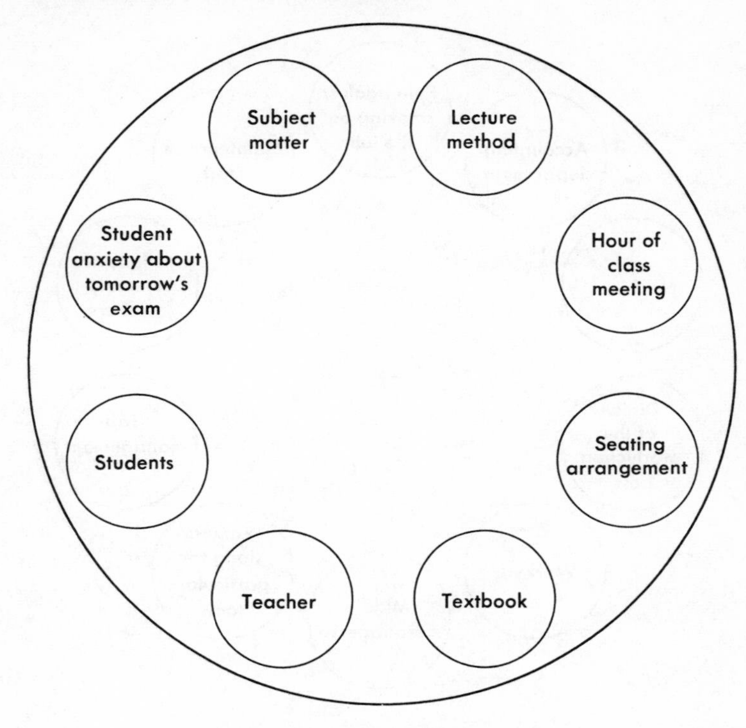

Figure 4. A Classroom System.

a joining with it so as to remove its danger. (12) Change that succeeds in creating negative feedback produces varying degrees of (13) system disintegration. This, however, is rarely final. New systems spring up from the ashes of the old through (14) resystematization.

The cybernetic concept of *feedback* is extended here to mean anything that influences a system's current action. That which keeps a system going as it has been or enhances its action in its present direction is *positive* feedback. Anything that serves to stop, slow down, or swerve a system from its present course is *negative* feedback.

Systems are thus *structural* patterns of senders and receivers,

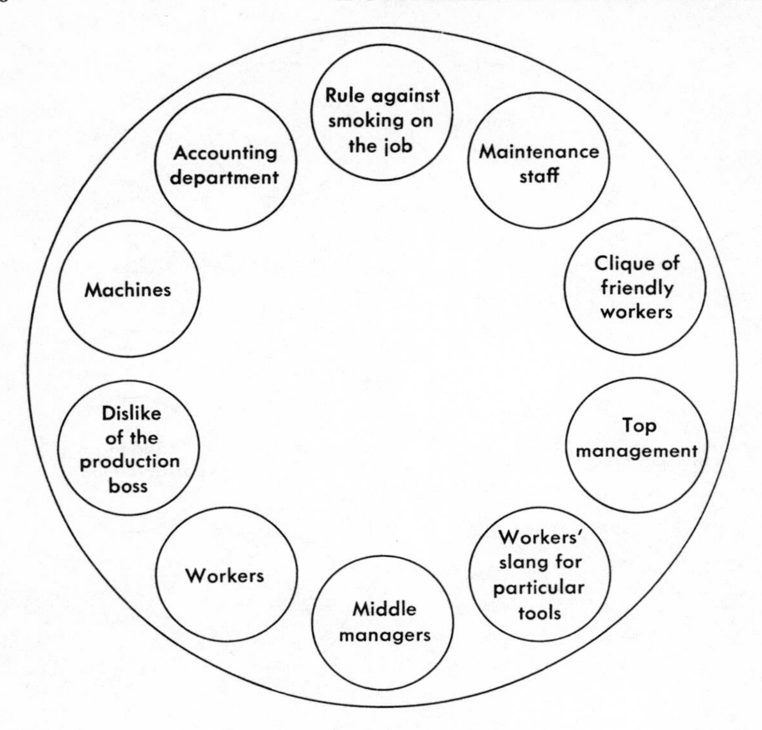

Figure 5. A Modern Factory.

and *content* patterns of what is sent and received. System components are the items of energy/information (including people) involved as either of the above.

People are, of course, of major interest to the social scientist because of their multiple capacity: (1) they are prime senders and receivers, (2) they may themselves be sent and received, and (3) they may move within, into, and out of systems relatively autonomously and "on their own steam." In the patterns of action involving one person as in those involving several, individuals are both major gateways of inflow and outflow (for ideas) and makers of system action. Other items of energy/information operative in system action—for example, artifacts, ideas, rules,

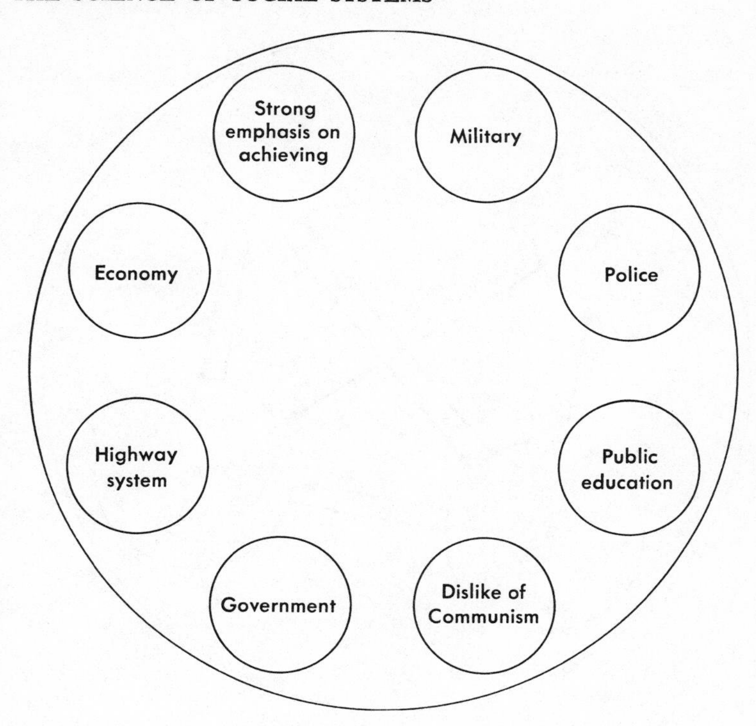

Figure 6. A Modern Nation.

emotions—do not themselves normally initiate their movement, but depend on people for their impetus. They may nevertheless be very important in system operation.

A crucial consideration in system study concerns what is to be regarded as a part of a system or an environment with which it regularly sends or receives. The decision depends wholly upon the system selected for study. A line may be drawn by the system analyst between those items treated as components and those regarded as environment. This line, for the study at hand, is the system's boundary.

An important part of this question concerns whether items of culture, material or nonmaterial, are to be included among

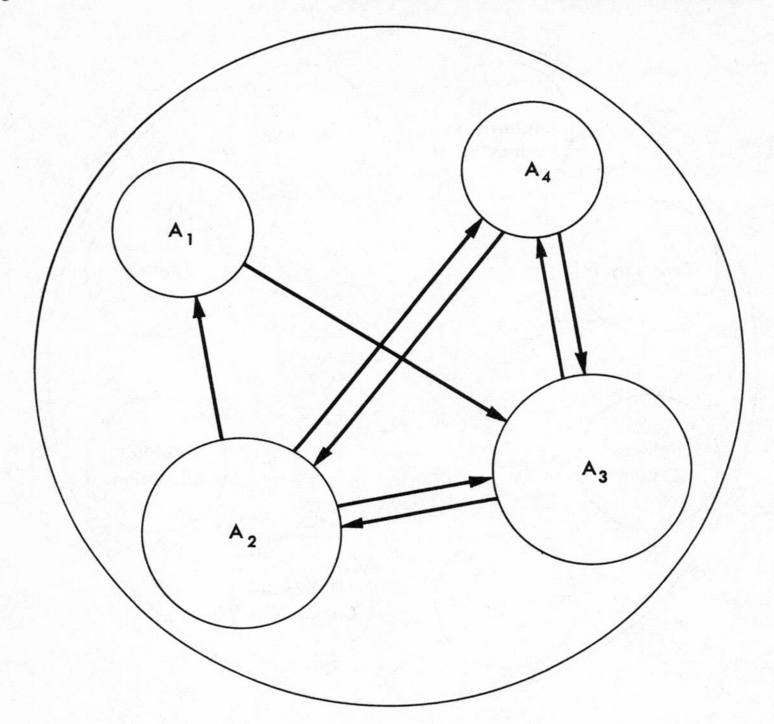

Figure 7. The Action Within System A.

the components of a social system or treated as external to it. Certain scholars (Parsons, for example), for purposes of analysis, have chosen to regard culture as external to a social system. As suggested, this is a legitimate choice resting with the analytic scholar. In the present book, items of both material and nonmaterial culture are treated as components when they operate as such, that is, when they send or receive with or move among the other components of the system under study. An idea—for example, the idea existing within a religious system of man's proper relation to God—may operate as a significant component of this social system and furnish the core of its identity. It may determine the major "doorman" of the system so that ideas or other items

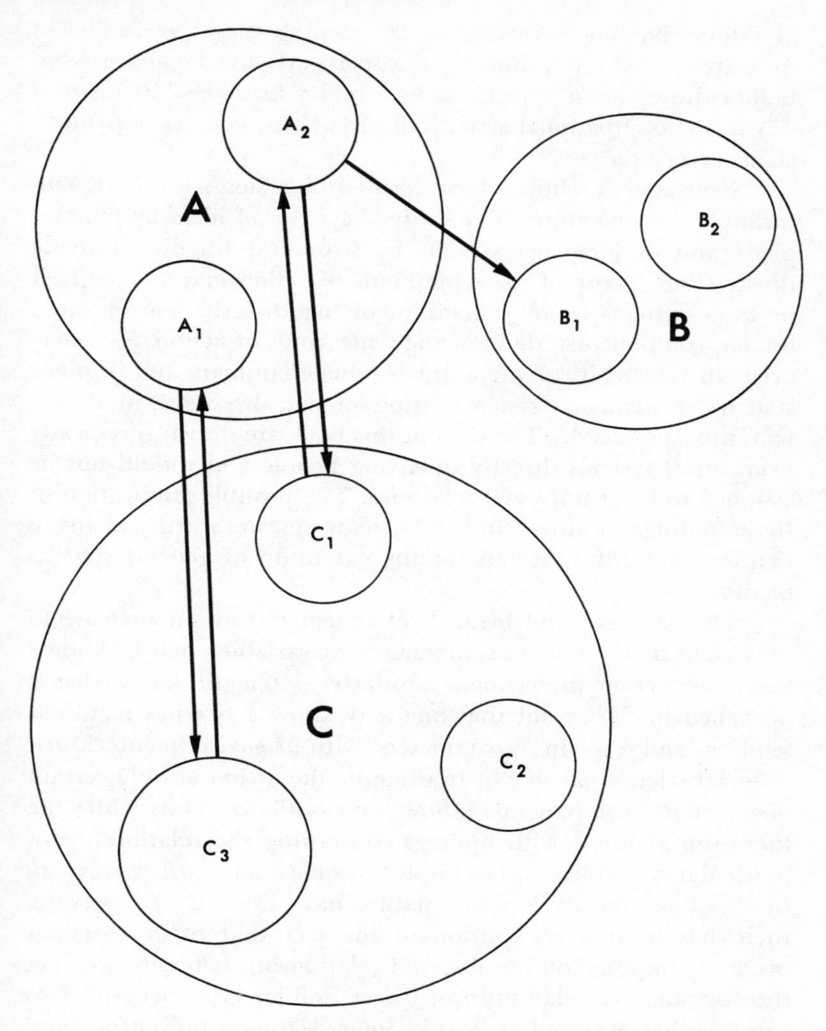

Figure 8. The Action of System A with Its Environments.

of inflow that are perceived as threatening (negative feedback) to it are denied entry. Similarly, a social system's language (symbolic culture) often appears to be a major feature of its identity —as in the occupational systems of physicians, lawyers, jazz musicians, or pickpockets.[2]

Some system scholars have focused on systems involving cultural phenomena alone. The study of systems of ideas by philosophers and of language systems by structural linguists provide illustrations. Many of the same kinds of action may be involved in these systems as in systems involving directly one or more human components. Many of the same kinds of action, also, may occur in systems involving animals other than man, and in plant systems, in planetary systems, in physiological systems, in all systems alive or "dead." The data of this book are drawn specifically from social systems directly involving people and should not be assumed to be of universal relevance. The possible application of these findings to other kinds of systems appears worthy of investigation and advantageous for the extension of general systems theory.

The accuracy and breadth of systematic insight increase to the extent that a system's components, or variables, may be known and their action understood. Similarly, systematic knowledge is deepened to the extent that one may know a system's manifold sendings and receivings (parameters) with its environments. Much of social science has sought to examine the action of only certain of a system's components, inflows and outflows. Thus while the literature abounds with findings concerning the relationship of particular variables, for example, income and fertility, few insights of specifically systemic nature have evolved. To be sure, there has been a recognition of the fact that other variables probably impinge on an observed relationship between two. Yet the focusing on relationships, direct and inverse, between two variables has operated at least in some degree to prevent a genuine system consciousness and orientation. The "relationship" way of seeing itself constitutes a system, and systems normally strive to prevent the intrusion from outside or the development within of items perceived as disturbing to their present action. As Kenneth Burke has observed, a way of seeing—including that of the present book—necessarily becomes also a way of non-seeing.

The present volume includes findings drawn from an examination of primitive societies, of non-Western societies, of non-American societies, of "un-American" societies, and of societies of the past. Nevertheless, the major data from which the present portrait of the normal social system emerges are data of modern American society and its various subsystems. Whether this portrait is universally representative of social system action is a matter to be determined by further empirical study.

Finally, the study of social systems has drawn impetus from an approach that has come to be known as structural-functionalism. The concept of system, to be sure, is not unique to structural-functionalism. It is rather an intrinsic feature of all science. Science is largely a search for pattern, probability, and predictability. It is a search for system within a mass of randomness, entropy, and chance. The study of social systems is thus neither synonymous nor coextensive with structural-functionalism. While the present book is basically not structural-functional, it does owe a debt to this school of thought and to some of its formulations.

CHAPTER 2

THE ACTION WITHIN

COMPONENTS

The focus of the present chapter is upon components of social systems and upon their action. Here social systems may be conceived as: (1) separate, without components in common, (2) overlapping, sharing one or more components, and (3) one within another.

Figures 9, 10, and 11 provide illustrations. It is important to note in Figure 11 that System A's gateways of entry and exit (in this case components A_1 and A_2) are specifically rather than diffusely open to inflow and outflow with environment (components B_1 and B_4 of System B). A social system is thus "surrounded" only at certain points of entry and exit.

Figures 9, 10, and 11, in any case, provide ideotypical rather than empirical portraits. In empirical fact, social systems that communicate at all with one another generally overlap in that they share at least some components—words or ideas or artifacts, if not people. It is only in regard to their human components that nonkin families in a modern American suburban neighborhood may be viewed as truly separate systems: they share many other components in common, such as desires, beliefs, television preferences, and a sometime fierce attachment on the distaff side to the ideas in Betty Friedan's *The Feminine Mystique*.

Overlapping systems (Figure 10) are most alike when they share many components in common. One way to study the impact of nonshared components, accordingly, is to note their ac-

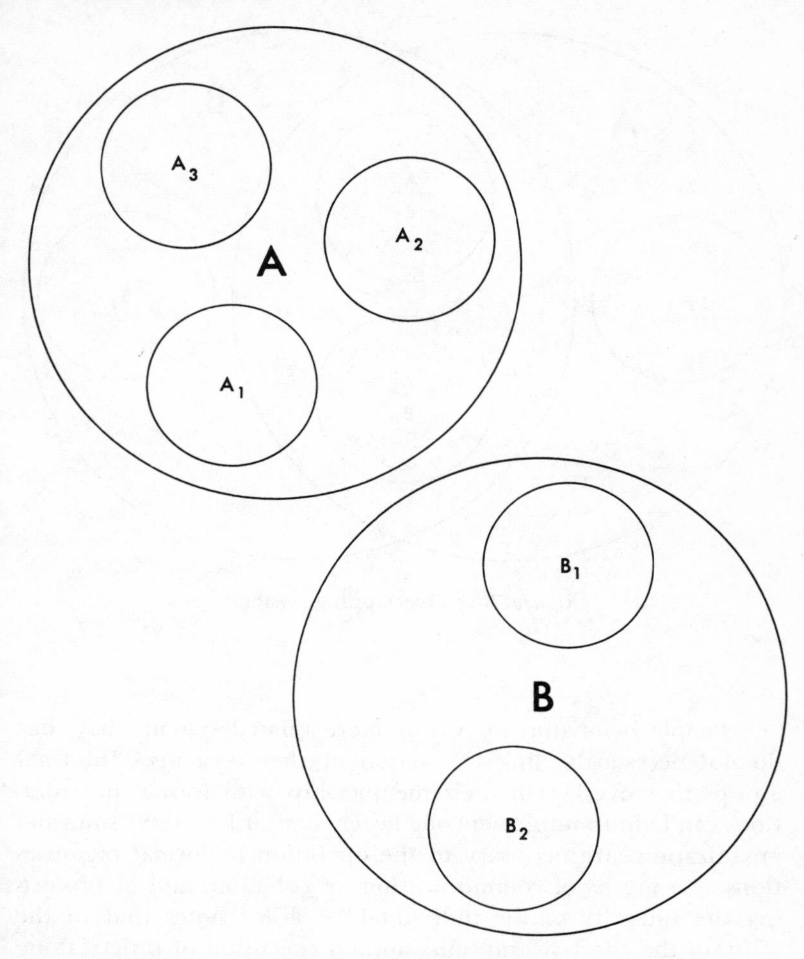

Figure 9. Separate Systems.

tion upon those that are shared. The man behind the steering wheel of a car ("Mr. Wheeler," part of an automobile driving system) may act quite differently from the "same" man in a pedestrian system ("Mr. Walker"); indeed, he may be hardly recognizable.

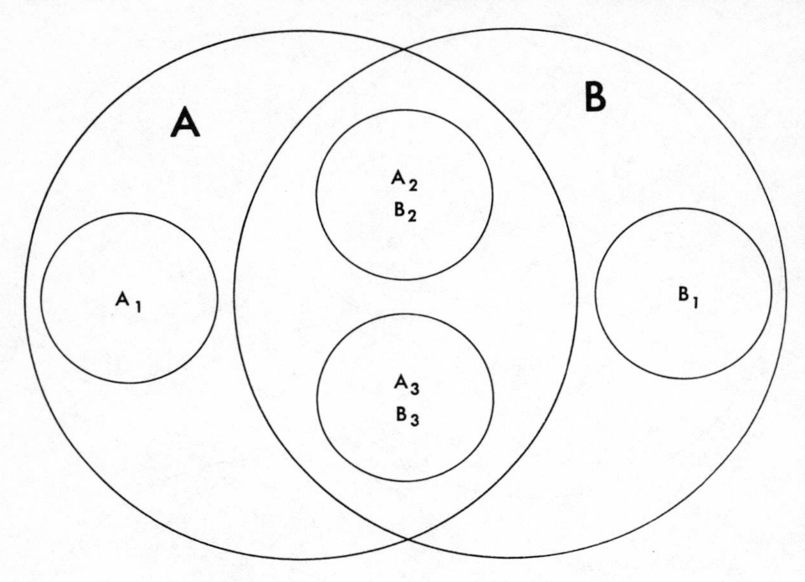

Figure 10. Overlapping Systems.

People belonging to two or more related systems may, but do not necessarily, link the action of these systems.[1] Informal groups that overlap in their membership with formal organizations can help to implement the latter. Barnard writes: "Informal organizations are necessary to the operation of formal organizations as a means of communication, of cohesion, and of protecting the integrity of the individual." [2] Shils [3] notes that in the military the effective transmission and execution of orders along the formal lines of command can be successful only when it coincides with the system of informal, primary groups. At the same time, these informal groups that overlap in human membership with the formal organization can damage the latter's operation if their values are far apart. Sayles [4] finds that management's desire to raise profits by reducing quality may be resisted by the workmanship norm of the informal work group.

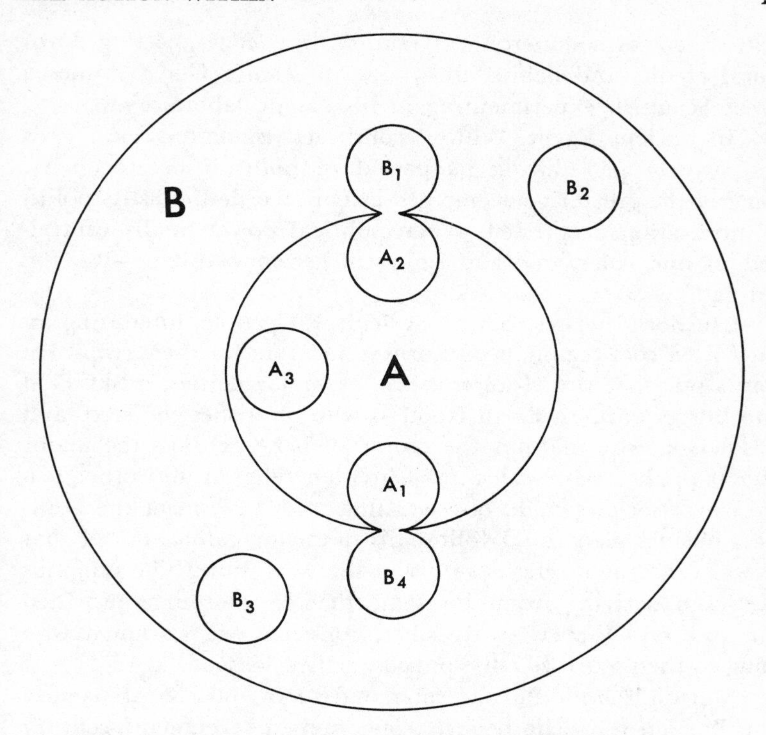

Figure 11. One System Within Another.

THE RECIPROCAL IMPACT OF SYSTEM AND COMPONENTS

Components appear to mold their social system—and one another—and to be molded by it. The reciprocalism of religion and other features of a social system has received much attention. White [5] describes the interweaving of a group's theology with its economic and other ways of life. A pastoral economy, he observes, may involve in its theology a Good Shepherd and his flock; a period of cathedral building finds God a Great Architect; an era of commerce sees Him with a ledger, jotting down moral credits and debits; in an age of science God becomes a Great Scientist, experimenting in his cosmic laboratory.

In ancient Egypt, White [6] continues, numerous local gods were worshipped during its period of political heterogeneity. Some of the greater gods emerged as national deities as its political unification progressed. When political power finally centralized in one ruler, one god similarly became supreme—Re, the sun god.

Murdock [7] writes that an agricultural people, inhabiting an arid, often cool region, need warmth and rain for their crops. He points out that the Hopi worship, as major deities, a Sky God who brings rain, an Earth Goddess who nourishes the seed, and a Sun God who matures the crops. Weber,[8] perhaps the major scholar of the reciprocalism of Christian religion and other features of a social system, observes that with Calvinism the bourgeois businessman could follow his quest for gain and feel that he was fulfilling a religious duty at the same time. The religious asceticism deriving from this same theological source provided him too, says Weber,[9] with sober, conscientious workmen who clung to their work as a life-purpose willed by God.

Merton [10] finds Puritanism powerful in the rise of science. The Puritan ethic, he believes, operated in seventeenth-century England so as to constitute one important element fostering the enhanced cultivation of science. He states that the religious interests of the day demanded a systematic, rational, empirical study of nature for the glorification of God and His works, and for the control of the corrupt world. While in the mid-seventeenth century the Puritans constituted a small minority in the English population, they composed sixty-two percent of the initial membership of the scientifically oriented Royal Society.[11]

SYSTEM DETERMINISM

A component's identity appears strongly dependent upon the social systems to which it belongs. A person's attitudes, for instance, tend to be those of the groups in which he holds membership: [12] his family, his friends, and his co-workers. This pressure of system upon its components may be called *system determinism.* It would include such other determinisms as economic determinism to the extent that a component may be molded by the economic systems of which it is a part. Should another system—a religious one, for example—pommel a component most powerfully, one might speak here of *religious determinism.* The determining agent in each case is the system, whatever its type, to which the component belongs.

Thus it is found that engineers and lawyers (usually parts of the larger business system of America) tend to resemble other members of this business system in the conservatism of their political views. University professors, while professionals in the same occupational sense as engineers and lawyers, have less frequently joined the business system; their political attitudes have consequently less often resembled it.[13] Similarly, business leaders who operate almost exclusively with other persons of the business community—executives in heavy industry, for example—resemble the business system in the conservatism of their political opinions more thoroughly than do business leaders who deal more with the public as in lighter industry and the distributional and processing trades.[14] Through system determinism, too, white-collar workers, who are usually resistant to unionization,[15] become unionized when they work in industries that are heavily unionized—for example, railway clerks, and clerical personnel in the printing industry.[16]

System determinism springs up in many contexts. With time, the components of a system, especially those of one category or type, become more alike. The United States military, as a part of American society, has become more thoroughly like other parts of America than it used to be. Janowitz [17] reports that at the time of the Civil War ninety-three percent of the Army's enlisted personnel had uniquely military occupational specialties for which no civilian equivalents existed. By 1954 the proportion had dropped to only twenty-nine percent.

The longer a component stays with a system, too, the stronger appears its deterministic clutch upon him. It is found that the longer a worker and his family have been workers, the more likely it is that he will support worker-oriented, political movements.[18]

It is essential to note that forces other than system determinism are likely to be operative here. Persons, things, ideas, and other items of energy/information that are similar to the present components of a system are most likely to enter and become new units of such systems. Systems attract and encourage the entrance of people and things like themselves. When new systems form through conjunction, they form largely of components that are already quite similar.

Through system determinism, in any case, a system's parts do move toward greater similarity. A person's decisions and choices of what to buy, for whom to vote, what television program to watch come increasingly to resemble those of other system members.[19] The peer system has been cited as especially powerful in American society. In teaching sexual practices and beliefs, for instance, the child's peer group carries more weight than adults.[20] Opinions, too, derive strength from their being shared. Berelson *et al.*[21] find the American voter's political convictions to depend upon the political homogeneity of his associates. Where his three closest friends are Republicans he will most likely be a strong Republican. Without the support of system homogeneity, attitudes are likely to change or be changed. In brainwashing situations men removed from their comrades are most likely to give in.[22]

Systems most deterministic of their components are those in which the latter are most frequently and intimately involved. The small intimate group of constant interaction, that is, family, work group, and close friends, and its norms tend to be more powerful than the large impersonal association.[23]

When a component follows norms different from those of his systems of ostensible affiliation, it points to the possibility of another system's determinism. Goldsen *et al.*[24] find that college students who go contrary to the political views of their fathers are really following the norms of other groups to which they feel an allegiance. Deviance from system norms may also reveal a component's systems of future or past adherence. For persons are found to take on the behavior and attitudes (or their perceptions of it) of the group or class to which they aspire.[25] Similarly, they may at times revert—under stress, for example—to norms of their past systems of membership. Seasoned pilots have crashed when in an emergency they have shifted back to a norm of their earlier flying days that was quite appropriate in airplanes of the past but disastrous with the present control system. To illustrate, when a plane is landing dangerously, "low and slow"—left hand forward on the throttle and right hand back on the stick—is the appropriate emergency response. But when the throttle is in the right hand and the stick is in the left, as in many aircraft, this action will produce a power-off dive instead of a full-power climb.[26]

It is because of the power of past socialization, that is, the tendency for old-system norms to persist so that they may interfere with proper component action in a new system, that students of industrial and other production often recommend a thorough change of personnel in a new system rather than a retraining of the old. In the switch of production from seamed ("full fashion") to seamless ladies' stockings it was found that so many values and habits of the old system were carried over to the new by old workers and old management that their retraining was unfeasible.[27] Of similar relevance are factory situations in which work norms of the past can block a change desired by management.[28]

The power of past-system determinism is likely to be greatest where components are forced out of their earlier circles of affiliation. For here the components are less motivated to take on the norms of the new circles.

Systems appear deterministic not only of their components' action with one another but of their environments as well. In America as elsewhere, it means something to belong to a particular system: to be an Episcopalian, a Negro, a Yale man, a Jew, a member of the lower class. It means not only that particular kinds of molding experiences will have been gained as a component of these systems. It means also that particular environments will act with components of these systems in particular ways—and vice versa. Lenski [29] examines these at length for Jews, white Protestants, white Catholics, and Negro Protestants in America. His findings reveal that membership in these systems means that a person will be more—or less—likely to:

	Order on each item
"Enjoy his occupation"	Jews, white Protestants, white Catholics, Negro Protestants
"Indulge in installment buying"	Negro Protestants, white Catholics, white Protestants, Jews
"Save to achieve objectives far in the future"	Jews, others
"Believe in the American Dream"	White Protestants, Jews, white Catholics, Negro Protestants
"Vote Republican"	White Protestants, white Catholics, Negro Protestants, Jews
"Favor the welfare state"	Jews, Negro Protestants, white Catholics, white Protestants
"Take a liberal point of view on the issue of freedom of speech"	White Protestants, white Catholics and Jews, Negro Protestants
"Oppose racial integration in the schools"	White Protestants and white Catholics, Jews
"Migrate to another community"	Negro Protestants, white Protestants, white Catholics and Jews
"Maintain close ties with his family"	Jews, white Catholics, Negro Protestants, white Protestants
"Develop a commitment to the principle of intellectual autonomy"	Jews, white Protestants, white Catholics, Negro Protestants
"Have a large family"	Negro Protestants, white Catholics, Jews, white Protestants
"Complete a given unit of education (rather than drop out)"	Jews, white Protestants, white Catholics, Negro Protestants
"Rise in the class system"	Jews, white Protestants, white Catholics, Negro Protestants

Belonging to an urban system, a rural system, or a regional system in America creates characteristic attitudes and beliefs.[30] American systems of varying nationality background, race, religion, and socioeconomic level, similarly, are found to differ in political and other opinions.[31] But *multiple* system affiliations lessen the clutch of system determinism. Where a person has only a few systems of membership—as in isolated communities—their influence upon him is likely to be steady and great.[32]

ORGANIZATION

Of crucial importance in system determinism is the cybernetic concept of organization. It pertains to intra-relatedness, the degree of impact of a component's action upon the action of other components. In systems that are highly organized, correlations of component action with the action of other components will be great.

The components of a system of *high* organization—for example, a family—are strongly interdependent. What one does is crucial for the others. A father's decision to take a job in another city is likely to have profound impact upon other family members. In systems of relatively *low* organization—for example, a metropolis—conversely, components are independent and autonomous. A low level of meaningful impact of one upon the other exists. A total absence of organization, of course, would mean a total absence of system.

A component may thus belong to more systems of low organization—many of which, moreover, may be quite dissimilar and incongruent—than to systems of high organization. For the latter involve deep attachment and a heavy expenditure of energy/information. While a component may "spread himself thin" over many systems of low organization, he is likely to "get with" only a limited number of high organization.

Depending upon the system, strong or meager attachment to it may be the expected norm. Whatever the expectation, a component's autonomy that is greater than it should be detaches him somewhat from system impact. To illustrate, persons in occupations that isolate them are found to hold deviant political attitudes: artists, writers, and intellectuals often support political movements deemed "radical." [33] Deviant labor-management relations marked by frequent strikes, similarly, characterize isolated, autonomous industries such as mining, lumbering, and maritime.[34] "Radical" political preferences and action likewise characterize these isolated and autonomous industries.[35]

Most of the data in this book derive from social systems of high organization. The greater visibility of action in these systems makes them more available to empirical study and the findings more likely to be accurate. Examples are informal work groups rather than "the economic institution," and families rather than "the family." Little rigorous data exist for social institutions as total systems, but quite a lot are available for the smaller, more highly organized subsystems within them.

SYSTEMS OF LOW ORGANIZATION

The relatively autonomous components of systems of low organization vary widely in their characteristics. A diversity, and a tolerance of diversity, in action and opinion are found.[36] Autonomy goes with heterogeneity, and both are especially likely in large rather than small social systems. Meaningful communication and reciprocal impact of components become less as the size of a social system mounts.

Minimal awareness of system and a low capacity for corporate action mark systems of low organization. American social classes, for example, lack clear-cut class consciousness and the thrust of concerted action.[37] Component autonomy reigns especially within the "new middle class" of salaried workers; they are individually more mobile, less attached to their community systems, and less distinct in political behavior than the old middle class of small rentiers and shopkeepers.[38] This is not to suggest that no class differences exist in America. Differences between classes in sexual behavior and ideas, in political and other attitudes have been extensively documented by scholars.[39] It is simply that with a higher organization of components within a class, greater uniqueness, class consciousness, and action as a system is likely. Similarly, while male/female differences occur in many spheres of social action,[40] little strong organization politically or otherwise by sex occurs in America. Nor does it occur in regard to age. Because of this relatively low internal organization, age and sex systems in America are often referred to not as systems but as "statistical aggregates." Their determinism as social systems upon the attitudes of their members remains minor.[41] Their gateways are wide open to input; their relatively autonomous units are mobile and interactive in a variety of other systems. As a later section reveals, a confinement of component sending and receiving to the limits of the particular system goes with high rather than low organization.

Again, this is not to suggest that no age differences in social action occur in America. They do, so that as elsewhere throughout the world age-grades represent a broad definition of capacities and obligations at given stages of life.[42] Every known society distinguishes among age groups and assigns certain appropriate behaviors to them. Especially marked is the line between legal childhood and adulthood.[43] Yet age *systems* as such in America exist at a comparatively low level of organization. Where the number of components within age-grades—children, adolescents, adults, aged—is small, conversely, as in primitive societies, age systems are likely to be more highly organized.

Components compelled toward autonomy in the early systems to which they belong, such as children in a family, appear unusually concerned about independence in their later systems of membership.[44] They also appear highly motivated toward achievement. McClelland *et al.*,[45] examining folk tales and childhood training among the Navajo, Central Apache, Hopi, Comanche, Sanpoil, Western Apache, Paiute, and Flatheads, conclude that independence training in a society ties in with cultural pressures toward achievement.

Cross-societally, certain system components carry a special autonomy about them. Technological similarity between societies generally means similarities too in the pattern of communication, in socialization, in marital relations, sex roles, and demographic rates. But political control, religion, art, and leisure preserve a characteristic independence and variability of their own.[46]

SYSTEMS OF HIGH ORGANIZATION

Families throughout the world are usually highly organized social systems. Psychological disturbance in one member of a family, for instance, carries a profound impact on other family members and upon the family as a system.[47] With increased autonomy of family members, as often happens in modern America, the less deterministic is the family system of the statuses and roles of its members in the larger society. It "places" them less thoroughly.[48]

Systems of high organization are generally marked by a homogeneity of components and an efficiency of output toward a particular goal. For systems prizing militancy, for example, "the more homogeneous the components, the higher the index of militancy. Herein lies the superiority of techniques of organization by separate and homogeneous milieux, such as are to be found in Communist cells." [49] In systems of high organization, the action of one member toward a particular entrant (a person or an idea, for example) is likely to trigger similar action by other members as well. Where Al and Bill are school chums and Al responds with cool indifference to Charley who has just entered their class, Bill is apt to show a similar coolness to Charley.[50]

When a system's activity norms depart significantly from the norms of the previous systems to which its components have belonged, its organization must remain especially high for its norms to be maintained and the power of past socialization to be minimized. The soldier isolated from his unit or poorly organized with it loses effectiveness as a soldier.[51] Here ideology by itself appears of little relevance for effectiveness in combat.[52] Its power depends upon its action as a component of a total, highly organized social system.[53]

A system's highest rewards go to its components of highest organization, to those who are most strongly involved in its action. Soldiers with strong positive feelings toward the army, with deep personal commitment to it so that they "get with it" rather than oppose it or withdraw from it are most likely to be promoted.[54] A component's rank, power, and prestige depend essentially on his attachment to system norms, his central involvement in sending and receiving,[55] his openness to system determinism, and on his provision of positive feedback to the system. This is true regardless of the kind of system involved. Where amiability and good fellowship are the system norm as in a recreational system based on companionability, components of most pleasing personality rank highest.[56]

It has been found, however, that high organization may sometimes be more apparent than real. Short and Strodtbeck [57] report that delinquent gang members are not so emotionally attached to the gang as they seem. According to these authors, the members feel little real loyalty to their gang. Each lives in a fantasy system of aspirations that is subject to ridicule if it is expressed when the gang gets together.

NUMBER OF COMPONENTS

The number of components in a social system strongly determines its action. The smaller its size, for example, the greater the homogeneity of its components is likely to be. Diversity marks the large urban system rather than the small town. The city stands more variegated ethnically, occupationally, politically, religiously, and recreationally.[58] The larger this diversity, the harder it is to maintain separateness of subsystems. Political and economic action begin to cut across racial and ethnic lines. Caste flourishes best in small, highly organized milieux, in villages rather than in large cities.[59] In the great and growing cities of India the boundaries of caste and the internal organization of its subsystems break down. Just so, the highly organized feudal system and the internal organization of its noble and serf subsystems broke down in large urban locales. Cities in the Middle Ages were places where serfs could lose their unfree status.[60]

The smaller the social system, the more frequent its internal communication and the higher its organization are apt to be. The more distinct will be its norms, the more rigid its gates of entry and exit, and the more clear-cut will be its identity as a system. The upper class as a small social system partakes of these traits more fully than the middle or lower, and the small town more fully than the metropolis.

As the number of components in a social system rises, increased differentiation is likely. In a formal organization this means a rise in the number of ranks of personnel.[61] A modern university, for example, has a variety of grades such as lecturer, fellow, research associate, and tutor in addition to the traditional professorial divisions. The American Army carries a greater variety of noncoms than it used to and it even has a rank beyond general. New departments are added to the Cabinet of the President of the United States. A split between big business and small also appears essentially a big-city phenomenon. In the small town little attitudinal difference is found between businessmen regardless of the size of their business. Boundary screens of separation are minimal. Businessmen of all kinds associate frequently and share a general political conservatism and an overall high status.[62]

As a social system increases in size, its components become more independent. The less does the action of one mean for any of the others and for the system as a whole. The less "concerned," similarly, will the system be regarding the action of any one component and the more "tolerant" will it seem; components and system will "care" less about one another and about system inflow and outflow. Not long ago a woman was murdered in New York City in full view of her neighbors to whom she cried many times for help. They did not come to her aid, they told reporters afterwards, because they did not wish to become "involved." A relative absence of component involvement is low organization. The greater involvement of the small town garage with the local automobiles brought to it for service, and with the owners of these cars, usually means more conscientious and "personalized" service than the large urban garage can provide with its staff of mechanics who rarely see or know a car's owner. Greater numbers reduce *esprit de corps*: the components will be less attached to the system, and it to them.

There appears in the large social system low agreement about who ranks where. Social perceptions become more difficult where internal communication and knowledge lessen. More discriminating and sensitive judgments are found for near things than for those farther away; [63] hence, the greater likelihood of accuracy for statements by system members about small than large social systems. Known personal characteristics such as family lineage and length of residence figure more prominently as bases of rank in the small than in the large community, in the small upper class than in the larger classes below.[64] Material wealth, often strongly visible, plays its ranking role most loudly where the social system is large.

Small social systems thus carry most distinct identity. When political parties broaden their base of membership and grow larger, they tend to lose their political distinctness.[65] The large Democratic and Republican parties of America are not very different. With increases in the number of components, too, a system's structure tends to become more formal. Chapin [66] finds that voluntary organizations move toward a formality of structure as they grow. Formal subgroups of separate specialized activity emerge within them. The spontaneous *esprit* of a truly "voluntary" organization disappears. Increases in formal structure with a growth in size are found also in informal groups of two to twenty members.[67] The larger these groups become, the greater the gap between the leader and the led, the more central the leadership and the greater the acceptance of manipulation by the leader, the more the differentiation into "active" and "passive" members manifested by the monopolization of energy/information flow by "active" members and the withdrawal from sending and receiving by the ordinary, "passive" members. Also, the larger the groups become, the less intimate the sending and receiving, the lower the level of member satisfaction, the slower the decision-making, the more tolerated (satisfactorily confined) the unresolved differences among members, the greater the number of subgroups, and the more formal the rules and the action.[68] Five to seven people appears a critical range. Beyond it, formality of structure and of leadership spring up rapidly and subgroups emerge.[69]

As a child grows he belongs to more and larger systems. The size of children's informal play groups varies directly with the age of the children involved. Preschool children first play individually although side by side, then in pairs, and then in larger groups.[70]

Social systems involving particular numbers of people show characteristic patterns of action. Highly significant for the individual, as will be shown in connection with sending and receiving, are the multiple *self*-systems he forms with himself as the sole human component: the individual and his fears, aspirations, material goods, and habits of thought and action.

Systems of two people, such as husband and wife, are marked by high tension and emotion, a tendency to avoid disagreement, a high level of energy/information transfer, a strong potential for deadlock and for instability, a tendency toward clear-cut role differentiation with one person as initiator of action and the other as follower with veto power.[71] A delicate balance prevails in that each has only the other for human support within the system. Mutual tolerance is crucial for system maintenance.

In social systems involving three people, two of them are found to combine against the other. These systems form a twosome, corner the flow of energy/information within the system, and isolate the one left out. Experimental studies of problem-solving, three-person groups substantiate Georg Simmel's proposition that a threesome divides into a pair and another.[72] Threesomes maintain themselves well although their internal coalitions may shift from time to time.[73]

Where the human components in a social system number four, six, or eight, patterns of internal action assume forms different from those in social systems involving three, five, or seven persons.[74] For the even-numbered systems tend to split into equal "sides," thus fostering internal strife. The system size found to be most personally satisfying to its members is five. It permits a relatively free flow of energy/information within. It is large enough for stimulation through diversity, and small enough for personal participation and recognition. It sometimes divides into subgroups of two and three, thereby providing support for the minority members.[75]

COMPONENT SIMILARITY AND DIVERSITY

The greater the similarity of system components, the greater will be the likelihood of positive affect (joy, happiness, or love) as an additional component of their interaction—

where positive affect constitutes a *legitimate* system component. This factor of legitimacy is crucial. Neither *increased component similarity* nor *increased component contact,* contrary to a basic notion of American middlelore, appear independently or jointly productive of positive affect in systems where hostility is the legitimate, expected component—such as a war. Escalation of the war in Vietnam appears to have increased both contact and similarity (in weapons, techniques of handling prisoners, styles of jungle fighting, and the like) of American and Viet Cong forces, but it does not appear to have generated an increase in affection between the warring factions. Among the Apache where son-in-law–mother-in-law avoidance and an absence of positive affect is the traditional and legitimate pattern, an increase in contact is not found to increase positive affect. Indeed, it may do just the opposite.

It has been observed along this line that when enemies learn to speak the same language they may also more readily insult one another. The essential point here is the irrelevance of actual, empirical similarity or difference as a factor in hostility. In systems where hostility must be sent, as in war, its sending often achieves legitimacy through a constructed belief (with no necessary basis in actuality) in the essential difference and moral superiority of the sender.

The close association of component similarity and positive affect where the latter is legitimate occurs in many social systems. In marriage, for example, where positive affect stands as a legitimate and expected component, homogamy appears conducive to it.[76] Similarly, college and university faculties—which are supposed to be friendly—that are homogeneous in attitudes actually have more friendly internal relations than do those of component heterogeneity.[77] "To like" and "to be like" thus appear closely related in systems of *legitimate component liking.* In therapeutic systems involving physicians and patients, the more similar these human components the greater the component of positive affect (which is legitimate here) in their interaction. But differences in class between therapist and patient lessen it. The presence of items of positive affect generally considered essential to the therapeutic relationship—mutual trust, respect, and cooperation—varies inversely with the social distance of the participants.[78]

A systemic composite of positive affect and component similarity commonly appears because positive affect is more frequently a system component than is negative affect. "Liking" systems are cross-societally more generally encouraged than "hating" systems. Component similarity—in a variety of social systems such as marriages, religious and political organizations, clubs, friendships, and the like—is more common than component dissimilarity. These factors condition the oft-noted coexistence of component similarity and positive affect. As indicated above, this coexistence should not be construed as proof that one necessarily produces the other.

The more similar the components of a system, at any rate, the more likely are they to interact in terms of their roles as components of this system rather than as components of other systems to which they may belong. Where physician and patient share the same class background, the more likely it is that they will perceive one another in terms of the ideotypical roles of professional and patient rather than as members of class systems.[79] It is found too that a therapeutic system will be more successful where therapist and patient share similar expectations concerning the therapeutic process.[80] The greater such similarity, also, the longer is the therapeutic system likely to be maintained.[81] For here it provides reinforcing positive feedback for both patient and therapist. Psychotherapists are more likely to find confirmation for their theories where they and their patients share the same middle-class background out of which psychotherapeutic theory evolved.[82] The tendency for systems involving similar components to last longer than those of component diversity may be noted too in marital systems. Divorce and separation appear to increase with diversity rather than similarity of husband and wife.[83]

Systems of component *dissimilarity* tend toward a formality of interaction with their environments. The more heterogeneous a nation's civil service, for example, the more rigidly bureaucratic its relations with contending political parties.[84] Where components are dissimilar, too, their interaction with one another appears motivated by extrinsic needs rather than a desire for companionship. Negro-white communication in America usually serves a specific economic or other purpose. It rarely centers around fun or a general exchange of ideas.[85]

Regardless of the initial similarity or dissimilarity of components, association in a social system increases their similarity. Both similar and dissimilar become more alike. Since the stoppage of large-scale immigration from Catholic countries to the United States, American Catholics have become increasingly like the components of other major religious bodies of America. Similarly, parents and children are found quite thoroughly to share political preferences;[86] they likewise share political indifference.[87] Economic status and action, and religious ideas and behavior tend similarly to be shared among family members. The impact of attitudinal similarity within the family system is likely to be reinforced by a similar attitudinal homogeneity in other systems to which family members belong.

So it is that a system's components of various kinds, such as persons, material objects, ideas and affect, grow increasingly alike as energy/information flows among them. Freedman *et al.*[88] point out that values, means of exchange, language, production processes, modes of transportation and communication, charity, religious practices, recreation, and other things tend to submit to the leveling influence of sustained interaction. National systems interactive as components of a larger international union likewise partake of this tendency toward similarity. By most standards the United States and Soviet Russia have become increasingly alike. A 1962 study by the economists Christopher Freeman and Alison Young[89] reveals that this similarity extends even to comparable expenditures for technological research and development—"R. and D."—and in the same fields, that is, space and military. In the United States at the time of the study 1,159,500 persons were engaged in technological research and development. In the Soviet Union the figure ranged from 1,039,000 to 1,472,000 depending upon the definition of "technological." About sixty percent of the American expenditure centered on space and military programs; the Russian percentage was comparable though somewhat less.

Tastes and beliefs similarly blend with increased contact.[90] An increase in attitudinal similarity is found,[91] and Homans [92] reports that the greater the frequency of contact, the more alike do both activities and sentiments become. This movement toward homogeneity appears in social systems of the freely conjunctive type, for example, in friendships and marriages in Western society, and in those dependent on external circumstances for their formation, such as members of a factory work-group. It is likely that the movement toward convergence in ideas and behaviorial norms is actually greater for components brought together through some external factor. In the self-impelled conjunctives, although increases in homogeneity also occur, members are apt to be quite similar to begin with in the realm of values.[93]

The process of component convergence has been demonstrated experimentally. Sherif [94] finds individual judgments shifting to conform to a group norm as internal communication heightens. People taken singly were asked to judge the movement of light (which actually did not move at all) in a darkened room. When they were placed together in a communicating system their individual judgments tended to converge, establishing a system norm generally regarded as "correct."

Strongly influencing the similarity/dissimilarity of system members is their tendency to agree with the opinions of other members they like. Their perceptions of member agreement with them are also determined by their liking; people believe that those they like share their opinions and that those they dislike hold opinions different from their own.[95] Those they like are also described as similar to the group norm while those they dislike are characterized as deviant.[96] Also, system members see themselves as more representative of their system and closer to its ways, if it is one involving positive affect ("our side"), than they really are.[97] Differences within are also underperceived by those who belong. At the same time the out-group is seen as exaggeratedly different. Political partisans fail to perceive their disagreements with their own candidate, or their similarities with the opposition.[98]

This tendency works to make "logical," and thus implement, the sending of positive affect within a system that demands positive affect as a component, such as a friendship, or a political party. It serves to heighten the necessary perception or misperception of *esprit de corps*. And it works to legitimize the sending of hostility to the "opposition" which is perceived as "different," often evilly so.

The expectation of positive affect as a usual component of communicative systems may be noted in the action of labor and management toward one another during a strike. At these times union leaders strive to avoid all except the most official and circumscribed contact with management lest they be exposed to criticism from their own members.[99] For easy, relaxed communication suggests positive affect, and possibly in this case a deal "selling out" the working stiff.

FEATURES OF COMPONENT ACTION

Overrating One's System

A prime feature of component action is to rate one's system higher than outsiders do. This system centrism ties in with ethnocentrism, the tendency to be culture-bound and rate one's culture generally superior to others. It is, however, a broader concept in that it involves the total system to which the person belongs rather than just its cultural features. Also, it is a tendency toward overestimation rather than an indiscriminate belief in superiority.

Caplow and McGee[100] call this tendency *aggrandizement effect*. In a study of fifty-five sets of six organizations of varied types, it was found that members of these formal organizations overestimated the prestige of their own organization eight times as frequently as they underestimated it.[101] A net overestimation by members of the prestige of their organizations could be discerned in each one of the sets. The kinds of formal organizations involved in the fifty-five sets included fraternities, sororities, teenage clubs, Protestant churches, Catholic parishes, public high schools, private colleges, dance studios, nursing schools, hospital services, chain hamburger stands, savings and loan asociations, pest-control firms, community centers, country clubs, dress shops, advertising agencies, Campfire Girl groups, branch Y.M.C.A.s, photography studios, Young Judea clubs, banks, chain supermarkets, printing firms, employment agencies, architectural firms, insurance agencies, foreign student clubs, skid row missions, trucking firms, department stores, religious youth organizations, and social science departments. Comparable study of informal social systems such as cliques and friendship groups appears potentially fruitful.

This tendency to overrate one's social system heightens component morale, implements the action of a system's "doormen," and helps maintain its unique identity. It is conceivably part of a general tendency to rate one's system well, whatever it may be, and to convince oneself of its essential legitimacy. Its defensive action is especially apparent in subsystems threatened by the larger milieu: criminals, jazz musicians, delinquent gangs, and the like. Words of praise for their way of life and disdain for the larger milieu and its institutions figure extensively in the special vocabularies of these subsystems.[102]

Aggrandizement effect serves also to legitimize various kinds of normally illegitimate action toward another system. Within certain American subsystems such as the KKK, that are strongly prejudiced toward ethnic minorities, hostility toward these minorities often becomes rationalized by an aggrandizement effect in which the prejudiced subsystem characterizes itself as deeply patriotic, religious, and nationalistic.[103]

Overestimation of Component Proximity to System Norms

A noteworthy characteristic of components is their tendency to overestimate their normality. To illustrate, they see their opinions as closer to system norms than they actually are. Kelly and Thibaut,[104] in noting this fact, speculate that it may be part of an attempt to allay anxiety about nonconformity by minimizing their actual deviation from group standards. It also suggests the essential irrelevance of actual, *empirical* deviance as a meaningful item in social control.

Component Clustering

A significant feature of component action is the tendency to cluster in particular areas of a social system rather than to be evenly distributed through it. Drug addiction, prostitution, homeless men, bohemianism, and many other subsystems have their zones within the larger milieu. While the distribution of urban residents varies considerably according to type and size of city, areas of highest density have been found to be (at least in the past) in and near the central business district. The declining density, however, is not uniform throughout. Along and near radial transportation routes, population density tends to be higher than in sections more remote from the major thoroughfares.[105]

Clustering heightens the action; the closer components are to one another, the greater their frequency of contact. An amplification spiral emerges as those who want a great deal of contact move closer to one another. While similar components are most likely to cluster together, dissimilar ones—racially, for instance—will associate more thoroughly when they are near than far.[106]

Within large social systems, such as nations, areas of component clustering and heightened action are common. Cities are more tightly packed than rural territory; certain railroad action concentrates in yards; marriages cluster in June.

Component Consistency

The identity of system components partakes of a general consistency. Components of a subsystem, for example, tend to share in the general status of that subsystem vis-à-vis the larger society of which it is a part, and to internalize this status. A person's self-evaluation appears strongly influenced by the ranking of his class so that upper-class people tend to feel individually superior while lower-class people tend to feel individually inferior.[107]

The identity of a component, moreover, is expressed generally and diffusely. The systems he enters or forms with other components have a basic consistency among them. To illustrate, politically oriented persons are found to be active in systems involving political talk, reading, and voting.[108] The barroom bully is more likely than Casper Milquetoast to "make it" as a commando, and the vegetarian is more apt than the butcher to be a pacifist. Whether self-directed or authority driven, one seeks and makes consistent systems. Studies of American and Italian fathers reveal that those who are pretty much on their own in their work encourage their children to be self-directed; fathers who are rigidly controlled on the job set up comparably authoritarian homes for their children.[109] Similarly, the highly active component, the "life of the party," tends to be so in a variety of systems; the "loner" is comparably inactive and autonomous in the systems to which he does belong. Union printers who mix a great deal outside the shop with others in their trade are also deeply interested in union politics.[110]

Participation in one social system leads to involvement in others that are congruent with it. When a worker joins a union and becomes involved in one kind of union activity, chances are strong that he will participate in a wide spectrum of union affairs before long.[111] In the development of agrarian socialism in Saskatchewan, similarly, organizationally active persons were the first to join up with the Cooperative Commonwealth Federation. The less active mass became Federation supporters only gradually.[112]

Thus some components remain consistently aloof, more autonomous than system norms dictate. Others tend to "get with" the systems to which they belong, to internalize and follow their norms, to be favorable toward their structures. Substantial correlations indicate that workers who are pro-union are apt to be pro-management while antiunionists are likely to be antimanagement as well.[113] In a study of a large plant, Purcell [114] found that fifty-seven percent of the foremen, seventy-three percent of the workers, and eighty-eight percent of the stewards kept up an allegiance to both union and management and felt attached to them both.

Several other kinds of component consistency may be noted.

Those who migrate once are likely to move again,[115] and spatial mobility goes hand in hand with class mobility.[116] Partners in happy, well-adjusted marital unions tend to perceive their parents' marriage as a happy one.[117] Tentatively, they create through conjunction the same kinds of systems from which they come; they may also, in consistent fashion, see the "bright side" of the social systems around them.

Components of systems of high economic power in consistent pattern tend to be components also of systems of high educational level, of strong political action,[118] and of high general prestige. Components of systems of low economic power, similarly, appear consistent through their membership also in systems of low educational level and low prestige.[119] Each of these congruent system affiliations provides positive feedback for the others and produces a self-perpetuating "virtuous" (or "vicious") circle of affiliative consistency.

A significant facet of consistency is a system's propensity for endowing all its components with its distinctive identity and tone. There appears here a *gilt* as well as a *guilt* by association. A component such as the speech of a high status social system itself carries high status. Hall [120] writes that before a single standard language arises in any nation the local dialects tend to be of equal prestige. In the early Middle Ages the speech of Northeast England, of Scotland, and of Southern England were all of comparable status and people spoke and wrote without hesitation in their own dialects. When the speech of a particular section comes to partake of a special prestige for political or other reasons, however, speakers of other dialects begin to feel inferior about their native speech and to use the dialect of greater prestige. Hall [121] states that Francien became the basis of modern standard French because Paris became the capital of France; Castilian provided the basis of standard Spanish because Madrid became the capital of Spain; the English of London and Middlesex became standard English because of London's rise to capital power.

Through component consistency, too, systems made up of the same or similar components are likely to be similar in their action. Systems of courtship and marriage, since they involve the same people, are apt to be very much alike. The sending and receiving of affect within them remain much the same. A smooth pattern of interaction during courtship goes along with a similar one during marriage.[122]

The congruence of system affiliations relates directly to overlapping system memberships. Studies of overlapping memberships, and of systems that never overlap, appear to be fruitful areas of system inquiry. Haitian peasants generally consider themselves both Roman Catholics and voodooists and maintain membership in both systems.[123] A Haitian folk expression even states that it is necessary to be a Roman Catholic to be a follower of voodoo. Rarely, if ever, however, is a Haitian Protestant also a voodooist.

A socioeconomic class is a composite social system based upon a multiplicity of congruent, overlapping affiliations (for example, family, residence, and occupation) by its components. Through knowing some of a person's systems of belongingness, accordingly, the fact of component consistency makes possible the prediction of others. To illustrate, Catholics and Jews in America have both shown a propensity to identify with the Democratic Party.[124] In similar vein it is unlikely to find a person belonging to both the KKK and the NAACP—unless he also belongs to the FBI. Certain systemic affiliations thus "go together," producing overlapping memberships. They tend to form a *compatible pattern.* Membership in certain social systems makes other system memberships more likely and more unlikely. Episcopalians in America frequently belong to other systems of high socioeconomic status while members of fundamentalist sects are affiliated largely with low socioeconomic groupings.[125] A great sharing of components among urban systems, systems involving high media participation, systems involving high literacy, and systems involving high political participation has similarly been found.[126]

The compatibility of Puritan and scientific systems has been noted.[127] The relatively meager affiliation of Roman Catholics in scientific systems has received comparable attention. In modern America, for example, Catholics appear underrepresented among scientists.[128] It is likely that this proportion will rise as Catholicism as a social system permits a greater entry of the viewpoints and perspectives of scientific and secular life, and as Catholics adopt increasingly the socioeducational perspectives of the middle class from which scientists largely are selected.

A component consistency may be found in several other systemic contexts. Persons with one highbrow taste, in music, for example, are likely to attach to other highbrow taste systems, such as painting and literature. A person who operates effectively in an intellectual system involving mathematics is found to be similarly effective in systems involving words and other kinds of mental components.[129]

Certain overlapping memberships conduce to high component efficiency and productivity in these systems. To illustrate, a genuine overlapping of the formal and informal organizations of industry so that certain values are shared appears to raise the output of industrial work.[130] Such overlapping systems are found to be important in military efficiency also. Transmission and execution of commands along the formal lines of military authority succeed best when they coincide (are mutually shared) with the informal systems of communication that develop within the army.[131] In the German Army, similarly, the more thoroughly a soldier belonged to an informal buddy system overlapping in membership with the larger, formal Army, the greater was his military efficiency.[132] The importance of achieving congruity between systems involving desires and realities is also well recognized in psychotherapy.[133]

Belonging to inconsistent, incongruent systems (see Figure 12) is thus rare. When it does occur it appears to hamper a person's capacity to make decisions. Overlapping membership in these systems subjects a component to cross-pressures stemming from contradictory system determinisms. Lazarsfeld *et al.*[134] find cross-pressures in the political realm likely to delay a final voting decision. A consistent bundle of values and biases, essential for clear identity, depends upon a consistency of the overlapping systems to which a person belongs. When normal component consistency breaks down and a person finds himself affiliated with incongruent systems, a choice is usually made between these norms so as to reduce the strain that would occur if he tried to follow both. A boy may come to follow gang norms

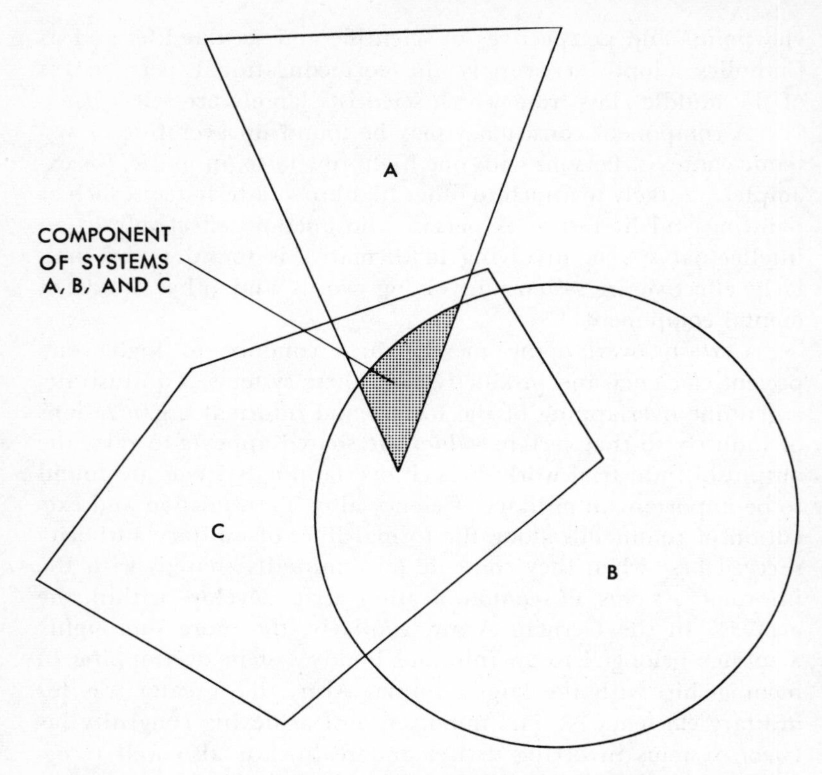

Figure 12. Membership in Overlapping, Incongruent Systems.

—indicating his greater organization and involvement in the gang system—rather than those of his family when the two are contradictory.[135] Choosing *one* of these congruent systems stops the "dissonance" they would otherwise create.[136]

For persons of incongruent affiliations, decisions are not only difficult but highly unstable. One system membership and line of action may temporarily take over, producing what may appear to be the dramatic change of "conversion." [137] Actually, his other systemic affiliations often linger latently in the background. One of them may later gain primacy as the most favored reference group. Reconversion is common among converts.[138] Where political incongruence marks the systems to which a person belongs, his choice of candidate for whom to vote is comparably susceptible to change.[139]

It has been suggested that the multiple and diverse affiliations common in modern democratic nations serve to reduce political emotion and conflict. A cross-pressured voter who finally makes his choice is not too disappointed if the other side wins for he is likely to have areas of affiliation and identification with the opposition. German data indicate that German Catholics voting Socialist were much less hostile to Adenauer, a Catholic Christian Democrat, than were socialist Protestants.[140] Similarly, manual workers voting Republication or Conservative in the United States and Great Britain are less liberal on economic issues than workers who vote for candidates of the Democratic or Labor Parties but they are more liberal than the middle-class supporters of their party.[141] The fact that a significant number of supporters of each party has ties with certain values of the other forces the leaders of each party to make concessions to retain these supporters [142]—and generally keeps them from extreme political postures. The departure from this norm in the Republican campaign of 1964 then cost the party heavily.

It should be emphasized that multiple, overlapping memberships cause difficulty only when they are incongruent and inconsistent. Where they have a basic similarity they produce little strain because the person never really "leaves home." The American tourist abroad who stays in American hotels wherever he may go is unlikely to be upset by incongruent system affiliations.

COMPONENT SENDING AND RECEIVING

The process of component sending and receiving is the core of system determinism and system control. It creates system norms, socializes toward them, and attempts to prevent their breach. Thus the voting preferences of a component's primary group are communicated to him and bring him to his "own" decision in general elections.[143] A work group sets productivity norms for its components and holds them to them—although these may often be different from management standards.[144] Even pairs of workers through the flow of energy/information between them set norms of output and maintain surveillance over them. These system-determined norms disappear when communication is shut off and the workers are isolated from one another.[145]

The greater the frequency of sending and receiving among system components, the more highly organized the system is likely to be. The flow of energy/information between them also tends to spread beyond its original boundaries. Task-oriented social systems are found to engage in much sending and receiving that is not task-oriented as time goes by. Argyle,[146] in noting Riecken and Homans'[147] explanation of this as due to a more permissive atmosphere developing within the group and allowing a broader variety of energy/information flow to occur, advances the possible alternative that such a broadening of communicative content might occur through the group's becoming bored with the task at hand.

Bales[148] finds a *phase-pattern* operative here involving a cyclic flow of instrumental and emotional items of energy/information. In a problem-solving group a high level of task-oriented activities is observed in the early periods of a meeting. But this heightens the level of tension and so threatens the system's action; the latter is adjusted through a later increase in social-emotional activities.[149] Those groups dealing with full-fledged problems show a phase-pattern involving (a) a relative emphasis on matters of orientation ("what is it"), (b) a relative emphasis on matters of evaluation ("how do we feel about it"), and (c) a relative emphasis on matters of control ("what shall we do about it").[150] A similar switch in content is found in psychotherapeutic systems of patient and therapist. Its pattern was observed to follow that of the problem-solving groups studied by Bales, above. Specifically, communication of an orientative nature, such as clarifications and confirmations, decreased during the first fifty hours of therapy. Evaluative communication, such as opinions, evaluation, analyses, and expressions of feeling, increased during this span and then reached a plateau.[151]

Often the sending of energy/information within a system is linear. That is, a member may send to another without receiving from him. In the pattern of displaced aggression the sending is A → B → C. A sends hostility to B which is passed on to C rather than being returned to A. It constitutes a social system because the sending of A to B gets passed on eventually to C, thus indirecly involving A and C. In such situations B is unable or unwilling to return hostility to A and so expresses it toward C—usually because C is unable or unwilling to return it to B. It is a frequent pattern in majority-minority interaction. Miller and Bugelski [152] have found increased hostility toward ethnic minority groups expressed by persons subjected to negative affect in the form of deprivation. Similarly, the lynching of Negroes in the southern United States was found to increase when economic indices—and especially the price of cotton—went down. Hostility unable to be expressed toward the price of cotton and the factors responsible for it appeared to be directed toward Negroes unable to mobilize retribution.[153]

Often such unilinear hostility finds expression long after its original implantation and in quite different social systems, suggesting that energy/information is stored and that during its storing exerts an additional impact upon the storer. An interesting subject for study would be the relative storing and transmission of certain kinds and amounts of energy/information that occur in particular social situations. For example, there appear long-lasting consequences of the negative affect received in the form of frustration (pain) during childhood. Maier [154] notes significantly more hostility during later life—in the form of frequent quarreling with friends, the carrying of grudges, and broken engagements—among persons reporting childhood frustration.

Part of the folklore—and sophisticated literate expression as well, as in Kierkegaardian existentialism—of Western civilization suggests the benefits to be derived from pain, suffering, fear, anxiety, and other forms of negative affect. The findings described above [155] indicate that these "benefits" are dubious to say the least.

A phenomenon comparable to displaced aggression that has received rather little attention by scholars may be called displaced *affection*. In it, positive affect sent from A (husband) to B (wife) gets passed on to C (children, or lover). The relative inattention to displaced affection is a phenomenon which itself might prove interesting of study.

PATTERNS OF INTERNAL MOVEMENT

Energy/information does not move randomly within a system. It appears to have distinct, normative pathways of movement among components. Both the amount and direction of movement, moreover, appear normatively ordered. Thus in studies of informal groups, component A, who is the recipient of twenty-five percent of the messages sent by component B, is also likely to be the recipient of twenty-five percent of the sending of components C, D, and E.[156] Similarly, the amount of a component's sending is found to vary directly with the amount of his receiving. High senders are high receivers. This is true both for his sending to the group as a whole and to particular members of it.[157]

Patterns of internal flow tend toward a greater informality than does a system's inflow and outflow with its environments. A social system such as a family or a corporation appears more likely to "let its hair down" internally; with outflow there appears more concern about its "image," and with inflow its power eye is especially watchful, often with formal apparatus, to prevent the entrance of what might provide negative feedback.

Pathways of internal energy/information flow may themselves operate as system components. An informal "grapevine" within a corporation, for example, is usually highly organized (mutually impactful) with other components of the corporate system. For this reason a "middleman" channel of internal flow may often be severely cross-pressured. Where components are of unequal status and power, especially, the position of the person who links them is replete with strain. He is subject to contradictory demands and expectations from those above and those below: typically, demands for heightened productivity from above, for more human concern and consideration from below. This is the structural position of such middlemen as foremen, head nurses, middle managers, noncommissioned officers, and the like.

A study in industry reveals that the ratings of foremen by their superiors and by their subordinates vary inversely. Foremen liked by the bosses are disliked by the workers.[158] In the American Army a noncom is valued by those above for being a strong military leader, by those below for being a "good guy." Officers want the noncom to maintain rigorous, official standards; enlisted men want him to be approachable and lenient.[159] Gibb,[160] in describing this dilemma, notes the multiple roles required of an intermediate officer in an organization. He must accept the values of top level authority and serve as an agent of the impersonal, coercive system of which he is a component. If he does this well his superiors will think well of him. At the same time he must hold the support of the men he directs so that he wields over them the authority which they give him—at least in a social system involving democratic ideology as a component.

The structural position of strain in which a middleman finds himself in systems involving democratic ideology, along with actual inequalities of power, appears eased somewhat if the people the middleman directs have had a say in his choosing. Downward communication appears to work best in these situations when moving through a middleman selected by those below. Communication from a central authority to a resident community, for instance, is more likely to have an impact in desired response if it operates through the informal leaders of the resident group.[161]

A system's media of internal communication, its newspapers and radio stations, for example, vary in the distinctness of their identity. Some have a strong, specific identity and significantly influence the energy/information passing through them. Others are more thoroughly "noise-free" so that little change in the message occurs. No channel of communication within a social system, however, appears completely passive and noise-free. While the Haitian peasant possessed by a voodoo deity is thought by believers to provide a noise-free channel for the voice and action of the deity, he is at the same time himself. What he says and does as a channel during possession is both a projection of himself and dependent upon his having learned the appropriate behavior expected of the deity, and of the person channeling that deity.[162] It is specifically this learning that enables him to be a proper channel.

Frequently the changes made by a middleman provide his essential *raison d'être*. Middlemen, such as labor-management mediators, implement the kind of mutually desired communication between components which fosters both component and total-system survival—and which could not easily be achieved without their intervention. Often they allow certain kinds of sending by the linked parties to blow itself harmlessly into the wind at the same time that it performs its face-saving function. Labor and management can bark ferociously at one another so that their constituents—and also themselves, thereby enhancing their self-esteem—may hear while the mediator quietly pursues the real business of peacemaking. Often the linked parties scream loudest at one another after a covert accord has been reached. National leaders can rage that they will never bargain with one another while official and unofficial diplomats reach an agreement acceptable to both. Diplomatic interpreters also are found often to soften the verbal exchanges of each side.[163] Coleman [164] notes a potential danger of violence between the "ins" and "outs" of a community where the mediating and compromising influence of middlemen channels is missing. Zimmerman [165] reports such a situation in certain rigidly dominated communities of Thailand and Mississippi. Hughes [166] describes a comparable situation involving the English minority in French Canadian towns.

As a communication link moves toward increased identity and specificity, its impact upon the materials passing through it becomes greater. The teaching of a college instructor not long out of graduate school tends to repeat the line of his recent professors. As his professional identity grows, more selectivity and change occur in the professional materials moving through him. He develops an ear, and a voice, of his own. With increased identity, too, a middleman channel becomes increasingly resistant to change in its action. It becomes resistant not only to the movement of nonnormative flow; it opposes also the redirection of this energy/information, enabling the components it has linked to (1) utilize another middleman or (2) communicate directly. Real estate agencies, sales representatives, and the native interpreter Sakini in "Teahouse of the August Moon" all have a vested interest in maintaining "linkage as usual."

Internal channels appear to vary in their formality. There are, for example, the official formal channels, or red tape, within an organization, and the informal "grapevine." There are the formal avenues of public welfare between donors and recipients and the informal mediation of the ward politician.[167] There are the formal channels of radio, newspaper, and television and the informal action of the "opinion leader" molding the attitudes of his associates.[168] The more formal a channel, the more selective and rigid it tends to become. Additional obstacles to communicative flow often develop. The greater ease of transfer frequently provided by informal channels may be resorted to by people who need to get things done quickly.

Worthy of note concerning movement within a social system is the action of internal "doormen" keeping certain features of a system apart. Often a large social system will include certain incongruities: for example, ideals of honesty along with the necessities of business, ideas of the brotherhood of man along with the existence of racial caste. Were these incongruent elements to meet head-on, this confrontation could seriously impede, that is, provide negative feedback for, the ongoing action of the system. The situation generally is handled by internal confinement and a blocking of communication between them. At the personality level this may be achieved by an internal "doorman" or a traffic manager's steering of certain items to the unconscious and confining them there, and by the development of "logic-tight compartments" separating certain kinds of ideas and behavior lest guilt, confusion, or other disarray accompany their association. Sociologists and anthropologists have long been aware of the closed doors between system components of "ideal" and "real." Myrdal[169] makes various contradictory items of America a central focus for analysis of Negro-white relations in the United States, and Hurlock[170] reviews several experimental studies concerning the action of internal doormen. These studies reveal that a belief in the rightness of honesty is bounded off from action so that children will cheat when a tempting opportunity for cheating presents itself.[171] Similarly, children who believe it is wrong to be aggressive toward their classmates are often aggressive in practice.[172] Delinquent children usually express the belief that delinquency is wrong.[173] Channels are thus often closed to traffic between ideas and their behavioral counterparts; [174] these two features of a social system frequently retain a high degree of *de facto* autonomy vis-à-vis one another. Mathematics too, despite middlelore to the contrary, appears to retain a high degree of autonomy. In an investigation holding IQ constant, Thorndike [175] found that the study of mathematics does not serve to spread its skills through other spheres. Students of mathematics were not significantly more logical or reasonable in their approach to other problems than were students who had no mathematical training.

PATTERNS OF INTERNAL POWER

Power is the manipulation of a social system or its components. It may originate within a system or outside; it may manipulate the system's internal action or its action (inflow and outflow) with its environments. Power means actual manipulation rather than the capacity or potential for it. It is *in practice* that power exists. Latent power, that is, without action, is irrelevant. A belief in a component's power, for instance, becomes meaningful when it is involved in system action, when people or other components act in terms of it.

The sociologic of viewing power as the manipulation of energy/information relates closely to the association of communication and component rank within a social system. In experimental studies of small groups, members of high rank dominate the communication.[176] They tend to oligarchize (center among themselves) the sending and receiving that occurs. Their interplay is less random and more task-oriented—hence more system implementive in the direction of positive feedback—than that of lower-ranked members; their sending involves a higher ratio of initiating to reactive communication, such as speaking without being spoken to; their sending has more impact on system action.[177] In these small task-oriented groups it is only where no member has special competence or where no clear-cut solution to the problem at hand exists that the amount of communication equals out.[178]

Top rank components' dominance of communication in these small experimental groups takes several forms. For example, they are more communicative with all other members than are components of low rank.[179] The direction of component sending is similarly reflective of their power. Normally, energy/information within a social system moves from equal to equal: from members of high rank to other members of high rank, from members of low rank to other members of low rank.[180] When components of varying rank are involved in communication, however, the normal pattern is for it to be sent by components of high rank and received by those of low.[181] This is especially true when the communication relates to the essential *raison d'être* of the system. Riecken and Homans[182] find that people in groups communicate most with high-ranking members in "task" situations, with equals in "social" situations.

An essential fact of power in a social system is the relative imperviousness of certain components to feedback from others. Components of absolute power need not be concerned about, that is, responsive to or influenced by, the reaction of those they manipulate through sending. Thoroughly immune from feedback, they may "get away with" anything. It is only in a completely democratic social system that all components are equally "other"-directed.

Dominance of communication—which in a *de facto* sense becomes unilinear sending without meaningful receiving in that the latter carries little feedback impact—is thus a systemically realistic measure of power. Where unequal statuses are clear-cut and legitimate (for example, queen and commoner, bona fide expert and layman), no threat to the one below is involved in a power component's dominance of communication. In a democratic social system, however, attempts to monopolize sending are resented ("he never lets anyone get a word in")—and precisely because of their illegitimate power implication. Letting the other fellow dominate the conversation, as Dale Carnegie intuited, is flattering through its implication of the talker's higher status, power, or expertise. It may so successfully "con" him that he will be unaware or permissive of being led to buy by the listener-salesman. A system involving true peers is thus one in which each member does "have his say," and where what he says has equal impact upon all other components.

POWER DIFFERENTIATION

Social systems of true peers are rarely reported. Power inequalities among components appear a basic ingredient of social systems regardless of their type, size, or complexity. Whether it be a marriage dominated by one spouse or a mental hospital manipulated by its attendant-staff,[183] social systems appear internally power-differentiated. "Other"-directedness does not mean *all* "others"—only those "significant others" with power.

An important contemporary trend involves the increasing centralization of power at the national level. When the United Nations Charter was signed in 1945 almost half of the fifty member nations were democracies in the usual sense of the word. Today only about one third of the members can claim this distinction. Most of Asia, most of South America, most of Africa and much of Europe presently live under totalitarian regimes—and the number appears to be increasing rather than decreasing.[184]

Davis [185] notes that there are primitive communities so small that no class strata appear, the social structure resting almost entirely upon age, sex, and kinship. Yet even here, he observes, the inequalities involved in chieftainship, individual prowess, and clan or family property introduce an incipient stratification.

The more generally differentiated a social system, which is apt to occur, for example, with a large social system, the more likely is it for there to be power and rank inequalities within it. Frazier [186] reports less class stratification within the Negro population of southern cities in the United States than in border cities, for example, and less in border cities than in northern cities—largely because of the progressively greater occupational diversity. Warner [187] also finds an increase in rank orders associated with a heightened heterogeneity of population and a rise in the division of labor.

Power inequality and a tightening of controls appear to heighten when environment threatens. Civil liberties are often submerged during wartime. Power inequalities, similarly, are extreme within the military which operates in a threatening, uncertain, anxiety-making environment of crisis. Janowitz [188] suggests that the greater the uncertainties faced by the military, the more manipulative its leadership: the more emphasis there is upon explicit orders, elaborate directives, and contingency plans.

It is found that the greater the power inequality among system components, the greater are the differences in characteristics other than power between those with power and those without. Lipset and Linz [189] explain this as a need by those in power to erect or preserve a style of life and a value structure that legitimize their claim to privilege.

FEATURES OF INTERNAL POWER

Where the manipulation of a social system originates internally, its power components take an active role in guiding it, directing its action, and persuading and coercing its other components. If the system's manipulation has its source outside, its internal leadership is found to operate as an agent of this external power.[190] The longer the life-span of a social system's leadership, whatever it may be, the more distinct appear the system's norms; the more clear-cut the patterns of internal communication, the more selective the system's pathways of particular kinds of messages, and the less likely the system's inventiveness in the solution of new problems.[191]

Research has focused upon the ramifications of particular *styles* of power. It has dealt largely with American society where a subtle, noncoercive, indirect manipulation, such as in advertising, is the style of greatest legitimacy. It is no accident that advertising has reached its greatest elaboration in America: our component of democratic ideology makes our society resistant to other kinds of power that directly "push people around." In various American subsystems a light leadership in which components retain much self-power vis-à-vis the leader appears more apt than authoritarian control to hold the system together over time, to satisfy its individual components, and to produce a high level of output on the task at hand.[192] The "friendly-helpful" boss is associated in the United States with low absenteeism, high productivity, positive feelings by employees about the organization and the boss, low conflict within the organization, and strong employee morale.[193] In similar vein, Adams [194] in his study of Air Force crews found that good performance (output) on training problems was associated with equalitarian treatment by officers. That this condition, however, is not a necessary universal concerning power in a social system but dependent upon the components of such a system (including ideas of what kind of manipulation is legitimate, and consequent behaviorial expectations in this regard) may be noted in the research. Gibb [195] finds that authoritarian persons prefer visible, status-laden, directive leadership, and regard the authoritarian leader as "better" than his more democratic counterpart. Any deviation from strong directiveness by the leader is regarded by them as "weakness." Equalitarian types, that is, those whose concept of legitimate style of power is one that is light rather than visibly directive, group-determined rather than leader-determined, on the other hand, are found to accept authoritarian leadership only when special circumstances require it.[196]

System components carry with them into their new systems, along with other features of past socialization, particular power expectations and statuses derived from systems of their past. A story circulates that a former German SS'er decided to study voice after World War II. At his first concert he strode to the footlights and screamed at his audience: "*I*, will sing; and *you*, will listen!"

The action of a system's power structure in setting its rules of proper behavior has been noted cross-societally. For example, proper behavior for children, adults, and the aged is normally assigned.[197] A system's power structure is its components who set up and enforce its rules, who send more manipulatively than they receive. It is the opinions of the prestigious, powerful members of the community that swing most weight in changing the political attitudes of newcomers to the community.[198]

The normal course of power within a social system moves from one based upon personal qualities (the "charismatic" leader) to one based upon administrative skills (the "bureaucratic" leader) as the social system enlarges and becomes generally more differentiated.[199] Weber[200] described the process as the "routinization of charisma." Selznick[201] points to its operation in the United Automobile Workers. He reports that militancy was a feature of this union's early action and leadership. After it achieved its initial aims, however, the militant methods of direct action and strong-arm leadership gave way to more subtle, negotiative techniques involving a change of leadership to one skilled along these lines. It may be noted also that as a social movement enlarges and moves closer to the norm (in this case bureaucratic) for the larger milieu in which it operates, it tends to move away from the opposition status which might have marked its charismatically led inception.

A "prestige lag"—whereby prestige lags behind power—has been observed. Power and wealth appear often to be attained before the commensurate prestige. For most ethnic groups in America, status has lagged behind economic gains and increased political power.[202] Baltzell[203] documents several features of this prestige lag, especially for Jews in America. Despite this prestige lag, however, prestige and power are generally associated systemically. Sayles[204] finds union leadership dominated by the more prestigious workers of the plant community, and notes that research on the coal mining industry of Great Britain has shown that top production workers, those carrying highest prestige, take the most active role in directing strikes in the industry.

COMPONENTS OF HIGH POWER

A system's components of major power wield this power diffusely rather than specifically. Of prime importance in this regard is the fact that power components manipulate the system both internally and in interplay with its environments.[205] No basic split is normally found here. Lyndon Johnson, Charles De Gaulle, and other national leaders determine both domestic and foreign policy. In like fashion, a juvenile gang's leadership rules within and leads in the defense of its "turf" from the onslaughts of rival gangs.

It is the energy/information sent by a power component which by definition manipulates the system. There is an interesting "gilt" by association here. Bales[206] notes that several studies have shown that a suggestion rejected or ignored if made by a low-status component may be accepted and acted upon (and thus carry power) if made by a high-status member. Components perceive and judge energy/information differently according to the structural position of the sender. The smaller the social system, also, the more thoroughly do its power components dominate it. The smaller the community, the more influential are its upper classes in matters of general community import—particularly in setting its "tone."[207]

A significant feature of genuine power is the capacity of power components to resist the revolutionary action of those eager for this power. Old-line American universities, of high power by virtue of their high-level political, economic, and other connections with top power segments of America, were on the whole quite successful in resisting the revolutionary action of McCarthy-type radicals, although attacks upon these academic institutions and their faculties were frequent. While such attacks were few toward colleges of lower power, these onslaughts were highly successful in manipulating administrations and faculty members there.[208]

In general, power components are found to (1) direct the system's action along lines of its established norms and to (2) follow these norms themselves so that their personal behavior is thoroughly "proper" for the system.[209] When systems have established norms it is extremely difficult for a new leader to change them.[210] He is more likely to be converted by these system norms, to be more manipulated than manipulative. Leaders are most powerful in initiating action where such norms are least established, as in new systems. Even here the "style" of the leader appears more determined by the expectations of the membership and the requirements of the situation than by his personal traits.[211] In a classic experiment children with traits of leadership were introduced into groups of children who had previously met sufficiently to establish system traditions.[212] The leaders were slightly older than the other children and were selected for their traits of initiative and directive will; the other children in the group were without these traits of leadership. It was found, however, that the "leader" *adopted* the habits and traditions of the children who were younger than he and who in the day nursery had been his underlings following his direction. He began to engage in the kinds of activities that the group had developed before he entered it. The things the leader initiated were either unsuccessful or accepted only after modification (conversion, routinization) to the traditions of the group. He was forced to accept these traditions. He thereby proved "weaker" than the system—more system determined than system determining—although he still managed to "play" the role of leader. It explains the situation of the revolutionary leader who looked out the window to see his party charging the ramparts. "Excuse me," he said, "I must join them; I am their leader!"

Power components appear strongly convinced of the rightness of the existent pattern of internal stratification and the legitimacy of their rule within it. Often they strive to explain it as due to ascription as much or more than to achievement, and due to factors extrinsic (God, fate, predestination) as well as intrinsic (ability, brains, muscle). The Divine Right of Kings is this sort of legitimization. Further examples may be found in the tendency for power components to identify the system and its welfare with themselves. Louis XIV stated, "L'état, c'est moi!" Charles Wilson appeared quite honestly to have believed that what is good for General Motors is good for America, and vice versa. And de Gaulle is reported to intone—conceivably to the tune of the "Marseillaise"—"Quand je veux savoir ce que pense la France, je m'interroge." ("When I want to know what France thinks, I ask myself.")

As a part of this desire for legitimacy, power components often strive to make their claim to power visible. In social milieux emphasizing the leader's ability to achieve the system's goals as the foundation of his legitimate power, leaders of small, informal groups are found to direct the system's action along lines of their special competence and to steer it away from endeavors in which they do not excel.[213] Where power inequalities are great, upper classes strive to legitimize their position through a style of life and a value system justifying their claim to privilege.[214] These rationalizations of legitimacy for the power structure, however, are sometimes not shared by components without power. While the upper class in a democratic social system believes it is on top because of ability and energy, the lower class believes this ranking depends also on connections and good luck.[215] The lower class most fully subscribes to the notion, "It's not whatcha know but *who* ya know that counts." Shils [216] observes that components of low status, even while acknowledging their lack of power, simultaneously resent and deny it. Radical ethics and revolutionary political ideas by out-of-power persons constitute forms of denial of the "superiority" of those with power. Often such ideology functions as a component of a subsystem opposing the larger milieu.

Components of high power see the social system in which they rule as highly extensive—and want it to be so. Stouffer's [217] data on this point are revealing. To the statement "A noncom should not let the men in his squad forget that he is a noncom even when off-duty," which in a de facto sense extends both the system and its power structure, eighty-one per cent of the officers agreed. The comparable figure for noncoms was fifty-four percent, for privates only thirty-nine percent.

A component belonging to one subsystem of high power appears likely to belong to other subsystems of power as well. Lipset and Linz [218] find that persons of high political status and activity usually come from groups of high education and economic status. Similarly, people wielding high power in one system are likely to exert comparable power in other systems to which they belong. Persons of high rank tend to be so in their manifold systems of membership. Lane [219] notes the generally higher power and activity of men than women in political systems. With exceptions the same may be said generally and cross-societally for the relative power of men and women in economic systems, in family systems, in religious systems, and others. Similarly, the middle aged tend to be of high power (throughout Western civilization at least) in a multiplicity of groupings. Lane [220] notes the high incidence among the middle aged of property ownership, of family responsibilities—and comparable power despite modern inroads of the adolescent—and of solid group status.

A considerable amount of the research concerning power has centered on human components. Other components—economic forces, for example—can similarly be powerful. A dramatic illustration is provided in the changed stereotype of the Chinese immigrant in California from welcome worker to despised competitor. Shrieke [221] writes that in the early period, when the Chinese people worked on ranches, they were regarded as "the most worthy of our newly adopted citizens," "our most orderly and industrious citizens," "the best immigrants in California." They were deemed "thrifty," "sober," "inoffensive," and "law-abiding." But in the cities, with time, they grew competitive with white labor in an increasingly large number of occupations. They became "unassimilable," they "carried back gold to their homes" in China, they "lowered the plane of living." They were "clannish," dangerously "secretive in their actions," "deceitful and vicious," and "filthy and loathsome in their habits."

The urban-industrial complex, a strong economic force, sets much of the tone for the society that houses it wherever this may be. Utilizing data for several nations—the Soviet Union, Japan, Great Britain, New Zealand, and the United States—Inkeles and Rossi [222] conclude that there is a relatively invariable hierarchy of prestige (in terms of occupation) determined by industrialism in these societies. The power of industrialism to increase class mobility and to move a system's base of internal stratification from ascription to achievement and from inherited wealth to earned income has likewise been noted.[223] Its power to heighten social mobility appears greatest where industrialism has reached a high level.[224]

Technology of all sorts appears a generally powerful system component determining many features of the work pattern such as the nature of the job, the scope of the working day, the recruitment and selection of workers, their training and retraining, the development of informal, on-the-job groups, and the manipulative patterns concerning superiors and subordinates. Its impact on noneconomic systems similarly holds strong. Simpson and Yinger [225] stress the importance of farm mechanization for landlord-tenant relations, for Negro-white population ratios in the rural South, and for migration rates and goals. Sayles [226] finds the type and quantity of technological equipment, skills, and plant layout impacting strongly on other system components: the degree of independence of workers in the flow of work, the number and similarity of jobs concentrated in any one location, the indispensability of any part to the whole, the extent to which work loads and output standards can be accurately defined, the promotional ladders and status relationships, and work group attitudes and action.

Technological growth within national systems has carried immense power. An increase in population, commercialization of the economy, heightened emphasis on contractual rather than status relations among persons, urbanization, stratification into working and middle classes, increased division of labor, and increased rationalism in human affairs have stemmed from it.[227] The impact of technology appears especially great when several items of technology combine to form a composite.[228] As with all change it is likely to wield most power where it is new on the scene. In societies with an already advanced technology the impact of additional increments of the same is relatively low; in less technologically advanced social systems the consequences of these new items are extreme.[229] Rapid economic expansion appears powerful in creating a heightened emphasis upon achievement within national social systems. A concern for achievement, as expressed in folk tales and stories for children, accompanies a rapid rate of economic elaboration.[230] This is true not only in Western democracies such as the United States and England but also in Communist nations like Russia and Bulgaria.[231] It is true also of several societies of the past: ancient Greece, Spain in the late Middle Ages, and pre-Incan Peru.[232]

The emotional component of a social system similarly packs

tremendous power. For this reason it merits intensive study by sociologists and anthropologists who have sometimes neglected it as a proper realm for the psychologist alone. Affect sets the tone of many social systems and it pressures other system components, such as beliefs and action, into line with it. Emotional investment in the outcome of an election pulls ideas and everything else into a tight bundle of consistency.[233] Rosenberg *et al.*[234] find that when the affect component of an attitude changes, there occurs a corresponding reorganization of beliefs around it. Affect thus stands high as a "prime mover" though its power in many social systems is obscured and even its study is often considered taboo. For example, an important cornerstone of American middlelore holds that communication can be counted on to spread emotional warmth, that any interpersonal or intergroup problem is really a lack-of-communication problem, that conflicts domestic and international will disappear when people get to know one another and "reason together." It is partially responsible for the popularity of books, research, and university courses in America devoted to "communication."

The amount of communication among components, however, appears to have little impact in either setting or changing a system's emotional tone. Increases in association do not in themselves yield bounties of affection; decreases do not necessarily deepen hostility. Personal contact with ethnic minorities, for instance, neither raises nor lowers tensions.[235] What appears essential is not the amount of communication and interaction but the total system in which they operate: the components (including affect) of that system, and the environment impinging upon it. Hostility may drop off with increased contact in a social system where this system's *legitimate norm,* generally agreed upon and enforced, is cooperation and liking. White American soldiers cooperating in battle with American Negro soldiers generally lose some of their anti-Negro hostility[236] because (1) the soldier system carries, as a legitimate norm, "comrade" feelings toward other soldiers who are on his side, and (2) an environmental threat such as war generally reduces hostility within a social system.

Similarly, heightened contact through living in an interracial housing project increases favorable attitudes toward Negroes among white American housewives essentially because the cooperative norm of such living encourages it.[237] Where the proper norm is one of prejudice and hostility this will just as readily be learned as association mounts.

The power of affect is covertly recognized in that it is often discouraged as a regular system component—even in such social systems as marriage. It is simply too strong, too hot to handle as a regular thing, and too wearing as a steady diet. Most social systems do not stand up well with high emotion as a component even when the emotion is love. Strong emotion of any kind involves large quantities of energy/information. Where emotion predominates there may not be much energy left for other essentials of system action. It is found, for example, that many marriages that begin with strong affection become "devitalized" with time.[238] In a very real sense they may have to—at least if they are also going to handle such varied energy-draining, business-of-life tasks as doing laundry, preparing income tax forms, having the car serviced, getting orthodonture for the children, and shopping for groceries. While social systems may for a while soar on love, they appear to have a hard time living on it. A covert recognition of love's impermanence accompanies the covert recognition of its power. Its fleetingness, indeed, may hold the key to its attraction.

Affect appears tentatively of a special and unique relation to power in America. This may stem partially from the low legitimacy of any manipulation in a democracy. It has been reported, for instance, that "Madison Avenue-ers" often feel guilty concerning their manipulation of the consumer. It is reported that President Johnson, possibly the most powerful President in the history of America, wants desperately to be loved by all. Positive affect here appears to reduce the guilt of the manipulator: people happy with their leader must really want to go the way they are being led. In studies of American informal groups, similarly, leaders appear highly sensitive to the affect they receive from other components; indeed, affect appears the action feature of feedback and "other"-directedness. It appears also a necessary accompaniment for manipulation in a democratic social order. When put to the choice, American informal group leaders are found temporarily to give up the instrumental, manipulative role in favor of being well-liked.[239] They are found to sacrifice program for good will, system direction for popularity. Since being liked relates closely to being elected in America, professional politicians appear likewise eager for a "nice guy" image. They appear highly sensitive too to the political popularity polls that abound in America.

Where affect operates this way in regard to power, it serves to limit the leader's manipulation of the led. It makes him responsive to their wishes and desires. In informal social groups involving the component of democratic ideology, the leader is followed to the extent that he makes possible the members' attainment of personal, autonomous goals as well as the achievement of system aims.[240]

In noting the frequent power of affect as a system component, the cross-societal quasi-illegitimacy of negative affect appears worthy of mention. Hate systems are generally considered "bad," something to be avoided rather than sought or encouraged. They appear less common than systems involving positive affect. To implement a conflict system, accordingly, components generally define one another as hostile, evil, and different so as to legitimize the sending of hostility to one another. Unfavorable stereotypes (concerning certain ethnic minorities, for example) are common techniques along this line. Similarly, to implement a system of cooperation, components utilize favorable stereotyping and normally define one another as friendly, similar, and a "good guy." The World War II American image of "Uncle Joe" Stalin was portrayed while the Russians were American allies; it later changed with Cold War necessities.

For systems involving positive affect (for example, a friendship system), the development of negative affect within is especially proscribed. If it lasts long or comes often in systems such as friendship and marriage where it is illegitimate and inappropriate, the system may break.

Significantly, positive and negative affect each generally appear in a "bunch." Negative affect often simultaneously involves hostility, anxiety, doubt, and fear. Positive affect generally combines together and at the same time love, trust, confidence, and joy.

COMPONENTS OF LOW POWER

Components of low power carry certain distinctive marks. These stand almost as stigmata of the kicked. In describing lower-class persons, Knupfer[241] notes their habits of submission, their isolation from sending and receiving through their limited access to sources of information, and lack of verbal facility, and their absence of self-confidence. While without authority and power, they are found to be highly authoritarian in personality, intolerant of civil liberties, hostile to radical political positions (including those designed to elevate them), antagonistic to the strivings of ethnic minorities, suspicious of the motives of others, and pessimistic concerning mankind's chances.[242] In a *de facto* sense they are usually a significant force of stability, of resistance to change, of maintenance of the *status quo* in power distribution and other features of the social system. Generally they do not organize as a revolutionary bloc. In America many of their leaders (such as heads of labor unions) adopt middle-class norms in several realms of behavior.[243]

THE ACTION OF A SYSTEM WITH ITS COMPONENTS

Certain features of system/component action have been treated under system determinism and the reciprocal impact of system and components. Here the focus is upon what the data point to be a basic determinant of a system's action with its components: the kind of component involved. The findings suggest that a basic division occurs here between *pro*components and *contra*components.

One way of defining pro- and contracomponents would be to judge those that yield positive feedback to a system as pro, and those that send negative feedback to it as contra. When hostile to its goals or methods, for example, strong informal groups within an organization are found to hamper its output.[244]

Such negative feedback could in one sense be said to constitute contra-action.

For an understanding of system action, however, it is more useful to examine the system's own definitions of pro- and contracomponents. Top power structure appears its major definer here. Procomponents of a social system are those which top power structure regards as providing positive feedback for the system, including the power structure's direction thereof. Its contracomponents are those which top power structure perceives as providing negative feedback to the system and to itself. Power units generally equate system welfare with its own.

Top power structure's definitions of pro- and contracomponents tend generally to be shared within the system. It is this sharing that lies at the core of legitimacy of the power structure. When a situation arises in which the power structure's definitions of pro and contra differ from those of the rest of the system, the power structure may be said to lack legitimacy. Definitions of environments as pro and contra (friends and enemies) are similarly the products of a system's power structure. Whatever the humanitarian motives involved, Americans sending blood to the Viet Cong are likely to be defined by America's power structure as contracomponents giving aid and comfort to the enemy.

Since pro- and contracomponents as such come into system existence when they are so defined by power units, they are likely to be in flux as power structure shifts. Some procomponents—family and religion, for example—have generally stood quite firmly as defined bulwarks of stability. But different power units are likely to feel threatened by different things. To illustrate, pornography in America has ups and downs of formally enforced definition as contra. Significantly, however, it has never really crossed the line to the pro side: those rallying to its support usually defend it on artistic grounds rather than as enjoyable "fun" that is good for a social system.

Pro- and contracomponents are often systems in their own right with components of their own. A person may thus be affiliated with prosystems or contrasystems that operate as pro- and contracomponents within a larger milieu. A third category whose numbers are claimed to be growing in America would include persons who attach neither to pro- *nor* contrasystems: the relatively unaffiliated and uncommitted.[245]

Where a power structure is heterogeneous or vague and its action accordingly ambiguous (America's loose, differentiated "power elite" in contrast to a smaller, more monolithic, totalitarian structure), there is a corresponding difficulty in clearly categorizing certain components as pro or contra. The various subunits of power will have their own definitions not necessarily shared by others. Thus while a recent Gallup Poll [246] reveals a rather clear definition by Americans of the KKK as a contracomponent (seventy-six percent of respondents classified it as "highly unfavorable," one percent as "highly favorable") and the FBI as a procomponent (eighty-four percent classified it as "highly favorable," one percent as "highly unfavorable"), other components of American society were less clearly defined. The figures for some of the latter were:

	Percent "highly favorable"	*Percent "highly unfavorable"*
John Birch Society	3	40
Americans for Democratic Action	13	9
Congress of Racial Equality	17	17
National Association for the Advancement of Colored People	17	22
Daughters of the American Revolution	19	4
American Medical Association	50	3

Comparable figures on a Harris Survey [247] show Americans defining as contra-active:

	Percent Americans unwilling to vote for
Communist Party member	93
KKK member	84
Admitted atheist	76
Member of John Birch Society	61
Admitted agnostic	59

The less clear-cut nature of top power structure in democratic social systems and its multiple, varying definitions of certain components have meant that its self-protection from contra-action has similarly lacked clarity and precision. Totalitarian thrusts arising within democratic nations have often not immediately been defined and opposed as contracomponents.[248]

Significantly, certain political action in America appears directed against the very vagueness and ambiguity of our power structure which is a basic component of a democratic social system. An intolerance of ambiguity appears to characterize potential contracomponents of authoritarian mien such as the Minutemen.

While a modern nation's power structure may at times decorate its heroes or publish a list of its most dangerous public enemies, thorough and *public* data concerning its pro- and contracomponents are understandably not available. In a legitimately powered modern nation under normal conditions one might expect a majority of basically procomponents, a small minority of contracomponents, and a somewhat larger minority (depending upon the heterogeneity or vagueness of the power structure and its concurrent tolerance of particular components) judged as "irrelevant." These proportions may, also, change with circumstances. For a nation with an illegitimate power structure on the eve of a successful revolution, the proportion of contracomponents would expectedly be much higher than where a well-established, legitimate regime holds sway.

Some of the major procomponents of a normal modern nation are: (1) the legitimate political structure, (2) the economic structure, (3) the upper and middle classes, (4) the legitimate church or churches ("sects," in their initial stages especially, are defined as contracomponents[249]), (5) families, especially those of the upper and middle class, (6) the public education structure, and (7) women (especially wives and mothers), who appear generally conservative and supportive of the *status quo*.

Some of the major contracomponents of a normal modern nation would be: (1) out-of-power political groups seeking power illegitimately. These would include such groups as Communists in a non-Communist nation, anti-Communists in a Communist nation. People who feel apart and "out of it" are those quickest to overstep the bounds of legitimacy and become disruptively hostile.[250] (2) Religio-political groups hostile to the established values of the current regime; in the United States this would to some extent include the Black Muslims. (3) Blue-collar criminals; these would include assaulters, robbers, and burglars. White-collar criminals are usually not defined as distinctly contracomponents.

Hence, social systems and their power structures appear to define their components generally as pro and contra and to operate with them accordingly. This division of pro and contra is similar to the basic split between negative and positive affect in that the subtypes of each—for example, hostility and suspicion as negative affect, love and trust as positive—appear less important than the major division between them.

Components generally share the definition of themselves as pro or contra and regard themselves in the same way as their system does. *Procomponents* tend to feel they are pro; *contracomponents* normally see themselves as contra—at least vis-à-vis the power structure if not the system. Withdrawal (nonnormative autonomy) by a component usually means being defined as contra.[251] While certain kinds of withdrawal are tolerated in various social systems (for example, monks in a monastery in America), systems and their power structures tend generally to regard those members not "with" them as "against" them.

The major action of a system and its pro- and contracomponents, accordingly, may be divided as follows: (1) The system's action with its procomponents, (2) the system's action with its contracomponents, (3) the action of procomponents with one another, (4) the action of contracomponents with one another, and (5) the action of procomponents with contracomponents.

The first two types of action may be summarized as follows: A system and its power structure support (send positive affect and other rewards in the expectation that they will serve as positive feedback) their defined procomponents such as legitimate political units, the basic economic structure, upper and middle classes, legitimate religions, families, the public education structure, and mothers and wives. They attempt to discourage (usually by sending negative affect in the expectation—frequently unjustified—that it will provide negative feedback) contracomponents such as radical political and religious groups, blue-collar criminals, and withdrawers such as beatniks, draft dodgers, alcoholics, and drug addicts.

The second two kinds of action listed above may similarly be briefed: Procomponents appear to "hang together" (such as a church and a family in a silent or expressed conspiracy of support) and to send positive affect intended as positive feedback to one another. Contracomponents at times send positive affect to one another (in a "my enemy's enemy is my friend" system) but not necessarily. Their load of hostility often generalizes toward the society as a whole, pro- and contracomponents alike. Also, they may single out certain other contracomponents for special attack so as to provide a visible sign of their own legitimacy. The hostility of the American radical right for "beatniks, Vietniks, and queers" provides an illustration.

The fifth kind of action listed above—that of procomponents with contracomponents—generally involves a reciprocalism of hostility. The sending of negative affect by procomponents to contracomponents, however, appears *diffuse:* from all procomponents to all contracomponents. Contracomponents will sometimes select specific pro-units of the larger system as major targets of hostility: for example, the established political order.

The question of pro- and contracomponents thus appears intimately tied up with the question of power. As noted, it is the power components of a social system who define its other components as pro and contra: its robbers and drug addicts as bad, its willing soldiers as good. Scholars have sometimes described norm conformity and deviance as if these fundamentally statistical terms were empirically meaningful in social action. They have at times used servo-mechanistic models such as a heating-system thermostat: suggesting, for example, that when the deviation from a norm reaches a particular scale point, the norm regulators come into play and restore equilibrium to the system.

Significantly, however, it is not the empirical fact of norm conformity or deviance upon which the classification of pro or contra appears to depend. Norms (modal action) in large social systems of low organization such as nations are frequently vague and ambiguous, and deviation from these norms in an empirical sense, poorly defined. Complicating the picture, too, is the factor of secrecy: much of what we do goes unobserved, even by ourselves. No one—not even "norm regulators"—can be empirically sure how much scale-deviation is actually involved in a particular situation. The cry of "norm deviation," when it occurs, appears generally to serve as a technique of control by power components or those desiring power. It is a social label without any necessary foundation in actual behavior of the conformer or the deviate.

Thus power components throughout history have at times been thoroughly deviant from existent norms and have gone unnoticed. It would be structurally a contradiction for power components to define themselves (or permit themselves to be so defined) as deviant and contra. There is evidence also that many components (quiet deviates, and funny deviates) are more tolerated because their deviance involves no open hostility toward the power structure or others. They are not regarded as threats sending negative feedback. While the servo-mechanistic model of the thermostat may be tentatively appropriate in system situations such as speeding (at fifteen miles above the speed limit on certain highways or in a radar trap, the patrol car is alerted, the chase made, and the ticket given), such automatic action by a power structure through its agents, or procomponents, appears quite rare in the totality of social system action. When it occurs it is generally in relatively insignificant areas of system action such as speeding. Even here it has been observed that certain deviates have been able to get such tickets "fixed" if they wished.

It is relevant in the present connection that the cry of "norm deviation" is often used by components seeking power to castigate those currently on the throne. Revolutionaries have frequently sought to paint the established power as behaving deviantly (former Senator McCarthy, for example, with his allusions to Communists in the State Department of the United States) while seeking for themselves the image of defenders-of-the-norms and the faith (one hundred and twenty-five percent American). Relevant too is the finding that components of a social system tend to be described as conformative by those components who like them, and as deviant by those who dislike them.[252] The inadequacy of empirically objective measures of pro and contra appears also in the fact that while certain components are defined as contra, their behavior may involve little if any real threat. Drug addicts, while generally classified in America as contracomponents, appear little motivated toward a seizure of political or other power. Pornography may reduce rather than raise social tensions; it may provide a withdrawal from crime rather than a precipitate. Similarly, much empirically real contra-action does not get defined as such. This is especially true where a power structure is heterogeneous or vague and where the contra-action is itself subtle, ambiguous, and unconscious. The basic antiestablishmentism underlying much "camp" and "pop" art goes generally unrecognized by America's power structure.

It is likewise worthy of note that components defined as pro are not always or necessarily *implementive* of system action; often they develop their own norms. These norms—while the mutual confidence game involved in a power structure's action with its procomponents keeps the process low-key and the power structure wears self-constructed blinders concerning it—may often impede total system action. The informal work groups that develop in a factory do often heighten output,[253] cohesion and ease of internal communication,[254] and do lessen absenteeism and turnover in personnel.[255] They are found essential too to the fighting efficiency of soldiers.[256] At the same time, certain norms of these informal subsystems (although the latter retain their general definition as procomponents) may effectively oppose the power structure's direction of the larger system. The Bank Wiring Room provides a vivid example.[257] Similarly, instances occur where management seeks higher profits by cutting quality but work-group norms resist the change.[258] Yet a power structure rarely defines as "deviant" the action of its usual procomponents. Its legitimacy depends on its support by such traditional procomponents; the measure of a legitimate and effective law is the law's adherence with the norms of the system's usual pro-units. The rigid enforcement of laws incongruent with these norms—as in the case of the Eighteenth Amendment in America and the United States Army's official ban on "fraternization" with civilians during the early days of occupation of German territory at the end of World War II[259]—places the power structure in a risky position difficult to maintain.

The flexibility of the label "norm deviate," in any case, makes it empirically of little utility as an accurate measure of system action and an unlikely basis for defining contracomponents. The significant thing in classifying pro and contra, as Humpty Dumpty pointed out to Alice in a comparable context, is *who has the power.*

It has been noted that large social systems appear especially unable to make empirically based judgments of pro- and contra-components. Stereotyped definitions of pro and contra—Jews are crafty and will "take over," Negroes are lazy and will slow down the work, blue-eyed persons are honest while dark-eyed persons lie—are found often to flourish in such large social systems of low organization. Stereotype composites normally strive for positive feedback confirming them. They appear most likely to disintegrate where the group is small and highly organized (for example, a friendship), where association occurs under nonstereotype norms, and where inflow from environments involving the old stereotype is avoided. It is important to emphasize that definitions of pro and contra are specific to the social system in question and to its power structure. For the United States as a total system the National Guard is a procomponent; its use to enforce Negro civil rights in Mississippi, however, can serve to be defined in this situation as contra-active by the local Mississippi power structure. Similarly, if the Negro poverty and civil rights movement, in frustration concerning the lessening of Federal interest and support for its program because of the Vietnamese War, should seek to oppose present American action in Vietnam, it runs the risk of being defined by the national power structure as a contracomponent. The Negro rights movement thus finds itself today in certain positions of structural tension.[260]

PROCOMPONENTS

Procomponents are doers, teachers, and enforcers of usual system action. For this structural reason procomponents such as police and teachers are normally discouraged by a power structure from having a genuine union involving autonomy from the power structure. For this reason, too, "academic freedom" constitutes an area of tension. The stability and manipulative force of a system's power structure require that its usual procomponents and agents of stability (especially such communicative ones as teachers) visibly remain pro and do not engage in political, sexual, or other contra-action. A withdrawal of teachers or students from institutionalized expectations in this regard is likely to create anxiety. The student-administered "para-colleges" and "free universities" that have recently arisen alongside the established universities in Palo Alto, Gainesville, Ann Arbor, Boulder, Austin, San Francisco, Los Angeles, New York, and Chicago have generally met various kinds of negative response from the educational and other power structures. Dr. John R. Everett, president of the New School for Social Research (in its early days somewhat radical, now more thoroughly part of the educational establishment), is reported as stating: "I doubt the free universities serve any academic purpose. It is a protest without a clear understanding of what they (the students) are protesting against." [261]

Where procomponents and their socialization toward system norms are relatively lacking, contra-action appears likely. Workers isolated from the impact of community subgroups, which are normally pro, are found often to show a political liberalism [262] of contra potential. Where family (normally a prime procomponent) ties are loose, the members are more likely to engage in contra behavior politically and socially, and they are more likely to become juvenile delinquents. [263] Suicide, a withdrawal type of contra-action, is especially high where procomponent impact is low—among the single, widowed, and divorced rather than the married, among those unattached to churches rather than the affiliated, and in the center of the city where other contra-action similarly flourishes.[264] Sykes [265] notes that if the individual lacks attachment to primary groups that support pro norms or identifies himself with other groups which place a value on violating the laws of the larger society, the likelihood of crime increases. Relatively more criminals and delinquents come from broken homes, from broken marriages, from families that have moved around and been poorly tied to community pro groups than from families that have been able to remain unified and attached to community pro groups reinforcing their pro socialization.[266] Marital conflict appears specifically disturbing to efficient pro socialization: there is evidence that the delinquency rate is higher for those whose parents have been separated or divorced than for those who have lost a parent by death.[267] The presence or absence of pro controls is considered by some scholars to be the fundamental factor in juvenile delinquency.[268] Power structure has to strengthen its formal enforcers, such as policemen and judges, where informal pro socialization and pro enforcement are weak—as among lower-class Negroes in America. Discriminatory action by formal enforcers against Negro delinquents is found to be common.[269]

Systems vary in their regulation of their procomponents. Significant are (1) the kind of procomponent and (2) the kind of system—and their conceptions of legitimate and desirable manipulation. As noted, procomponents of authoritarian type generally desire strong direction from the power structure. A relatively light direction conduces to morale among procomponents more democratically oriented, as in most American social systems. In a study of American office work groups, for example, supervision by the larger system was varied as follows: for two offices there was close supervision from "above," in two similar offices there was a delegation of authority to the office staff itself. It was found that morale and satisfaction with the company increased in the "autonomous" offices and declined in the "hierarchically controlled" offices.[270] In a study of an American national health organization, similarly, a greater autonomy for its local units in the spending of funds helped to heighten the "vitality" of these local units.[271]

Productive of both procomponent morale and system output is a procomponent's perception of his own goals as synonymous or identical with those of the larger system.[272] The true organization man thoroughly equates his personal welfare with the organization's welfare. (It will be remembered that power units do the same thing.) His private goals are system goals. Riecken and Homans [273] suggest that the aims of pro members must be partially submerged to the requirements of total system action. Their full emergence would hamper both system output and pro-component welfare because of the effects of task failure (and a consequent dearth of external rewards) upon member satisfaction.

Pro-units hang together in clusters. Much of their strength lies in the fact that they do not stand alone. They form alliances, formally and informally, with other procomponents. In the taming of the American West, "law and order," established religion, and wife-and-mother women helped to convert it from a place of wild drunkenness, harlotry, and quick-on-the-trigger action to one of greater stability. However, old systems rarely die and thoroughly fade away; parts of them hang on in new configurations. Remnants of the old Wild West may still be found today in the radical political movements and song-and-dance senators of California.

The clustering of procomponents of top power constitutes an *establishment*. At the national level there generally appears a formal or informal alignment of the established political order, top economic leadership, the religious hierarchy, upper-class and upper-middle-class families, and a system of private education that provide support and positive feedback for one another. Members of top level ethnic and religious bodies are found to support the established, conservative political parties.[274] Generally, too, persons attached to one pro-unit will be attached to others as well. Devotion to stable family life is found to go along with attachment to established religion.[275] The proper Yale man is traditionally supportive of God and country too. It is the complex of pro-units that sets overall system tone and provides the realm of study for "culture and personality." Authoritarianism within one pro-unit such as the family, for example, is likely to be duplicated and triplicated within the established religion and the political order and to set a distinctive tone for the system as a whole. Adorno *et al.*[276] have studied this composite in Germany.

CONTRACOMPONENTS

The greater the heterogeneity among components of a social system, the greater appears the likelihood of contra-action by some. In cities characterized by great ethnic diversity, for example, crime rates are high.[277] Contra-units, however, appear to tolerate little diversity within themselves. This probably depends essentially upon the hostile environment they perceive to surround them. The data suggest that the more thoroughly a contra-unit is a "minority," the more solidly unified and organized will be its ideology.[278]

Contracomponents appear more variable in their diachronic action than do pro-units. With time, contracomponents sometimes move or are moved closer to pro norms. The greater rewards generally accruing to procomponents, however, appear to hold them more thoroughly to behavior as procomponents; they seem rarely motivated toward contra-action.

A description of contracomponent fluidity along this line comes from American labor union action. While often quite contra in its original action, as a union grows it becomes more like management and other bureaucratic pro-units of the larger milieu: it takes over certain traditional functions of management such as recruitment, discipline, and promotion, adopts management points of view and practice, such as a desire for professionalization of its staff, and it develops a bureaucracy of its own as its leadership changes from charismatic to organizational. It centralizes its practices, lessens its demands upon management, and loses the active participation of an increasing proportion of its members who consider it less and less as "their" union;[279] hence, it becomes converted by the larger system.

The greater the perceived opportunity for upward mobility within a social system, the less appears the contra-action within it. Lipset and Linz[280] find that a society's lower classes are least contra-active where a strong emphasis exists on the possibility of upward movement.

Contra-action involving withdrawal, as in "beatnikism," appears less threatening to a system's power structure than does active opposition. While it is generally discouraged it meets with less severity than overt political revolt. Lipset[281] suggests that withdrawal can serve as a somewhat more legitimate functional alternative to political extremism. Organized radicalism in politics, he notes, made little headway during the Depression in

America. But small religious sects offering other-worldly rewards grew rapidly.

In the same way as pro-units encourage the learning of pro norms, subsystems of contra-action teach contra norms. Delinquent gangs move their members toward delinquency in several ways: [282] by promoting hostility toward procomponents such as community agencies of social control, by teaching techniques of crime and a general pattern of destructiveness, by setting up a status system awarding top prestige to criminals of highest daring and skill, and by serving as a medium of contact for beginners in crime, more experienced juvenile offenders, and adult criminals.

Men appear the major contra-actors. Biological factors, such as the greater male strength and agility, as well as social factors are probably involved. While official statistics carry a bias in favor of women,[283] the general preponderance of men among criminals is still basic. Cressey [284] considers sex status to be of greater statistical significance in differentiating criminals from noncriminals than any other single trait. Even allowing for the statistical bias in favor of women, men are probably six to seven times as criminal as women.[285] This favorable prejudice toward women in regard to crime—their lesser likelihood of arrest, indictment, conviction, and sentencing than men for the same offense—suggests further the essential irrelevance of empirical deviance as a definer of contra-action. A power-unit overlooks a lot of deviance by its generally bona fide pro persons such as women, especially wives and mothers. Often it chooses not to believe the evidence of female contra-action as this would mean negative feedback for its usual expectations. Powerful in the acquittal of church-going Lizzie Borden for the axe-murder of her parents was the jury's belief in the utter unlikelihood of the offense.

There is some evidence today that as women extend their sphere of social participation their criminal activity will increase [286] and their pro image commensurately lessen. It is worthy of note that in social systems where criminal contra-action is high—in cities, for example, and among low-power ethnic minorities such as Negroes in America—women appear more contra-active than they do in systems where contra-action is generally low, as in the upper and middle classes. The difference in crime rate between men and women narrows in large cities and among Negroes.[287] While the generally harsher treatment of lower-class Negroes of both sexes by official enforcers[288] is conceivably a factor, there may be other forces at work as well.

The relative immunity from prosecution of the white-collar criminal has received significant attention.[289] It may relate essentially to the usual high-level pro position of white-collar criminals (corporation executives practicing fraud, for example) and the reluctance to define their behavior (whatever it may be) as contra-action threatening to the power structure. But lower-class delinquents receive harsh treatment by agencies of pro control (police and juvenile courts) and figure disproportionately in the official statistics of crime.[290] Out-of-power ethnic minorities such as Negroes,[291] Puerto Ricans, Mexicans, and American Indians in the United States are subjected to similar harsh treatment. At the same time it is likely that their out-of-power position does drive these groups toward more actual contra-action in the form of crime.[292]

A clustering of blue-collar crime in the late teens and early adult years marks Western civilization.[293] These are the years normally freest from the usual pro impact of family. The individual is detached from his family of orientation, not yet formative of his family of procreation.

The lessened impact of organized religion likewise functions in much blue-collar crime. Rates are generally lower for persons belonging to a church and attending services regularly.[294] Blue-collar crime abounds in slums where family and church are weak[295] and contracomponents hold sway as socializers.[296]

Contra-action lessens when environment threatens. In times of war, disaster and physical calamity, crimes and suicides, divorces and community conflicts dwindle in number.[297] Within a military organization a sudden reduction in internal tensions and delinquencies occurs when war comes.[298]

Large social systems accommodate contra-action most readily. Cities rather than small towns tolerate strongholds of crime within, as in slums.[299] A greater tolerance of religious and political radicalism similarly marks the urban milieu.[300] Cities are generally of lower organization than small towns. Contra-action has milder impact, may more readily be hidden from view, and is less easily regulated by enforcers. What passes as the virtue of tolerance is more properly a structural correlate of low organization. A comparable rise in tolerance toward unresolved differences and conflicts marks small, informal groups as they grow larger.[301]

While less so than procomponents, contracomponents sometimes do get together. For temporary political advantage, hostile contra-units such as Communists and fascists may work as a team to upset an established regime. Professional criminals combine too in treating all insiders of crime as "right" and all outsiders as "slaves." [302] But on the matter of honor, thieves are probably no better than the rest of us. They do "rat" on one another. And defectors from the Communist Party and the KKK "sing."

CHAPTER **3**

THE ACTION WITH ENVIRONMENT

THE MOVEMENT OF ENERGY/INFORMATION

A social system is normally *open*—that is, engaged in action with its environments. From them it receives; to them it sends. This movement in and out may involve any kind of energy/information: people, things, ideas, and affect. Inflow moves in, outflow leaves. These comings and goings move through system components serving as gateways. Moreover, components serving as gateways of inflow are often at the same time gateways of outflow as well. A secretary-receptionist may perform both duties, letting certain people and things in to see the boss and moving others (for example, letters) to various environments outside. Cities, too, are apt to be channels of both inflow and outflow. Important cities have sprung up at transportation breaks (for example, land-sea).[1]

All things entering and leaving, it should be emphasized, are *total*-systemic in their impact. They get with, or out of, all system action—directly on their own steam and/or indirectly through the gateway component they influence and the latter's impact on the system. In the oral hygiene system portrayed in Chapter 1, Figure 2 for example, a new type of dentifrice that enters through the person's buying it may quickly influence other parts of the system: the stiffness of toothbrush, the frequency of brushing, and the interest in brushing.

Regular action with any environment gets normatively structured. Thus people tend to behave in the same way toward all kin they call by the same name (for example, "brother," "sister," and "uncle").[2]

Gateways

Inflow and outflow with environments do not happen indiscriminately. As noted, specific gateways of entry and exit occur. And there are keepers of these gates. In self-systems (those involving one person only, together with relevant ideas, emotions, artifacts, and the like) the gate protectively responsible for a particular "lack of insight," into a trait of one's personality, for example, is specific to one thing rather than a blocker of all inflow.[3] Gatekeepers, moreover, do not arise on their own steam. They depend on a system's identity and leadership for their action. The more clear-cut this identity and leadership, the more rigid will gatekeepers be. To illustrate, the patterns of action of both upper and lower classes in America are more clearly defined than are those of the middle. Also, upper and lower classes are residentially most rigidly segregated.[4]

Norms of gateway action develop. Often they coincide with comparable norms of other systems operative with the system in question. A rather constant movement of about thirty percent of each generation out of the nonfarm working class and into the middle class has been found—and vice versa although somewhat less. This holds true, too, for the United States, Germany, Sweden, Japan, France, Switzerland, Denmark, Great Britain, and Italy.[5] Systems with much movement in, too, are likely to have much movement out.[6] (This relates interestingly to the finding in Chapter 2 that big senders within a system are big receivers as well.) Systems of easy "come"—unskilled occupations, for example —are also systems of easy "go." They are moved into and out of a great deal.[7] Their gatekeepers are minimal.

Large systems generally have rather lax doormen. Gatecrashing, for example, is easier at large parties than at small, intimate gatherings. Where the system numbers few components the new entrant is most likely to have an impact, and to be noticed. The more different are social systems, too, the more closed will they be to one another. Along with the more clear-cut differences between classes in village than city, for example, are stricter doormen at the gates. Class mobility is less in the small town than in the metropolis.[8] Similarly, the military's separate patterns of action for officers and enlisted men go along with rigid gateways permitting only certain kinds of communication between these groups.[9] A like situation of communication restriction exists between different ranks in government bureaucracy.[10]

When systems are unlike, this difference hinders movement between them. The lower-class person—handicapped by habits of submission, little access to information, a lack of both verbal facility and self-confidence—is often afraid to enter many social systems (for example, higher education) of middle-class America.[11] The *closedness* of gateways to inflow from a system that is different can also set an amplification spiral in operation. Each increase in dissimilarity amplifies the rigidity of doormen; each increase in doorman rigidity heightens the imbreeding and dissimilarity. The relative openness of gatekeepers to inflow from a system that is *similar* may similarly set an amplification spiral going. For the movement of energy/information among any systems heightens their similarity.[12] The frequent movement of energy/information between systems that are already similar increases this similarity. And this further widens their gateways, producing still more similarity.

Berelson *et al.*[13] find an intensification of difference between rival parties during a political campaign when members of each party erect stricter gatekeepers restraining their contact with the opposition. This solidification of gateways accompanies a heightened frequency of contact within each party—and a heightened specificity and homogeneity of opinion within. A comparable situation occurred in the industries of mining, lumbering, fishing, and shipping. Physical factors isolated them and blocked their contact with the larger milieu. Their identity developed separately and uniquely along specific lines because of their isolation from the heterogeneous cross-pressures of the larger system. Often they grew in politico-economic ways defined by the latter as radical contra-action.[14]

Where the ratio of farm laborers to farm owners is low, similarly, gatekeepers are few. Contact between farm owners and laborers is easy and frequent. Farm laborers tend to share the farm owner's house—and his values. They are less likely to identify with a farm-labor class group and to be reached by leftist appeals.[15]

Gatekeeper action thus varies by type of inflow and outflow, and by type of system. In marital systems, regardless of their form, gateways to and from environmental sex tend officially to be closed. Only five societies out of one hundred and forty-eight that were studied by Murdock [16] freely allowed adultery. Similarly, gateways influence *quantity* as well as *type* of inflow. Some systems are thus more open than others to ideas, artifacts, or people from outside. A larger quantity of inflow from a greater number of sources reaches them. This applies to self-systems as well as to those involving many people. Lazarsfeld [17] and Riley and Riley [18] find that moviegoers are also radio listeners, magazine readers are also television fans, and nearly all of them also read newspapers regularly. Broad spectrum gateways of inflow, through their action as opinion leaders,[19] tend to be relatively open gateways of outflow as well.

Gatekeepers are a major bulwark of system stability. The barriers imposed by the gatekeepers of marriage—so that exit through divorce is costly in time, energy, and money—do lengthen the time-span of marital systems. These gatekeepers of pro-unit (the family) stability, when not imposed by the pro-unit itself, are generally set up by the larger system's power structure. The early "mistake" of the Soviet regime whereby divorce was made easy and frequent after the Revolution of 1917 gave way to the more normal situation of strict national guards on the borders of matrimony.

The more elaborate and rigid a gatekeeper, the more does an aspiring entrant (or exiter, as in escape from a prison camp) prize getting through. Entrance to an exclusive club brings greater joy than successful entry into one whose doormen (with uniform and without) are less selective. Festinger [20] finds that a person exercising great effort to reach an objective tends to persuade himself of its special desirability. What is or has been hard to attain becomes valuable. The evidence here relates to the *labor theory of value* which suggests that the value of an item varies directly with the effort, or labor, expended in its production. Persons paying an emotional price for admission to a group found its meeting more stimulating and its members more likable than did persons who had no difficulty entering.[21]

In a large and heterogeneous social system where power units compete, each strives to be or dominate the gatekeepers of the whole society. For this, it is at least covertly recognized, means genuine power and control. Censorship Boards normally do not seek specifically to censor entry or circulation within their own committee. They aim to be the city's or the nation's gatekeeper.

Gateways of Inflow

A system's major gatekeepers are those of inflow. Social systems are generally more concerned about what comes in than what goes out because the former more visibly involves the threat of negative feedback. Environmental threat alerts gatekeepers to keep it out. Along with—if not as a result of—this shoring up of the barricades against a hostile presence in the environment, internal hostility drops. It drops not only in systems involving people but in those of other animals as well. Konrad Lorenz [22] reports marital peace between a pair of cichlid fish only when the male's hostility was directed toward another male in an adjacent part of the tank. When the male's vision of this other fish was obscured by algae growth on the glass that separated them, he picked on the female. Similarly, a child may in some cases promote husband-wife "togetherness" by providing them with an outside target for the hostility previously hurled at one another.

At any event, systems that remain peacefully intact longest generally have an environment that threatens. Enemies outside raise friendliness within—and joint efforts at defense. Where people in a voting district feel politically threatened by the population groups which surround them, they devote themselves assiduously to politics.[23] Similarly, where a social system's opinions are threatened from outside, heightened bonds of mutual identification develop among its members who share these opinions.[24]

Gateways—of inflow and outflow—are generally dependent variables of a social system. They are normally built by power structure or those seeking it. They are customarily designed to encourage the entry of items which the power structure perceives as providing positive feedback to itself and to the system (friends) and to discourage the entry of items which the power structure regards as negative feedback for itself and for the system (enemies). To illustrate, the good gatekeeper-secretary lets through persons, telephone calls, and information helpful to the boss and the company while restricting others. Crime and violence in the mass media, similarly, are normally permitted or prohibited entry to the extent that they reinforce or inhibit a basic line of system action.[25] For self-systems in which they provide no feedback and are thus neutral items, they are generally unattended to as irrelevant.[26] But where they do get in and no other foci of identity exist, they may serve to establish one that will then seek reinforcement. As a system develops a more clear-cut identity, as it takes stands vis-à-vis an increasingly broad scope of action and opinion and erects gatekeepers accordingly, less and less inflow will be neutral.

While gateways are normally agents of a system's power structure, they often elaborate as systems in their own right. Here they may develop a power structure and identity of their own which could move them toward a relative autonomy from the larger system's manipulation. Should this occur, they become potential of contra-action. A system's power structure, to retain effectiveness, must carefully police its doormen and keep them from "going into business for themselves."

Chapter 2 noted a power structure's tendency to equate itself and its welfare with that of the system. It is important to emphasize that definitions of environmental "friends" and "enemies," along with definitions of internal pro- and contracomponents, are creations of a system's power structure. It is not the empirical, objective action of an environment that determines its definition as friend or enemy. It may in a real sense provide positive feedback to a system and its power structure and still be defined as an enemy—and vice versa. Moreover, it is often the power unit's line of action rather than the power unit itself that receives maximum protection. Custer's action as director of his men at the Battle of the Little Big Horn was personally and systemically catastrophic, but consistent with his normally headstrong style of leadership.

Doormen of inflow tend to be tighter the higher the status of the social system. To illustrate, occupations that rank high are hardest to enter. And while an upper-class person may enter a lower-class pub and be served, it would be difficult for his lower-class bar friend to follow him into his exclusive gentlemen's club.

A system's doormen selectively expose it to environmental input along lines of its existent action.[27] Farmers involved with strong opinions tend not to hear the radio material with which they disagree.[28] Similarly, congenial rather than uncongenial rumors are permitted entry and passed on.[29] For systems, it will be shown, achieve positive feedback through their sending as well as their receiving. From its environments, in any case, a system's doormen of inflow select what the system can use in reinforcing its present action and then harmonize it with their present action. From the Lone Ranger's activities, children deeply involved in peer-group play chose those items that implemented this play. They related their reading of Westerns to "playing guns" in the woods afterwards.[30]

Gatekeeper action sometimes takes the form of a decreased awareness of environment that is threatening.[31] At other times a mechanism of repression appears to operate.[32] Jews in Hitler's Germany often ignored the signs of impending catastrophe. The line of present action, not welfare, was given protection. Advance warning of a coming natural disaster such as a tornado or a flood can similarly be repressed or distorted. Many people will deny or disbelieve information that such danger is at hand. They seize upon any vagueness, ambiguity, or contradiction in the warning that makes it possible for them to interpret the situation optimistically. Often they continue to interpret heralds of danger as signs of familiar, normal events (hence positive feedback) until it is too late to take effective precautions.[33]

The selective action of system doormen is vividly portrayed in the gatekeeping done by the pupil of the eye. When pleasant objects (those involving positive feedback) appear in the environment, the pupil dilates measurably. Distasteful materials produce contraction.[34] Acknowledged male homosexuals could be distinguished from normal heterosexuals of both sexes simply by their different pupillary response to photographs of male and female pin-ups. In one experiment none of the heterosexual males showed a totally negative response to the pictures of women. Conversely, no male homosexual or female heterosexual showed a positive response to the pictures of women. And while the female heterosexuals and the male homosexuals gave similar responses, the male homosexuals showed a much greater rejection of the pictures of women than did the female subjects.[35]

Gatekeeper action, in any case, is a general feature of social systems. It makes scientific as well as other objectivity difficult. For gatekeepers tend to ignore, disregard, distort, or denigrate environmental data not providing positive feedback, and to be especially alert to that which does. The researcher seeking external confirmation of his hypothesis is likely to find it in the same way as the pathologist searching for a particular microbe under a microscope is more apt to find it than is the person for whom the presence of that microbe represents no positive feedback.[36] In hypochondriacal systems, similarly, there is an acute sensitivity to sensations that most people ignore.[37] Interviewers bring back responses which support their biases.[38] And it has been suggested that psychotherapists may reinforce their particular brand of psychotherapeutic action by a special openness to patients' responses of the desired kind, and a selective encouragement of these responses.[39]

What is needed from the environment for positive feedback thus appears at the forefront of doorman attention. As advertisers have discovered, the presentation of information relevant to the satisfaction of needs is accepted more fully after than before these needs are aroused.[40] Hungry subjects report more food objects in vague "pictures," which are actually just smudges, than do less hungry subjects.[41] Persons involved systemically with rigid stereotypes of ethnic minorities are found in laboratory experiments to react in stereotypic fashion to a wide variety of environmental inflow.[42] This may reflect less an intolerance of ambiguity *as such* than a normal seeking of positive feedback. For vague, ambiguous inflow generally is twisted to provide reinforcement.[43] It is found that when they involve a stereotype as a component, systems through their doorman action either (1) block out, (2) twist to fit the stereotype, or (3) judge as vastly different and thus irrelevant to the stereotype any inflow which departs significantly from this stereotype.[44]

Various gateway devices are utilized to shut out the possibility of negative feedback. Rotter[45] notes Rubinstein and Parloff's[46] observation concerning a professional meeting of psychologists and psychotherapists: "Although one of the prime purposes of the conference, as described in the original plan, was to provide 'a comprehensive picture of the status of research on the effects of psychotherapy,' as if by some tacit agreement the issue of outcome was skirted by the conference." Such resistance to the possibility of negative feedback has been a major force impeding the objective study of social systems and their power structures. Researchers have usually found that the "evaluation" most social systems really want is praise. It is a basic factor in the late entry of science into the study of social systems. Not until the late nineteenth century did the empirical, experimental, systematic, operational, scientific investigation of human behavior really begin.[47] For the study of any system is incomplete without an examination of the power structure which manipulates it and its components. The more potentially threatening along lines of negative feedback the study of any system to that system and its power structure—or to a related system's power structure—the less likely will be such study if the relevant power structures (or those striving for power) are capable and desirous of preventing it. Such was the case in the hue and cry raised in Latin America to the attempted study of power and insurgency by the now famous *Project Camelot.*

It is no accident, then, that analytic, objective investigation has fared best under conditions of low authoritarianism in the power structure. The more potentially threatening a particular area of study, the later and the more difficult has been its development. Sciences most intimate to man and thus most frightening for power structures have come last. Astronomy developed before geography, physical science before biology, medicine before psychology—although in each case the availability of data was in the reverse order.[48] The more extensive and clear-cut a system's power structure, too, the more directive it is of system operation and concurrent gateway action. The more rigidly selective will be its doormen of both inflow and outflow. Even in America, entering the ranks of the business elite from lower echelons rarely occurs. Only ten-to-twenty percent of American business elite have risen to it from below.[49] The sons of men at the top of the economic structure in the United States have five-to-eight times more chance to succeed their fathers than would be the case if the top level were completely open to entry from below.[50] Realistic acceptance of this gatekeeper may be a significant factor keeping the vocational aspirations of children of various social classes in line with it. A Midwestern study shows seventy-seven percent of adolescents from the upper economic structure aspiring to professions and business while only seven percent from the lower structure indicates this vocational aim.[51] Where power components have a low birth rate and are thus least able to replace themselves through reproduction, significantly, their gatekeepers to entry from below appear to relax.[52]

Deep involvement—what French existentialists have labeled *engagement*—in an issue means a clarity of system direction and action, a heightened gatekeeper capacity to distinguish environmental friends and enemies and to permit or deny them entry. The more thoroughly is a person tied to an issue, the more resistant will he be to the entry of items out of line with it.[53] In one experiment Boy Scouts were exposed to a speaker who criticized their basic program of camping and outdoor life. When queried privately later, those Scouts deeply involved in scouting were found most likely to disregard this attempt at negative feedback and to retain their high evaluation of scouting.[54] Similarly, political partisans involved deeply in an election campaign seek most thoroughly the positive feedback involved in their own party's propaganda.[55] And they retain it longest [56] because it coincides best with their action, while rejecting and forgetting easily the other side's arguments. People already active in a cause, too, are most likely to notice the material designed to recruit additional volunteers.[57] Star and Hughes,[58] evaluating an intensive campaign to inform the people of Cincinnati about the United Nations, concluded that the people reached by the campaign were those least in need of it and that those missed by it were the new audience it had hoped to gain.

Much of this gatekeeper action is unconscious. Those who report themselves as undecided on a controversial political issue still manage to expose themselves predominantly to the side their class and other affiliations would normally lead them to support.[59] Whether he is aware of it or not, a person hears what he wants to and reads the things that support what he wants to believe.[60] Once a line of system action is formed, whatever this may be, gatekeepers of inflow arise to protect it. Even a newly acquired opinion will be immediately protected from inflow that challenges it.[61] "Facts" that dispute it are as easily protected against as other kinds of inflow.[62] When any two items of contradictory information are presented, the item presented first will dominate the impression received because doormen are immediately built to protect it.[63] The first-in-time position provides especially great protection for highly "desirable" items, those of strong positive feedback; [64] it provides enhanced protection also for highly "relevant" items [65] because they do the same thing.

This first-in-time factor is of far-reaching significance. Because of it the young child's early inflow from environment—and the gatekeepers that arise to protect it—carry lifelong power. Psychiatric observations, experimental work with animals, and systematic data on socialization in human subjects all point to the power of early experience.[66] The child's early receiving from parents, siblings, and peer-group, which reaches him while he lies open and unprotected, remains with him as the essential core of his adult identity. The ghetto has provided a certain protection for the young Negro child from hostility by particular segments of the white environment. As the ghetto goes, it could mean that he will be exposed earlier, and thus even more profoundly, to the trauma of racial prejudice.

This is not to suggest that new systems are necessarily amorphous in identity and unprotected by gatekeepers. Many systems, new political parties, for example, begin with a rather clear-cut line of action only to grow increasingly entropic as their numbers grow; their heterogeneity mounts and their internal organization lessens. As they move toward majority position they strive to become all things to all people.

Changing a system is most difficult where its action and inner direction are clear-cut. Here its doormen are most protective against negative feedback, for the latter is easiest to perceive. The mass media are generally ineffective against staunch gatekeeper action. Regardless of the issue—vote intentions, tendencies toward or away from delinquency, general orientation to life and its problems—Klapper [67] finds the mass media more likely to reinforce than to change. The media are more effective in reactivating a latent taste, for instance for good music, than in introducing it.[68]

Generally, environments that are similar to the components of a system are perceived as most likely to provide positive feedback for it and are thus most apt to be permitted entry by its doormen. People tend to talk to others of similar political and other persuasion [69] so as to reinforce their own ideas and action. Gatekeeper operation has meant that in American immigration policy, immigrants from the Protestant and Caucasian nations of northern and western Europe, who are most similar to and thus perceived as least threatening by American power units, have been admitted most freely in the past. A reshuffling of immigration barriers to the United States at the present time suggests a concurrent reshuffling of the traditional power structure of America; some recent power changes here have been described by Baltzell.[70] Evidence of doorman openness to inflow similar to the existent system appears also in the movement of sons into their fathers' occupational systems. In the United States sons are more apt to take up their father's occupation than any other single one.[71] Similarly, unskilled workers, when they are moving upward, are more likely to enter the ranks of semiskilled workers than those of professionals.[72]

Gatekeepers have often been more permissive of artifact entry than of items of nonmaterial culture. Tools and clothing generally find their way in more readily than do religious ideas or new forms of social organization.[73] Systems thus appear able to adapt many artifacts to their present line of action so that they constitute positive feedback. Religious ideas and new forms of social organization, however, are likely to require a profound change in existing structures.

Systems distinct in their action, with comparably rigid doormen, tend toward a high level of organization. Lasswell and Kaplan [74] find in these systems a tendency for members to identify strongly with one another and to be mutually impactful. Here, too, gatekeeper action can be cumulative and mutually sustaining. For example, gatekeepers of higher education have required entry qualifications of proper secondary schooling and tuition money. Gatekeepers guarding well-paying occupations have required a college or professional degree. The poor are involved in a vicious circle of multiple gatekeeper action in which poverty means early working and an inability to complete secondary school, thus preventing entry to higher education. This in turn prevents the taking up of well-paying occupations which means continued poverty and early working.[75]

Where normal gatekeepers relax, items of negative feedback may enter. Chapter 2 noted the internal walls which occur within a social system, separating certain of its features. In this connection, social systems in which hostility is illegitimate, such as a friendship or a marriage, may temporarily erect internal screens preventing all communication when disagreement occurs lest hostility flourish. Should this barrier to communication be lifted, a quick increase in hostile communication may result.[76] It is important to note that gatekeepers do not in themselves produce a particular emotional response. Hostility, for example, is likely to arise only from gatekeepers' perceivedly illegitimate action. The normative, legitimate, relatively rigid caste barriers of the past in India and in America's Old South produced little hostility. Similarly, the normative, relatively light, class barriers of America have generally occasioned little interclass hostility.[77] It is this presence or absence of legitimacy for gatekeepers which appears crucial. The externally induced removal of caste barriers in communities of the Deep South, where these barriers still carry a great deal of local legitimacy, has at times erupted in racial violence. Where a relative openness of gatekeepers has been the legitimate norm, similarly, a tightening appears creative of stress.

An organization's management that tries to reduce conflict with lower echelons by establishing more rigid regulations and barriers often creates additional hostility.[78]

Where a system's line of action and concurrent doormen are clear-cut, environmental items of potential threat seeking entry may utilize various techniques of getting in. Sometimes they strive to disguise themselves so that their features of threat are invisible. This "wolf in sheep's clothing" process has been observed by psychoanalysts in the movement of *id* items, wearing symbolic, nonthreatening guise so as to get through the doorman represented by the *superego* and into the *ego* of everyday behavior. Gatekeepers of inflow appear most capable of selectivity and discrimination where visible difference occurs. Ecological segregation within a city is greatest for ethnic minorities such as Negroes, who are most visibly different.[79]

A "gilt" by association technique may be utilized whereby a letter of introduction or recommendation by a trusted and prestigious system member paves the way for successful entry. Similarly, the marketing technique of positioning—whereby a new consumer product is characterized, for instance, as a speedy and tasty breakfast food—signifies to system doormen its suitability for basic system action and thus its rightness for entry. An item desiring entry may also choose the course of changing itself toward greater similarity to system components. When Utah wanted to become a state it renounced Mormon polygyny. It is found, too, that the longer a minority group has lived in a society and assimilated the values of the larger milieu, the greater are its opportunities for upward mobility.[80] Calling attention to an actual similarity of the inflow item with existing system components may similarly help to gain entrance for it. A teacher who indicates the congruence of Latin and English words during Latin study serves to enlarge the student's English vocabulary.[81] Emphasizing the broad similarity of principles involved in shooting at underwater targets of varying depths significantly improves shooting skill at all depths.[82]

Ritual affords a further technique of gaining passage through a gatekeeper. In primitive societies the line of action involved in the adult role for each sex is comparatively clear and distinct.

The doorman guarding entrance to it is accordingly rigid. Rituals, or *rites de passage* that occur between childhood and adulthood or between adolescence and adulthood publicly proclaim "Here is a person on his way to performance as an adult!" [83] They test and/or certify his competence to provide positive feedback for adult systems—for example, the economy and the religion. Various requirements that the aspirant must meet are frequently part of this gatekeeper action. *Rites de passage* may also involve ceremonial circumcision, the imparting of certain secrets and similar practices which make the prospective entrant physically and cognitively similar to adult systems so that upon entrance he may fit into the established system with least disturbance. But in large, heterogeneous societies, such as America, where adult roles are numerous and where they are entered at varying chronological ages, little occurs in the way of general *rites de passage* that are the same for all. Each adult system, for example, occupational and marital, depending on its clarity, here has its own gatekeeper—and they vary widely in their action.

Where power structure is weak, gatekeepers are minimal. Persons of low self-esteem, lacking distinct self-direction, are found especially susceptible to a variety of propaganda.[84] Indiscriminate television viewing, movie attendance, and radio listening are also more common for psychologically insecure children who lack self-direction and identity.[85] Studies of adolescents find too that confirmed scholars or athletes use the mass media least indiscriminately.[86]

Middle-of-the-roaders of any sort have indistinct doormen guarding their self-systems and may be most easily manipulated by propaganda which establishes an identity for them. In a study of wet-dry sentiment many more middle-of-the-roaders were changed by either wet or dry arguments than were those who were strong wets or drys.[87] The mass media, similarly, exert genuine influence only where no strong preexisting opinions are found.[88] Here, too, the power of a prestigious communicator is extreme.[89] But when the communication is deeply relevant for basic action, the need for positive feedback will cause the communication of even a prestigious and well-liked communicator to be twisted into line with this action.[90] It will also produce a special doorman alertness to additional environmental cues of positive feedback. In one experiment,[91] subjects from a modern teachers' college heard a recorded speech by a person identified as a professor of education. The speech was interrupted several times by applause. For one group of subjects the applauders were identified as faculty members of the college; for the other group they were identified as townspeople. The speech argued for a return to more authoritarian teaching methods, in strict opposition to the educational philosophy of the subjects' college. It was found that all of the subjects attributed to the speaker more modern views than he actually expressed. But those subjects listening to what they believed was "gown" applause used this cue to distort the speaker's views toward congruence with their own college-trained philosophy more fully than did those who heard what they were told was "town" applause.[92]

Where no clearly defined opinions exist, the power of "opinion leaders" in implanting opinion is extreme. Opinion leaders are more deeply involved in election systems than are those they influence. They are better informed and they are more partisan.[93] Their influence is profound where rigid opinions are unlikely, as with children. Here the father of the family clearly sets political attitudes.[94]

Where a system's power structure is heterogeneous and its action accordingly multilinear, its gatekeepers of inflow are likely to be comparably multiple and often competitive. Power units may battle for control of all gatekeepers, such as immigration services and passport offices. Inflow providing positive feedback for one power unit and line of system action, moreover, may well provide negative feedback for another. Eisenstadt[95] reports a study of Oriental Jews in Israel in which contradictory inflow from parents and schools created mixed identity in children. Often in such situations a dominant line of action "takes over" and alerts doormen to protect it; sometimes, several incongruent lines of action are protected by gatekeepers' stopping all relevant entry.[96] But when these techniques are ineffective (as may occur with a young child), the reception of contradictory inflow can heighten internal conflict. In the case above reported by Eisenstadt [97] there were extensive school dropouts, poor grades, and poor school attendance by these children.

When doormen permit contradictory inflow the system is sometimes referred to as cross-pressured. Cross-pressured systems are found to be especially susceptible to attitude conversion and to reconversion.[98] A comparable condition holds in heterogeneous milieux having many different subsystems. Thus a major problem in reaching a mass audience is to provide positive feedback for all the subsystems within—a feat difficult to achieve.[99] It is for this reason that *consensus,* which in a *de facto* sense means a disintegration of internal subsystems and their differences, is important for the mass advertiser and the mass politician.

The desire for environmental inflow along usual lines appears in experiments in which people were confined in a cubicle blocking their usual sources of input.[100] They wore goggles to eliminate visual variability and had their hands cuffed in cardboard to reduce tactile stimulation. Tests during and after these isolation periods showed an impaired functioning verbally, mathematically, and in spatial skills. During these isolation periods, moreover, hallucinations occurred—possibly as a kind of substitute for the subjects' normal environmental reinforcement.[101] Cosmonauts confined experimentally in space capsules report similar fantasies, delusions, and hallucinations as substitutes for usual environment.[102] These fantasies and hallucinations may serve as functional equivalents of genuinely external, reinforcing inflow. Similarly, the schizophrenic who finds little reinforcement in his actual surroundings may shut them out and create a self-system involving extensive fantasies. Cosmonauts who remained "healthy" during the confinement experiment reported above did so by involving themselves in overt action and authentic sensory perceptions: they kept busy, they sang songs, and they talked to themselves.[103]

Gateways of Outflow

Gateways of outflow screen the energy/information that leaves a social system. Like doormen of inflow, they are normally molded by a system's power structure. They are designed to ensure that items leaving a system do not through their leaving create negative feedback for the system as perceived by its directive units. Gatekeepers of endogamy, for example, prevent outmarriage of a type defined as potentially disintegrative for the group.

The more manipulative a system's power structure and also the more specific its action, the more selective appear its gatekeepers of exit as well as entry. Dictatorships are frequently restrictive of emigration. Doormen of outflow appear especially rigid where a system's power structure strives to keep outside environments unaware of the system's presence or screened off from certain features of its action—as in the case of the CIA, FBI, KKK, or Mafia. Gatekeepers of outflow are its guardians of secrecy. Since contracomponents—political subsystems such as the Communist Party and Nazi Party in America—are opposed by the larger society's power structure, certain kinds of secrecy ensured by rigid doormen of outflow are a characteristic feature of these subsystems.

RECEIVING

The Receiving of Energy/Information

Energy/information successfully passing through a system's gatekeeper is fitted into the receiving system. It becomes a component, pushed toward congruence with and reinforcement of general system action and identity. It is organized into meaning and relevance. Thus, the letters

c f i
b e h
a d g

are generally ordered by users of our alphabet as abc/def/ghi rather than cfi/beh/adg.[104] Items of ambiguity that enter are similarly given meaning and ordered into congruence with basic system action.[105] Items of special meaning for system operation loom large in consciousness so that children are found to overestimate the size of coins as compared with discs of the same size; poor children exaggerate more than do rich children, conceivably because of the greater meaning (positive feedback) of these coins in their self and family systems.[106] A similar overestimation of the size of poker chips which are redeemable for candy is found in another experiment with children.[107]

As systems push and shove items of inflow into line with their basic action they will frequently give quite different meanings to these items than their sender might anticipate in terms of the latter's own identity. Primitives receiving alarm clocks from traders often hang the clocks around their necks as fetishes; this, of course, may not really be too much of a change if one regards time as a fetish of Western civilization. When receivers are allowed to "draw conclusions" from information, similarly, their conclusions are apt to be highly variable and often far different from the sender's expectations. Propagandists have found it more effective, in achieving a particular interpretation of information, to provide the desired "interpretation" along with the "facts" rather than to expect receivers to arrive at it on their own.[108] To feel absolutely sure of getting their message across, preachers may first tell their congregations what they are going to say and mean, then what they are saying and meaning, and finally what they have said and meant.

Judgments of inflow thus depend essentially upon its receiver. Inflow becomes what a receiving system makes of it, and it is relevant only in these terms. Thoreau states in *Walden,* "only that day dawns to which we are awake." Yoga philosophy expresses it as "when the pupil is ready the *guru* (teacher) appears." Without a receiver, energy/information has no impact and thus exists in no meaningful sense. It is not what parents do but what children perceive them as doing which carries weight in socialization.[109] What is negative and positive feedback, too, depends upon the receiving system. Deprivation has no necessary, objective basis in poverty but is a learned response of the deprived. Advertisers are more properly merchants of deprivation than of products, sending an awareness of deprivation to receivers who will let it in. A mounting sense of relative deprivation through the dangling possibility of still greater gains surges when things are getting better so that revolutions tend to flare up after rather than before reforms. It is possible that American Negroes feel more deprived today than before the civil rights program and its gains.

In the movement of energy/information from one system to another, the pull of the receiver generally appears greater than the push of the sender. The data on migration indicate that economic conditions in the country of reception are usually primary in motivating movement.[110] A comparable condition holds within a nation in the attraction to the urban of rural young people, especially women.[111]

The Impact of Inflow Upon the Receiving System

Where clear-cut system identity and gatekeepers are relatively absent, items of inflow may establish a system's action. For a system becomes what it receives and what it sends.

Inflow received during a system's formative stage is thus of immense impact. Childhood holds major significance for adult identity. Early parental pressures on a child to achieve carry lifelong power.[112] Children receiving rejection, hatred, and hostility, similarly, tend to become these things they have received. They come to see themselves as unworthy of love; and they become incapable of loving. The hostility received by members of ethnic minorities,[113] aggravated sometimes by *self*-directed hostility in Jewish and other subcultures, in which a child's feelings may be utilized as a technique for his control, often takes its toll in a lifelong incapacity to love. Conversely, children who consistently receive a great deal of love see themselves as lovable and are able to pass it on.[114] This happens too with animals other than man. Harlow and Harlow [115] report that monkeys rejected as infants often exhibit masochistic traits, biting themselves and engaging in other forms of self-punishment.

The impact of inflow of a particular kind is heightened when it is received from several sources, such as home, school, and peer-group.[116] Here immediate environments—specifically, components of the intimate systems to which one belongs—carry greatest weight. Caring applies to what is close at hand. When inflow comes from afar in geographic space it is more likely to concern things with which a system is not intimately involved and thus does not care very much about. When it comes from afar, also, its message is more likely to be distorted because of intermediary systems along the way and their multiple reformulations of the information. Studies by Fritz [117] and by the National Research Council [118] of various kinds of disasters such as floods, tornados, and large explosions reveal that the farther away people are from the scene of a disaster, the less their concern for the victims and the less accurate their information about the disaster itself.[119]

Where two kinds of positive inflow are available and a choice must be made between them it can be made quickly and easily.[120] Similarly, two kinds of potentially negative inflow are normally responded to by the simple expedient of blocking out or withdrawing from both.[121] In situations, however, where a receiver is subject to mixed, contradictory inflow from a sender, it positions itself vis-à-vis the sender. Beyond a certain distance the positive aspect gleams and the receiver moves closer to the sender. But when the receiver moves closer than this point the negative feature predominates and the receiver withdraws. A kind of cybernetic oscillation occurs within this range of approach-withdrawal, similar to the oscillation of temperature in a room and the action of a thermostat.[122] Its operation may be noted in systems involving a person's vacillation about marriage or indecision in the purchase of a luxury item. Repeated approaches in the latter case—window shopping, inquiries, and haggling over price—often stop just short of buying, conceivably because the negative features, such as guilt and fear that the item cannot really be afforded, loom large as the "moment of truth" approaches, while they recede in immediacy and the positive features, anticipated joy in ownership, for example, come to the fore as distance increases.[123] It is in such systems that absence can "make the heart grow fonder."

Level of aspiration may operate as a part of this pattern. Goals are received and become meaningful at a point where their challenge and their opportunity for realization balance. Systems involving fear of challenge choose the safer course; those involving confidence accept riskier, more stimulating, more challenging tasks.[124] Experiments with laboratory animals suggest possible extensions, too. It is found, for example, that the attraction of a positive item increases only slightly as it is approached. The tendency to withdraw from a negative source, however, rises steeply as the space to it narrows.[125]

When the attractiveness of a mixed, that is, a positive and negative item is increased or its negative feature reduced, a receiver will move closer to it.[126] Much of modern advertising suggests that its product will accomplish this. "Use our deodorant," it says, "and men will flock around." (It usually says this to women.) With two negative items of environment, however, and no possibility of blocking out or withdrawing from either, a receiver will seek to position itself at a point where the two negative items balance.[127] It will strive to shield itself from as much negative reception as possible. And it will often cultivate a kind of objectivity that bears a striking parallel to that of the scientist or the critic watching a drama. Sixty-nine percent of World War II combat flyers reported that they experienced at times a sense of detachment from their flying systems, a feeling of unreality which made it seem that what was happening was not really happening to them.[128] Bettelheim,[129] a clinical psychologist, writing of his Nazi concentration camp experience, states that his survival depended largely on his capacity to reconstruct reality so that the degrading treatment somehow did not happen to "him" as a subject but only to "him" as an object. It was as if he watched things happening in which he participated only vaguely and from afar. Later he learned that many surviving concentration camp prisoners shared this capacity to detach themselves from the present and look upon it as unreal.

Confusing a receiver by presenting it with mixed and ambiguous energy/information has been carried out experimentally in the laboratory. It is found that cats both fed and shocked at the same sound develop deep anxieties and a tendency to withdraw from the mixed inflow.[130] Dogs subjected to mixed, ambiguous inflow similarly show neurotic tendencies.[131] Comparable confusion occurs every day as a consumer receives multiple, often contradictory messages from a plethora of smiling advertisers competing for his dollar.

A hostile environment, it has been noted, reduces hostility within a social system. Crime, suicide, mental disorder,[132] and community conflict drop off during wartime and when external disaster threatens.[133] Within the military, war brings a lessening of internal tensions and delinquencies.[134] But a word of caution here. Where environmental hostility does get through the gate-keepers, as in the prejudice received by ethnic minorities, it may take a toll in self-hatred and intragroup conflict. There are high rates of homicide and assault of Negro against Negro in America. Some of this, too, is likely to be displaced hostility unable to be expressed toward its white environmental source.

The Impact of Entry Upon the Entrant

Movement from one social system to another often appears productive of stress and strain for the mover. In addition to the structural fact of leaving and entering is the meaning of such movement. Expulsion or withdrawal, for example, are likely to involve some hostility on both sides: for expeller and expellee, for withdrawer and those withdrawn from. Moreover, movement often means a rise or fall in status, both of which can require some adjustment. New recruits entering an established military unit feel inferior to the "old guard" which wears the badge of veteranship, shares intimacies, and "knows the ropes." [135]

Entry into a new system involves the learning of new norms and the unlearning of old. These are often difficult, especially for entrants of clear and established identity. The greater the difference between entrant and receiving system, moreover, the greater appears the likelihood of stress and strain for both. Problems of the immigrant have been extensively documented.[136] Rapid social mobility likewise disrupts the mover, predisposing to neurosis.[137] Persons moving up or down in America are found to display more hostility toward ethnic minorities—a common form of displaced aggression—than do those who remain stationary.[138] In Germany, too, it was the downwardly mobile middle-class groups, "squeezed out" from their former ways of life, who became the major followers of Hitler. The secure and static middle-class segments uninvolved in downward mobility were less likely to espouse extremist nationalism and anti-Semitism.[139]

Moves from the parental home to college occasion varying degrees of change and possible strain. Upper- and middle-class girls going to Bennington College, avant-garde in its orientation, were found in one study to develop modes of progressive and liberal thought. Boys of the same socioeconomic level who went to Williams College developed no new orientations of this sort, and conceivably suffered less strain, because of the attitudinal similarity of Williams College to their parental homes.[140]

Pre-entry may itself carry impact. Persons moving up take on the political attitudes of the social class to which they aspire.[141] They also take on the sexual practices of this class—and they do so early in life. Indeed, early attachment to particular sexual norms may be used as an indicator of eventual socioeconomic class status. An American's sexual behavior concurs with the pattern of the social group into which he ultimately moves rather than with that of the group to which his parents belong.[142]

With heightened mobility occupationally and residentially in America, with increased movement in and out of various schools, churches, marriages, and sexual unions, a growing number of Americans pass through a series of temporary systems. Their action in these milieux, the operation of temporariness itself as a system component, and the impact of such entrants and exiters upon a social system and it upon them merit intensive investigation. It is conceivable that the resort worker's "Sure I love ya, honey, but the season's over!" approach, or farewell, may in some cases become a way of life.

Feedback

Intimately involved in receiving is the cybernetic element of feedback. As noted in Chapter 1, the concept of feedback is broadened for present purposes to cover any influence upon system action. Positive feedback encourages current action; negative feedback discourages it. The receiver is crucial here. For it is the response of the *receiving* system—what it does in terms of stopping, slowing down, or accelerating—that determines whether what it has received is positive feedback, negative feedback, or no feedback at all.

Systems and their power structures normally strive for positive feedback and seek to avoid negative. This stands as a fundamental law of system action. Through gatekeepers and internal enforcers, systems strive to perpetuate "business as usual"—or more so. When they can they surround themselves with mirrors. They hire yes-men of various shapes and forms. They close their ears to the disharmony of nay-sayers. It has been noted that opinionated poll takers consistently bring back information in line with their biases,[143] and that psychotherapists find validation for their theories in sessions with their patients.[144] They also give more time and attention to upper- and middle-class patients, who are more likely to tell them what they like to hear, than to patients of the lower class who for various class-based reasons do not make the right noises.[145]

Receivers often receive what they wish by selectively encouraging the sender's "proper" sending. Even a reinforcement as mild as an "uh-huh"—indicating yes, go ahead—can do the job. The quest for positive feedback as a subsystem, similarly, is the essential core of a system component's action. It is the social cement that glues self-systems to systems involving many people.[146] Reception of positive feedback marks systems which last. Here mutually reinforcing spirals of positive feedback often occur. The formation of "secular" groups, for instance, fosters impersonality which in turn increases the effectiveness of these "secular" groups.[147] Where receivers find certain input unproductive of the feedback they crave, they turn to other sources. Television and other mass media often provide satisfying input for those who for various reasons do not receive it in overt-action systems: the dull, the emotionally insecure, and the students without recognition as scholars or athletes.[148]

It is to be stressed that positive feedback is craved, not necessarily positive *affect*. Persons of low self-esteem seek evidence of their inadequacy. Neurotics strive to confirm their neuroses, making psychotherapy aimed at change very difficult. Systems involving authoritarianism crave harsh, authoritarian command as positive feedback; democracies normally reject it.[149]

Full success or full failure are equally catastrophic for a social system. Completion of its goals may mean its demise. Victory can produce an army's dissolution. Moore writes: "For the leaders, the people who become committed to the organization and identified with it, success in the organization's finite mission is disastrous. For the continuity of such organizations, nothing succeeds like failure or perhaps, near success, a close enough approximation to victory to keep the issue or the party alive and to keep a sufficient number of supporters to justify associational activity. . . . Entering a contest in which the organization is foredoomed to defeat . . . is a risky strategy" [150] if the defeat means dissolution. "The strategy may not withstand an unrelieved succession of collective defeats." [151] A story circulates that the leader of an organization devoted to racial peace was once approached by someone who claimed he had found the practical solution to racial strife. "Shh!" was the leader's response.

The desire for reinforcement is well recognized. It is the basis of flattery. Thus the sending from below to above, that is, from subordinate to superior, is usually intended as positive, and praise abounds. Conversely, messages moving down a hierarchical line are often meant to convey negative sanctions. Argyle [152] reports studies showing that subordinates in an organization hold back criticism of those in high places and also bad news lest they be blamed by top leadership.

The Difficulty of Negative Feedback

When a receiver receives the same brand of energy/information it sends—love or hate, for instance—it generally means positive feedback whatever the intention of the sender may be. Responding with love to an expression of love will normally keep a social system of affection going. Hostility given on the eye-for-an-eye principle, similarly, amplifies a system of hate. Escalation of conflict—in Vietnam, for example—meets comparable escalation. Nations' stockpiling of arms creates reciprocal stockpiling by the other side, and neither appears to be a deterrent of eventual war.[153] Nor does the pain of imprisonment bombarding the hostility of crime serve to deter the criminal. Its impact appears instead to be positive feedback, fostering bigger crime. About three fourths of those who enter prison have been to prison before.[154] Detention institutions for juvenile delinquents likewise show high rates of recidivism.[155]

Other punishment similarly appears of little use as a provider of negative feedback; it usually creates positive feedback instead. Mothers who punish their children's bedwetting produce chronic bedwetting; mothers who punish dependency get highly dependent children; mothers who punish aggression severely create aggressors.[156] Delinquent gang boys often show a history of severe punishment at home.[157]

The threat of death as punishment similarly wields no deterrence. Comparative data for states and nations with and without the death penalty for murder reveal that murder rates are about the same where a death penalty exists as where it does not.[158] Certain scholars have suggested that a death penalty may actually encourage murder among those who crave a dramatic, attention-getting way to die. A belief in punishment and the threat of punishment as effective negative feedback may itself, however, constitute part of an on-going system resistant of factual evidence to the contrary. Despite the actual ineffectiveness of the death penalty in deterrence, American police claim that their lives are safer in states that have the death penalty for murder.[159]

The difficulty of changing on-going action appears throughout many social systems. Organizational leadership that tries to reduce employee hostility by tighter regulations usually finds that these increase rebellion. An amplification spiral of more regulations and more conflict commences.[160]

Largely through their gatekeepers and internal enforcers do systems and their power units protect themselves from negative feedback. The everyday action of a mental hospital, for example, is dominated by attendants. It is they who run the show, manipulating patients and doctors. A "good" doctor, to them, is one who does not interfere with the way they run the ward.[161] The on-going system of United States air strikes in Vietnam appears similarly self-protective from negative feedback. Despite or possibly because of its ineffectiveness as an instrument of victory (several strategists—among them Major General Edward G. Lansdale, USAF [ret.] in *Foreign Affairs,* October, 1964—believe that it encourages Vietnamese villagers to join the Viet Cong), it probably does furnish positive feedback for the American Air Force as a social system.

When systems fall down in self-protection and negative feedback arises or enters, the results to the system are usually catastrophic. Even when total collapse is averted and the system goes on, it goes on often as a weakened and mixed-up unit. Negative feedback exacts a lasting systemic toll. The behavior patterns of adults whose activities as children (when bulwarks against negative feedback are minimal) met strong parental rejection and criticism are marked by generalized anxiety and a lessened capacity for attachment to other people.[162] Weaning, modesty training, training in heterosexual inhibition, and independence training, when by their sharp imposition they constitute traumatic negative feedback, take a comparable toll cross-societally. Their early entry before the young system has the capacity to "routinize" them effectively means an adult system ridden by guilt.[163]

Because many social systems protect themselves from negative feedback, creating it when desired can be a difficult task. It is the problem confronting system therapists and other power personnel: psychoanalysts, executives faced with increasing tensions within a corporation, United Nations leaders seeking to insert effectively the olive branch of peace into an on-going system of war. For most efforts at negative feedback, as noted above, create unintended positive feedback instead. It has therefore been suggested by some scholars, such as Skinner, that we give up trying to create negative feedback and work at the easier task of positive feedback instead. Here, on-going systems which we do want to maintain are encouraged and amplified while those we wish to end are allowed to die through a lack of reinforcement. Wolpe [164] in this way substitutes a "virtuous" circle for a "vicious" one. His patients who are in a bind of unsatisfactory sexual relations creating a withdrawal from sex, which in turn creates further unsatisfactory sexual relations, are instructed to participate only in those sexual unions which are distinctly pleasurable. When they do, sexual responsiveness rises. Moreover, it spreads to new avenues of potential sexual pleasure. The range of situations in which the patient is capable of satisfactory sexual performance is thereby extended, and with each extension his sexual confidence grows.

The effectiveness of positive feedback as a teaching device in a variety of social systems is extensively documented by Skinner,[165] Hilgard,[166] Isaacs,[167] Filby,[168] Holland,[169] Jenkins and Stanley,[170] and other scholars. It is found, too, that a reinforcement of on-going action may occur even when sender and receiver are quite unaware of it.[171] It happens all the time in normal conversation.

Thus it is *positive* feedback that most fully solidifies system action. When this reinforcement assumes the shape of love, as it often does cross-societally, it appears especially potent. Its early input is found to create and encourage loving action. A parent-child relationship that builds strong positive ties of affection encourages the lifelong affiliative tendencies of the child.[172] Rewards of parental affection, rather than the pain of punishment, work best in creating happy, loving, successful children of strong self-esteem.[173] The more love-oriented the parents' approach to their child, moreover, the more effective is their control over his behavior—directly, and indirectly through the enforcer of conscience.[174] Physical affection, hugging and kissing, contains special power as a reinforcer. Parents who give a great deal of physical affection as a reward for achievement condition a strong achieving drive in their children. One study shows a need-for-achievement score for sons hugged and kissed when they achieved well to be double that of sons unrewarded in this way.[175]

The power of emotional warmth as a reinforcer appears greatest for action systems that have been deprived of it. One experiment gave children a choice of two holes in which to drop marbles. The experimenter said "good," "fine," and other expressions of warm approval when the children dropped them in *one* of these holes. Some of the children were first "socially deprived" by keeping them isolated for twenty minutes; another group was "satiated" by lots of warm and solicitous behavior by the experimenter on the way to the laboratory; the third group, the controls, went directly into the experiment. Results showed the "deprived" group most responsive to the experimenter's warmth during the experiment. More than the others, these children were eager to place the marbles where they got an emotional reward. Next in line came the controls, with the "satiated" last.[176]

Like negative feedback, positive feedback coming early in life carries long-range impact. Parental reward for achievement and a high ratio of successes to failures condition a lifetime drive for achievement.[177] Mothers appear especially powerful here as reinforcers.[178] A consistency of child and adult cultures is found, too, in that childhood rewards for independence and achievement are matched by an accompanying emphasis upon achievement in the adult culture. Examining the Navajo, Central Apache, Hopi, Comanche, Sanpoil, Western Apache, Paiute, and Flatheads, McClelland *et al.*[179] find that strong cultural pushes upon *adults* to achieve are closely associated with extensive childhood training and rewards for independence and achievement.

Learning that lasts, somewhat surprisingly perhaps, thrives best on feedback that has been intermittent, unusual, accidental, and inconsistent rather than steady. Both for people and other animals, rewards that have come now and then keep action going longer after all reward has stopped than do rewards that have come one hundred percent of the time.[180] Hope beats longest where reward has been unlikely. The reinforcer making its appearance inconsistently reinforces best.[181] One parental "yes" to a child's demand may undo many weeks of "no." Indulging a former habit now and then—an occasional cigarette for last month's heavy smoker, an occasional drink for the former alcoholic—is likely to keep it going and may lead to its revival. Occasional reward becomes especially attractive when its cost is high. People value strongly the things for which they have labored long and hard, or for which they have suffered pain.[182] Girls who had to endure embarrassment to enter into a social group thought highly of the group and its meeting.[183] Children for whom the cost of playing with a favorite toy was high (the threat of severe punishment) were more likely to do so than children for whom the cost (the threat of mild punishment) was low. Indeed, the favorite-toy-playing system could be given either positive or negative feedback depending on whether it was threatened with severe or mild pain. Contrary to "logical" expectation, severe threat kept this system going full steam while mild threat slowed it down.[184] Laboratory experiments find that rats who have had to work hard to get food make more later, unrewarded attempts than do those who have had easy access to a meal.[185] Thus highly tenacious values lasting long after reward has stopped can be created by sporadic rewarding—once after five minutes, again after twelve, next after two, and so on—during a training period.[186] Slot machines and rain dances may retain their attractiveness precisely because they pay off irregularly. Negative feedback works similarly. It stamps out action best when it is inconsistent rather than steady. Rats punished now and then were more effectively inhibited from a pattern of behavior than those punished regularly.[187]

SENDING

The Sending of Energy/Information

A system's sending to its environments, as its receiving, is determined by its internal action and its wish to implement this action. It normally sends in ways meant to yield positive feedback for itself and its power structure.

The sending of a social system—whether it involves propaganda, buying, love making, or whatever—is, in a broad sense, the manipulation of a receiving environment. Sending is its impact upon the receiver. In a systemically meaningful sense it does not become sending or anything else until it is received. The act of reception creates it: places it, gives it meaning, and makes it what it is. While a sender normally sends what he *means* to be —through its reception by a receiver—positive feedback for the sender's internal action, whether it actually constitutes positive, or negative, or no feedback in this regard ultimately depends on what the receiver does with it—and the latter's impact upon the original sender. Receiving is thereby the more significant process.

A social system sends what it *is* (components), what it *produces* (output), and what it has *received*. As noted earlier, a receiver becomes what it has received. And both in degree and in kind it passes this on—often long afterward, suggesting its capacity to store and to be what it stores. The unloved are the unloving toward themselves and others.[188] Parents isolated from affection as children appear unable to send it to their children, thereby perpetuating emotionally deprived families from generation to generation.[189] Both love and hate get passed on. They may be reflected to their source [190] or displaced.[191] They may be sent outward or inward. The more consistently affectionate the child's parents, the more friendly will be the child in his sending.[192] The greater the rejection and hostility he gets as a child, similarly, the more marked will be his aggressive tendencies.[193]

Among animals other than man the same pattern holds. Harlow and Harlow [194] find that poorly mothered female monkeys become poor mothers. In one experiment four female monkeys were maternally deprived. One was raised in a bare wire cage, three were raised with artificial mothers made of cloth. Later on when they became mothers none of them treated their infants well. They ignored them, rebuffed them, struck them, mouthed them roughly, and pushed their faces into the wire-mesh floor.

Leaders likewise lead as they have been led,[195] and parents rear their children as they have been reared. They reenact what happened to them during childhood although they are usually unaware of it. Hilgard [196] finds mothers re-creating with their children many of their old feelings that have never been "worked through." The mother identifies one of her children with herself, another with her old rival, herself with one or both of her parents and sets the stage to reenact her old family drama.

What a sender will send in any situation depends largely on the cues he receives. When a respondent in an interview is asked a question set up to reveal stereotyping and is steered to reply in this way, he is likely to oblige.[197] Other reception appears similarly significant in sending. In much of middle-class America where pressures to achieve are strong and "wasting" so many hours watching television is likely to produce guilt, a displaced hostility toward television and its programs has been found.[198] The sending of hostility specifically toward *low-status* ethnic minorities similarly stands as a learned pattern for certain senders. A consistency of sending is found here, too. Persons displaying one form of ethnic prejudice are likely to display other forms as well, and the sending of hostility toward one low-status ethnic minority is generally accompanied by a comparable sending to other low-status ethnic minorities.[199] Senders of this sort appear broadly rather than narrowly hostile.

As with receiving, sending stands as a significant creator and reinforcer of identity. A sender becomes what it sends as well as what it receives. If after hearing one side of a controversial issue a person publicly proclaims his agreement with it, a gatekeeper becomes alerted which reduces the effectiveness of subsequent presentation of the other side.[200] The sending involved in role-playing carries the same impact.[201] We remember best what we recite.[202] One must choose carefully the roles he plays, for he is likely to become them. We as well as others receive what we send. Indeed, we are our most important and appreciative audience. In self-systems involving only ourselves as human components—along with our thoughts, our tools, our emotions—we run an on-going, powerful conversation. When we talk out loud we speak essentially to ourselves although others may be listening too. Through our wish for positive feedback we say what we want to hear. Both the professor's lecturing from his favorite notes and the golden, stentorian tones of the professional orator are likely to provide excruciating pleasure to the speaker. Writers too (including this one) love to read themselves, and sometimes rewrite themselves over and over again in book after book. A test of change may be whether we still read our writing of yesteryear.

This receiving of our own sending means that we normally send pleasant things to our ears and to our minds. For we like to receive positive feedback. So too the things we expel make us feel better; through the sending involved in expulsion we rid ourselves of the abrasive.

Senders eager for positive feedback in the form of approval from others are likely to send what they believe will produce approval. There appears a tacit recognition that people enjoy hearing what they already believe. Arguments favoring a raise in teachers' salaries are remembered especially well by those who believe they will be talking later to a teachers' group.[203] Others who were told they would be speaking to an economy-minded group of townspeople remembered best the arguments against a raise in teachers' pay.[204]

Systems vary in their awareness and initiative of the outflow from them. Much borrowing—of ideas and artifacts, for example —happens without conscious awareness. On the other hand there are missionary systems eager to pass on "the word" to others. A broader range of sending than receiving, however, generally holds forth. A receiver lets in a narrow spectrum of hopefully positive feedback; its sending is comparatively diffuse. To illustrate, no equivalent of expulsion—the sending of people, things, and ideas that have been damned as negative feedback—occurs in connection with inflow.

The Sending of Specific Energy/Information

In the movement of people out of a social system, the distance they go depends largely on which receiving systems beckon. Stouffer[205] has found the distance of migration to vary directly with the distance of a potential receiving system offering appropriate economic opportunities.

A person leaving one social system generally enters another. Rarely does he "leave home" with no place to go. Norms of the old system lose their hold as he learns to adjust to the requirements of the new. Parental ways diminish in their impact as a child grows up and moves into systems having other norms. Goldsen *et al.*[206] find that when a college student adopts political attitudes different from those of his parents it represents less a rebellion than an attempt to "get with" the norms of his new systems of allegiance.

In the sending of emotion, the general illegitimacy that has been noted for negative affect requires certain kinds of adjustment by those who send it. Allport and Kramer[207] find that prejudiced people ordinarily underestimate the extent of their prejudice. They tend to be unaware of the deep hostility they send and are likely to feel no shame. What hostility they do recognize in themselves they frequently legitimize as "natural" and fully justified because of the misbehavior of those they dislike. They further disguise it with patriotic and nationalistic sentiments.[208]

Hostility appears not only of low legitimacy cross-societally; it appears also of *negative* value—something to be avoided rather than sought. A fear of reciprocalism serves to inhibit its sending. Hence it is more often directed to receivers of low status and power than to those of high standing who can reciprocate.

Norms appear in the sending of affect. Scandinavians are reported to invert hostility and to have a high rate of suicide in consequence.[209] Mediterraneans are more apt to express it outwardly in high rates of murder and assault.[210] These norms are inversely related so that where one flourishes the other is rare.[211] Kluckhohn,[212] citing the work of Benedict and Jacks, notes that the hostility of the "primitive" psychotic is likely to be directed outward while that of the person reared in the Jewish-Christian tradition will more frequently be pointed inward. Depression appears rarely in "primitive" societies; it is especially uncommon among African Negroes.[213]

CHAPTER **4**

SYSTEM IDENTITY AND CHANGE

SYSTEM IDENTITY

Identity is the core of a system's uniqueness. It is what sets it apart from other systems. It provides its distinctive tone.

System, norm, and identity interweave intimately. A system, as defined in Chapter 1, is a regularized pattern of action. This pattern is its norm and the basis of its identity. The clarity of all three—system, norm, and identity—depends upon power structure and its firmness of direction. The more powerful a system's power units, the less random will be the system's action. The more distinct will be its norm and its identity.

Three major ideotypes of system identity may be drawn: (1) monolithic (Figure 13), (2) vague (Figure 14), and (3) multiple (Figure 15). Monolithic and vague identity are related to, although not synonymous with, high and low organization.

(1) *Monolithic* identity requires a strong power structure. The system's norm is accordingly distinct, rigid, consistently repeated, well enforced internally, and well protected by gatekeepers. An illustration would be a "good-night" pattern followed each evening in the same way, involving Mr. Clarity's winding the clock at 10 P.M. with precisely four turns, setting it to ring at exactly 7 A.M., brushing his teeth with the same toothbrush, dentifrice, and number of arm motions, placing his suit upon the same hanger, saying the same prayers to the same deity and turning out the light at 10:15 P.M. to sleep—and perchance to dream, in the same way. Factory belt-line production portrayed *in ex-*

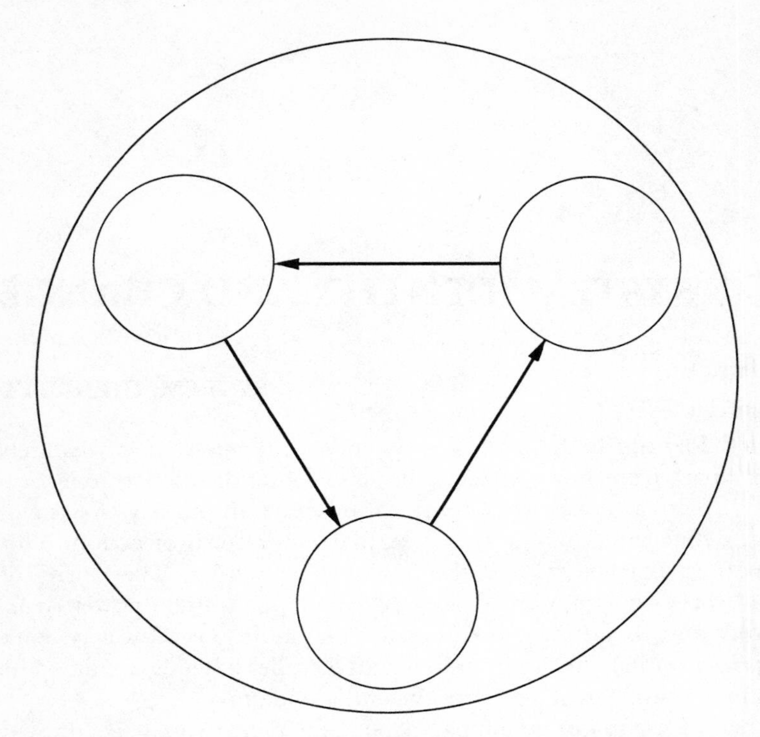

Figure 13. Monolithic Identity. Single line of action, repeated over and over again. Example: Mr. Clarity's precise going-to-bed system.

tremo by Charlie Chaplin's *Modern Times* provides a comparable case.

For monolithic systems, items of potential positive and negative feedback are readily apparent and the system's power units respond decisively. Persons involved in monolithic systems of religious thought and action, for example, are found to be strongly intolerant of ways different from their own, and also hostile and punitive toward criminal and other deviates from the rigid patterns they adhere to.[1]

Monolithic systems thus send and receive decisively. When

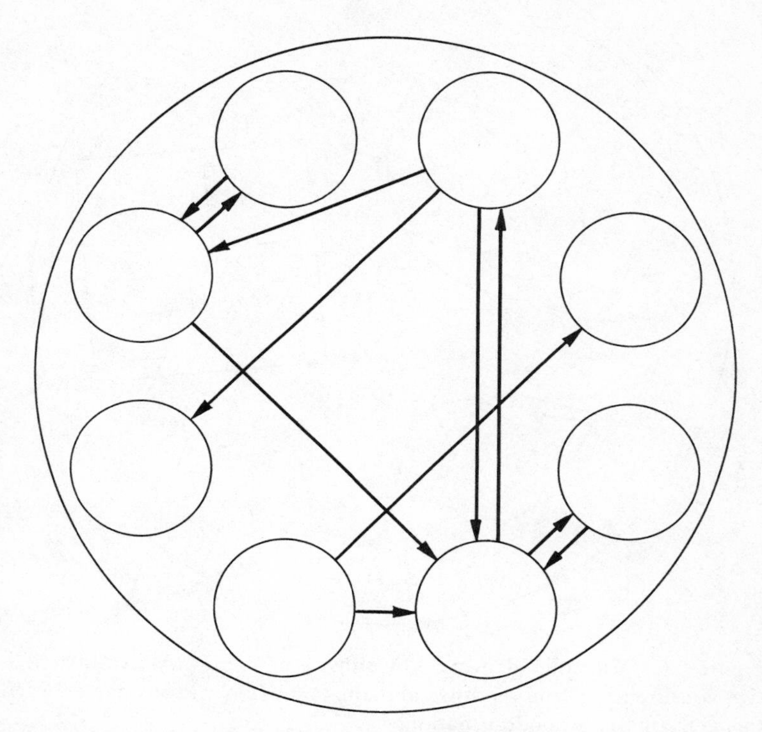

Figure 14. Vague Identity. The sendings and receivings occur over a unit of time. Each is infrequently repeated. Example: The student lounge of an impersonal, large-city, American university.

involved strongly in partisan politics, persons make their final voting decision early.[2] Those but mildly, vaguely involved avoid making these decisions. Often they postpone them until Election Day. Many never make political decisions at all.

The attachment of a person to opinions tightens as he grows older.[3] Gatekeepers become more specific, and less tolerant of a broad range of inflow. Action becomes "set" with time and repetition.

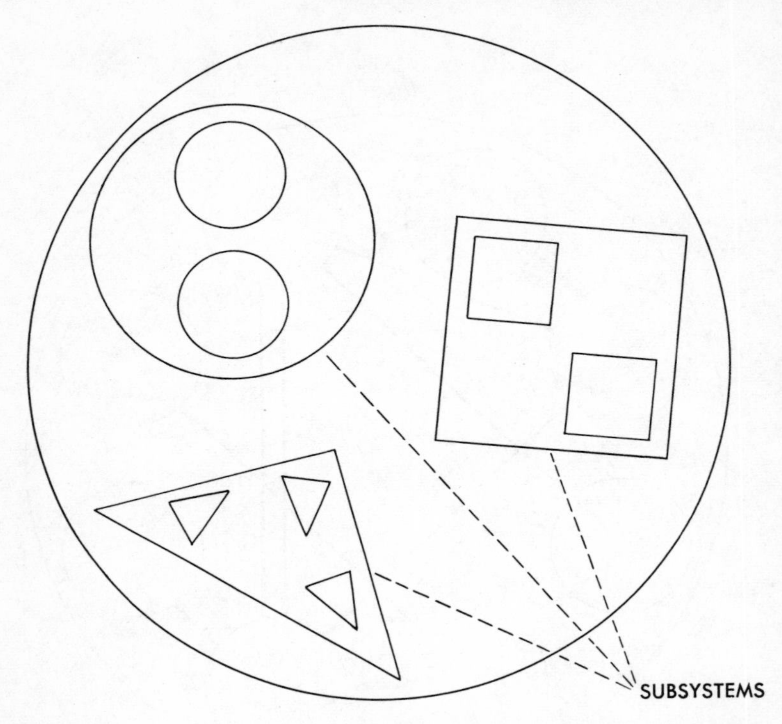

Figure 15. Multiple Identity. The subsystems may vary in the repetitive consistency of the sendings and the receivings within and between them. Example: A modern nation.

A comparatively monolithic system of sexual action marks the lower class of America. In groups of higher educational and socioeconomic level, a greater diversity of sexual practices appears.[4] (2) *Vague* system identity involves a fuzziness of internal power units, line of action, internal enforcers, and gatekeepers. Components move rather randomly and without clear direction. The norm is blurred, indistinct, entropic. Systems in process of becoming, such as new friendships, new marriages, and new fraternities, often partake of vague identity. So too do the systems created by the infant and the young child. Of similar vague identity are social systems of unconcern to their components, systems about which they do not care much one way or the other, such as casual acquaintanceships.

Components of systems of vague identity often move to create or enter those of clearer line, as in the case of the maturing child. Meaningful change here means attachment to specific patterns of thought and action, and the rise of enforcers and gatekeepers to guard them. It is the movement away from "freedom," autonomy, randomness, and ambiguity. It is the movement toward organization. Societies, while varying in the number and type of possible subsystems—job, marriage, church, friendship—with which a person may affiliate strongly, normally press him to choose some for clear attachment. Bell [5] believes a major problem in America to be the pressure to choose subsystems—in careers, styles of life, and friends—without clear standards for making these choices.

(3) *Multiple* identity characterizes systems containing subsystems, each with an identity of its own. Each has its line of action; each has its power structure; each has its internal enforcers and watchers at the gate.

Large social systems such as nations are marked by this sort of multiple identity. At times certain of their subsystems may cluster as an establishment of politics, church, and economy dominating the larger milieu; others may struggle competitively as in the case of political parties jockeying for power. Positive feedback for some may be severely negative for others.

Systems of multiple identity present a complex picture in regard to change. Meaningful change here may take the form of a realignment of their subsystemic power units, an increase or reduction in their capacity to manipulate, the emergence of new power forces, or the cyclic swing in what Pareto called a "circulation of the elite." Each modification will make an impact upon subsystem action and each subsystem in turn pushes upon the larger milieu.

To illustrate, with change in the form of an environmental threat such as war, systems of multiple identity mobilize into a more monolithic line. Action takes a straighter, narrower path, gatekeepers tighten and operate less competitively. Internal enforcers muster a joint and steady hand. Action and organization within heighten; action with environment dwindles. The inflow and outflow that do occur take a more specific shape.

So it is that an election with the potential threat that the wrong candidate (any outside one) might succeed produces a greater unification in the ranks. Political campaigns intensify political homogeneity within parties, within religious groups, within socioeconomic strata; and they rigidify the differences between them.[6]

Norms

System components are especially deterministic of their system norm when they are isolated from such environments as scientific evidence, objective reality, or the norms of the surrounding community.[7] What is correct here depends thoroughly upon what the system creates as correct. As noted, when a group of persons was asked to judge the movement of a light in a darkened room—a light which really did not move at all—their perceptions combined to produce a group norm as to the "correct" amount of movement.[8] Other groups made up of persons who individually and by themselves first made judgments of the light's "movement" also developed a group norm after they joined together and operated as a social system. Their consensus involved a blending of their individual judgments—but it still showed a greater modal range than where no separate, individual perceptions were first allowed.[9]

A system's norm has been defined as its line of action. In a large social system with subsystems and thus multiple norms within, the lines of action of these subsystems are generally more or less congruent. As Sumner observed, there is motion toward consistency in the mores. There is usually a consistency too in the person's (or other component's such as an idea's) multiple systems of belonging. A person affiliated with several of a society's subsystems, such as family, job, and community at one time, or moving seriatim from one to another, does not generally undergo much strain through inconsistent norms. Societies having strong sex taboos in their childhood systems tend to have strong sex taboos in their adult systems a well.[10] An emphasis on achievement, similarly, occurs consistently within certain societies over a broad range of their subsystems from those involving folk tales and stories for children to those involving electrical output.[11] This consistency, moreover, occurs not only in Western, comparatively free enterprise democracies like England and the United States but also in Communist nations such as Russia and Bulgaria.[12] A comparable consistency in achievement emphasis throughout its subsystems marked several achieving societies of the past: ancient Greece, Spain during the late Middle Ages, and pre-Incan Peru.[13]

Norms grow increasingly "set" with repetition. Continued action along the same line more firmly cements the pattern for components remaining in the system. Scientific disciplines that have existed for some time, such as chemistry, have a more clear-cut, consensual norm as to what are relevant data, what methods of study are proper, and what constitutes reliable proof, than do younger disciplines such as sociology. Through time and norm-making a system moves toward organization and away from entropy and randomness. Its components come to move in narrower, more consistent circles. Summarizing the results of several studies, Rogoff [14] reports more homogeneity of values among students at the end of their four years of college than when they begin. While it is possible that some of the more variable students are more likely to have dropped out along the way, the norm at any event assumes a more definite shape over the college years; the senior norm in values and beliefs is more distinct than that of the freshmen.

With an increase in contact of components, the norm becomes not only itself more distinct but the members' knowledge of it similarly deepens and becomes more accurate. For example, they come to know the opinion of the group.[15] Components thus achieve a system consciousness, an awareness of norm.

Component welfare appears enhanced where norms are clear and components are aware of them. The system here becomes predictable; expectations are possible; the consequences of component action shine clearly. Children reared in homes of norm clarity are found to be happier and more successful in adjusting to the norm requirements of school and play.[16] Exposed to clear norms and expectations, also, they are more likely to judge the parental discipline they have had as fair and deserved.[17] Children from homes of norm ambiguity considered their discipline generally unfair and capricious. And they liked their parents less.[18] Positive affect appears an unlikely component of a social system where negative affect in the form of norm anxiety holds forth.

The Learning of Norms

Components learn the norms of their social systems: the proper, expected ways of action within, and with various environments. Where no previous norms have been learned—as with a very young child—Piaget [19] reports a progression whereby the child moves from (1) a nonrecognition of an expected pattern to (2) a perception of the pattern which is taught by power components (parents, for example) as absolute and morally correct to (3) a perception of pattern as something that is agreed upon by components to (4) a perception that this pattern may be manipulated by himself and others.

Values and prejudices are part of norm learning for a child. These are acquired within the family and other social systems to which he belongs. He learns ethnic attitudes as he learns other proper ways for these systems. Much of this learning is quite unconscious. Few parents, for example, formally and directly and consciously teach norms of racial prejudice. Yet their attitudes and behavior, their restrictions on the child's playmates, their tendency to stereotype all persons of particular races and religions with certain physical, behavioral, and mental characteristics nevertheless do constitute norms which their children pick up.[20] Community patterns of segregated schools, buses, and waiting rooms are learned by the child as proper norms.[21] White persons' attitudes and behavior toward Negroes in the South have stood as institutionalized, expected patterns.[22] They bear no relation to intelligence, sex, degree of maturity, size of home community, or occupational level.[23]

Persons moving from one social system to another take over in varying degree the norms of the group to which they move. Recruits during basic training, for instance, learn many of the norms of the soldier system, including the proper mild hostility toward officers while in the buddy group of enlisted men.[24] While downward mobility produces less change of this sort because the person hangs on to certain norms of status, upward and horizontal mobility conduce significantly to the adoption of new ways of thought and action. Northern students at a southern college gradually move closer to the normative racial attitudes of this milieu.[25]

Learning the norms of a new system depends essentially upon three factors: (1) The person or other component learning (jibing with, converting to) the norm, (2) the norm itself, and (3) the norms of the person's other systems, past and present. Learning the new is easiest where the new stands most like the old and the current. It is easiest where the person is separated from his other systems of affiliation. It is easiest where it is "better" (higher status and more fun) than the past. It is easiest for people who are not long and deeply established in other systems. It is easiest for those whose learning of new norms is itself a norm. And it is easiest for those capable of high organization; "loners" maintain their pattern of autonomy.

Thus, Stouffer *et al.*[26] found that learning the expected, good-soldier norms in the American Army was easiest for the (1) better educated; a possible explanation is that these men were used to learning new things, (2) sociable and nonneurotic, coming from stable homes and healthy childhoods; these men had no severe "loner" traits and were able to "get with" the Army as they had "got with" their social systems of civilian life, (3) young; these had no deep-set norms from long action in another system, and carried less likelihood of high status distinct from the lowly position of the new G.I., (4) unmarried; the marital tie not only meant a pattern quite different from a soldier's life, and attachments to a system now often productive of G.I. anxiety, but the contrast of sexually and otherwise comfortable married life with Army life added to the married soldier's feeling of deprivation, and (5) those not in constant personal contact with their homes; isolation from these other systems meant that there was only one present, soldier norm to follow.

Norm Conformity

It is conformity to a line of action that creates a norm and makes possible the concept of deviance. Even in large, heterogeneous social systems such as modern nations, many norms of general conformity appear. The connotations of words, for example, bear a remarkable similarity throughout a total society.[27] The way various conceptions of objects, such as "leader," "church," and "Marilyn Monroe," are placed on a scale between good and bad, strong or weak, active or passive shows far-reaching agreement.[28] Even in the heat of a presidential compaign it is found that the opinions of Republicans and Democrats on a wide variety of political matters show a basic similarity.[29]

It is these far-reaching norms that give nations any distinct identity they may have as total social systems. They make possible the national characterizations found in such works as Seymour Martin Lipset's *The First New Nation*.[30]

Conformity within a large social system appears most easily achieved on matters with which components are not deeply involved. Social issues not of immediate or deep concern are amenable to conformity pressures; personal tastes and preferences, however, are resistant.[31] The norms to which a person conforms, regardless of what they are about, hold the key to his actual social systems of reference. It is the norm supported by his source of social approval which he generally follows.[32]

Present system norms—those of the milieu in which a person operates here and now—generally carry most weight. In a biracial coal mine (one is tempted to suggest that racial discrimination is understandably less likely in a dimly lit mine where all dirty faced men look black, or at night when all miscegenating cats look gray) Negro miners were generally accepted as equals whereas in the outside community patterns of segregation were the norm. White miners shifted their interracial action according to where they were. Minard [33] writes in this connection that about sixty percent of the white miners had no personal prejudices or antiprejudices, and that they were simply adjusting their role upon passing from the mine's mouth into the outside world. In a study of industrial workers in Chicago, similarly, no evidence appears to support the widespread belief that persons who show a high degree of acceptance of Negroes on the job will also be acceptive of Negroes in their home communities.[34] The significant point is that both personal attitudes and behavior follow the norms of the social system in which they occur.[35]

Norm conformity stands as a general, universal social value in all times and places. This is a basic law of social system operation. It is equal in stature to that concerning a system's normative quest for positive feedback and resistance to negative. Norm conformity is rewarded by system members; deviance not only carries no group reward, but usually precipitates the opposite. Members of social systems, accordingly, tend to view their own opinions as hewing close to the system norm; actually, they are more deviant than they think they are. It has been suggested that this may reflect an attempt to allay anxiety about nonconformity by minimizing one's actual deviation from the group standard.[36] It is found experimentally, for example, that first-born persons, who are unusually high in anxiety,[37] are exceptionally apt to conform with group judgments rather than to take an independent stand.[38] Norm conformity reduces anxiety because it assures the person of group support.[39]

Social systems of exceptional norm conformity—and thus a clarity and distinctness of line—are able to present a secure front to the outside world[40] and a home base of security and identity for their members from which confident forays with environments may be made. Morale is good among soldiers highly organized in informal groups and strongly attached to the latters' norms. They appear less fearful in battle, more confident in being able to perform well, less likely to resort to prayer under danger, and to surrender under stress.[41]

Norm conformity, moreover, goes with success in a social system. The more closely a member holds to his organization's values, the more likely will he be promoted within it. Conformity with army standards in both attitude and action marks recruits who advance.[42] Those who are or become group leaders are those most attached to its norms.[43] New leaders that enter are molded to old-system ways. They come to accept the group's traditions.[44] Where system norms are well established, a leader who tries to change them is not likely to remain a leader for long.[45]

Especially high levels of norm conformity appear characteristic of several kinds of system components. Highly authoritarian personality types, for example, appear strongly conformative to the norms of their group.[46] Conformity is comparably high for persons who value deeply their membership in a group.[47] Where the rewards of membership are great,[48] where the person wants to remain in the group,[49] where pressures toward conformity are strong and augmented by a rigid ideology as in a Communist cell,[50] and where the issue is perceived as important, the levels of norm conformity are raised. Festinger *et al.*[51] find that if a person wants to stay in a group, he will respond to pressures from it and abide by its rules. Components having least contact with other systems, and thus with other norms, likewise score high in conformity. Women of an ethnic minority in America, for instance, are likely to have a more pronounced ethnic accent because they "get around less" in a variety of economic, recreational, and other nonethnic systems than do the men of their group.

In systems made up of components who like one another, conformity is high.[52] Visibility of action figures importantly too; conformity holds firm where a member's deeds are readily apparent to others of his group.[53] Great frequency of contact [54]—common in small informal groups—generally means this sort of visibility, high organization, and a mutual policing of one another's behavior. Persons centrally and visibly located as active crossroads of communication within a group are especially conformative to its norms.[55] Pairs of workers can control one another's output when this output is visible. Control disappears when each worker works alone, separate, and unseen.[56]

In small informal American groups, where equalitarianism is generally prized as a social value, contact on a basis of equality appears especially meaningful for conformity. Uniformity of thought and action lessens when some members "throw their weight around" and exercise more authority than others.[57]

Strong component interest in the stability of a social system heightens conformity to its norms. It is a significant factor in the adherence of pro-components—mothers and wives, established religions, the political order, the basic economy—to expected, proper patterns. Civil service employees, who have a strong stake in political stability, rarely take extremist positions in politics. Lipset and Linz [58] report that civil servants are among the most moderate political elements of a society. They identify closely with the existing system of political arrangements; the latter might be changed by an extremist party.

Deviance

Conformity creates deviance, for a norm must exist before one may speak of deviance from it. By definition, too, empirical deviance can never be *modal* for the system in which it exists. Only about ten percent of persons in a wide variety of occupational fields, for example, music, geology, chemistry, and gerontology, are "deviantly" creative, accounting for fifty percent of the total creativity that occurs.[59] Noncreativity here, as elsewhere, stands as the modal norm.

The focus here is upon actual, empirical deviance rather than upon the label "deviance" that may be foisted upon people, things, and ideas which are defined as contra-active by a power structure. Sometimes, to be sure, actual deviance marks those who are defined as contra-active. But the two are in no sense identical and it is important analytically that they not be confused.

The deviance involved in crime may thus mean quite different things depending on who does it. It is generally defined as contra-active if a low-status person does it, and it is severely handled by the agents of power structure.[60] Upper-class persons, because of their pro and power positions, seldom are defined as seriously contra-active. Whether they commit blue-collar crime which is empirically deviant for their class or white-collar crime which is the proper kind when they are criminal, they are often treated lightly rather than as dangerous felons threatening to power units and to system action.[61]

There appears, similarly, a tolerance of eccentricity when a high-ranking eccentric is involved.[62] The lower-class mental deviant receives especially rigorous treatment. He has been found more likely than the upper-class mental patient to be put into the electric shock machine or to be operated on, less likely to get psychotherapy.[63] He is generally defined as sicker than his psychiatric equivalent of higher status.[64] He is more apt to be confined in an institution.[65] He is often more avoided than treated,[66] and he is more frequently described as antisocial, immature, and organically diseased.[67] The label "mentally sick" attaches to him more readily than to an equally disturbed person of high socioeconomic level.[68]

The deviance of the low-status person, then, is most likely to be defined as contra-active. Significantly, too, his own low-status systems permit him no special deviance from their norms. Regardless of class, for example, a person whose aspirations are out of line, that is, either higher or lower, with those of his family is likely to be treated as abrasive to family action.[69]

Deviance and conformity are generalized for a component regardless of his affiliations. They are features of component consistency. The "misfit"—the abnormally autonomous loner, for instance—tends to be so in the many systems to which he belongs. Certain kinds of deviance, moreover, predispose toward others. The person unattached to a steady job is apt to be comparably unattached as well to community, church, and marriage. Deviance in the form of exceptional autonomy may thus unfold into a total way of life for the deviant.

Yet it is the true reference group that must always be kept in mind for an accurate appraisal of deviance. The lower-class adolescent who is deviant from middle-class norms in being a school dropout is likely to be comparably deviant from these norms in his recreational, sexual, and other patterns, although he is thoroughly normative in terms of his true, lower-class reference groups.

The lone deviate can frequently be pushed into conformity with group norms. He is unlikely to hold out against the weight of otherwise unanimous group opinion even on matters where his perceptions tell him the group is clearly wrong—at least if he is a normal American and not a habitual deviate for whom the unpopular side is the one to be on. In a series of experiments,[70] a group of eight male college students was instructed to match the length of a line with one of three unequal lines. Each subject was asked to announce his judgment publicly. In certain trials, subjects were faced with purposely incorrect judgments by the others. Only one fourth of these held out for their own stands against the majority view when they were the only deviant in the group—even when the total group was as small as four: that is, three in the majority, and one deviant. When they were joined by one more deviant who took the same view as they, however, most subjects held firm against the rest of the group even when six others were arrayed against them. At least two human components in this case appear essential for a deviant social system to be *internally* reinforcing. A comparable study with school children provides similar findings.[71]

Deviance is low where the system carries great momentum, sweeping its components along with fervor. The rate of psychiatric withdrawal drops measurably in an army with the momentum of full advance and full retreat.[72] Withdrawal from all kinds of systems rarely occurs. The schizophrenic, the hermit, the painter engrossed in his work have extensive self-systems in which they operate as components.

Major factors in deviance are (1) the inadequate learning of norms and (2) an isolation from norm enforcers. These factors lead to the development of self-systems and self-norms, or to outside attachments and a learning of "strange" ways. They explain such things as the fact that new business deviates more fully than old from the "proper" political norms of the business community; unaffiliated, free-lance intellectuals display more variability from the "proper" political norm for intellectuals than do intellectuals who are connected with universities; youth run a wider gamut of political nonconformity than do the aged; unskilled workers, who move a great deal from system to system, show more political variability than do skilled workers; and the isolated industries of mining and maritime have often been marked by a wild deviance from the usual political modes of America.[73] Strikes in these insulated industries of mining and maritime are likewise heavy of incidence.[74] Political norms carry less weight, too, for those with small vested interest in the status quo: farm laborers and poor farmers rather than rich farmers, the unemployed rather than the employed, and the uncommitted rather than those deeply involved.[75]

The creatively deviant—artists, research scientists, and inventors—display a similar pattern.[76] They learn the usual, noncreative norms poorly. They attach to, and construct, a multiplicity of systems of thought and action. Their norm deviance—from occupational interests [77] to political ideas—stands generalized and diffuse rather than specific. Their inflow involves a broad spectrum of energy/information including much that is contrary to the norm of the occupational and other systems to which they belong as minimal members. Norm regulators of various sorts wield lessened power over them. And quite distinct from the usual tendency to rate oneself closer to the system norm than one really is,[78] the creatively deviant appear quite willing to accept themselves as deviant.

One study of industrial chemists [79] finds the creative ones thoroughly aware of their attitudinal difference from others, unattached to organized religion and its dogma, comparatively free from the norm enforcer of anxiety,[80] uncontrolled by the fear of failure and the chance of blame. A study of architects [81] reveals the most creative of them to be marked by an exceptional openness to a multiplicity of experience, a freedom from petty restraints and inhibitions as norm regulators, an independence of thought and action, and a commitment to creativity as a self-norm.

The creatively deviant stand as new-system makers and thus relatively apart from old norms. Throughout their work may be found the metaphorical process of conjunction: new combinations, new patterns, new organizations of materials, and new orderings.[82] A passion to encompass all in one comprehensive system marks them. Their Rorschach inkblot perceptions combine all details in one massive, synthesizing image.[83] Among the systems they make are patterns of humor,[84] thereby revealing a highly developed sense of humor.[85] They relate things of here and now to a wide variety of there and then; a study of their responses to pictures indicates a broad spectrum of associations.[86]

The highly creative escape the norm regulator of absolutism by viewing authority as conventional rather than absolute.[87] Group consensus similarly exerts little control upon them.[88] Their inattention or active opposition to norm enforcers when the latter are around often gets them into trouble with agents of authority.[89]

Deviance, as Chapter 2 indicated, is not necessarily defined as contra-action. The quiet, unabrasive deviant may "get away" with much. The funny deviant may be enjoyed. The high-status deviant may be followed.

Significantly, deviance generally draws most hostility only when it serves as a vehicle of hostility. It is this *vehicle-of-hostility* feature which alerts norm regulators and the policemen of social order. Indeed, certain deviants may strive to alert them. To thumb one's nose at a norm regulator and to let him know you are doing it may be, for a lower-class delinquent, his only chance for impact, for recognition, for existence in a middle-class society which ignores him and denies him power. The gang is often his instrument of raucous, hostile tune. And enforcers appear to set radars for such deviance of hostility and threat.[90]

Yet there are norms here, too. Delinquency and violence are normative expressions of hostility for the lower class although deviant by middle-class standards. Involvement in political activity, such as belonging to the John Birch Society, is the proper, gentlemanly way of expressing hostility among middle- and upper-middle-class persons. Frustrations stemming from being forced into "second choice" professions are sometimes channeled into a support of political parties hostile to the status quo.[91] During depressions and other circumstances limiting their opportunities, middle-class university students likewise take radical political stands.[92] Were the John Birchers of lower-class status, it is likely that their hostilities would find expression in personal violence and other channels normative for this class. Political and economic programs by organizers of the lower class such as Saul Alinsky are essentially attempts to swerve the illegitimate (by middle- and upper-class procomponent standards) hostility of riots, delinquency, and violence to the more proper, gentlemanly (again by middle- and upper-class standards) antagonisms of politics.

Enforcers

Enforcers strive to police a line of action. They guard a system's internal pattern, its gatekeeper operation, and its interplay with environment. They are normally a system's power units or its representatives, but often they develop norms and a certain autonomy of their own. They vary widely, too, depending upon the system in which they operate: whether it is what Etzioni [93] has called a "normative" one, for example, such as a religious or political organization with a strong ideological component; a "utilitarian" one, as in economic bureaucracies; or a "coercive" one, such as the army and custodial institutions.

Where enforcers are official agents of a power structure (although their norms may at times clash with this power structure's expectations), they tend to be given a wide berth of permissible action. An attorney for the American Civil Liberties Union has complained that vagrancy statutes are "purposely drawn vaguely so police can sweep large groups of people under them." [94] Similarly, draft boards have been reported as using their power to enforce conformity with United States government action in Vietnam by threatening to draft students who protest the United States' policy.[95]

When acting as agents of a system's power components, enforcers such as police and prisons exert greatest impact on out-of-power units. Mayer [96] notes a class bias in the administration of justice and legal protection in America so that out-of-power units are most frequently arrested, indicted, convicted and sentenced. Rarely do controllers of blue-collar people control white-collar people as well. Much white-collar crime—illegal corporate price fixing, for example—goes largely unattended to by enforcers of this kind. Often blue-collar crime by white-collar people, when it occurs, is regarded by these enforcers as "surprising." Shoplifting, burglary, and robbery by those who do not need the money raise questions of mental aberration as they are so unlike the proper norm for this group. When they reach blue-collar enforcers such as police and judges, their unexpectedness and thus their appearance as one-time aberrations and other factors, such as the efficient attorneys of rich, high-status deviates, generally means that they are dealt with leniently. As items of incongruence they present problems of thought and action for those who deal normally with blue-collar action by blue-collar people. They are sometimes most easily handled by making believe that some mistake occurred and that they really did not happen at all. A comparable though reverse problem—gentlemanly behavior by a criminal—was similarly intolerable to Police Inspector Javert in Hugo's *Les Miserables.* Indeed, the incongruence was so traumatic that he could resolve it only by suicide.

Out-of-power units of a social system are generally aware that the power structure's enforcers single them out for specific attention. Hollingshead and Redlich [97] report a deep-seated distrust of authority figures within America's lower class. From childhood to old age, suspicion and resentment are directed toward police, clergymen, teachers, doctors, public officials, public health nurses, and social workers. Politicians are regarded as exploitative of poor people. Some lower-class persons believe they are housed in slums because the state is taking advantage of them.[98]

When a system's action is unpleasant for components, stimulating entry to it generally requires strong pushers. A draft is often necessary, for example, to gain needed recruits for a military system. And police are necessary to catch criminals for a prison system. Within such systems, moreover, enforcers tend to be formal and rigid. Prison regimen has been notoriously strict. Military administration and command, similarly, are predicated on the implicit assumption that most soldiers will be either indifferent to or nonoriented to the army.[99] Enforcement of military expectations is accordingly mechanical, rigidly structured, and inattentive to personal variability.[100]

Formal enforcers of large and formal systems may be significantly strengthened when duplicated by informal ones operative in the person's immediate, intimate systems of interaction. Stouffer [101] writes along this line that the critical problem in the United States Army was to mobilize informal pressures of the soldiers in support of their fellows who conformed to Army standards and against the nonconformists, and to heighten the internalization of controls through habitual action. The individual recruit seeks solace in the company of his fellows who are as new and bewildered as he. With all escapes blocked by formal enforcers, soldiers can foster each other's adjustment to the inevitable by applying sanctions of their own to those who cannot "take it." Stouffer [102] notes that the fear of being thought unmanly by one's buddies can be as powerful an enforcer as the fear of the guardhouse. When these informal controls coincide with the formal, the Army has begun to build a soldier—a process that continues through internalization and automatization in the form of conscience.[103]

Enforcers work best on visible, clear-cut, well-known lines of action. Where entropy and randomness are high, enforcers are similarly entropic and random. In cases where a system's norm is perceived by its members as modally wide, or where members' perceptions differ greatly as to what the norm really is, it will exercise little control.[104] The widely touted "tolerance" of the city, as noted, is more properly a combination of such mixed perceptions, an absence of deep emotional involvement in norms that are vaguely defined, and the indifference that accompanies the low organization of urban living.

Where enforcers are strong the deviant has a difficult time. Suicide appears high in societies rigid in action and intolerant of misfits.[105] Yet rarely is suicide a legitimate "way out." Pressures on a person to stay with a social system are many and strong.[106]

Within small, informal groups, communications to deviants are at first heightened so as to bring them back to the fold.[107] In one experiment this was found to vary directly with the extent of their deviance.[108] Disapproval of dissenters and a lowered ranking for them within the group follows next.[109] When there finally appears no longer any chance of enforcing their conformity, communications to deviants fall off sharply and they are in effect isolated or expelled from the group. Both the rise and fall of these sendings to deviants are more pronounced in groups of high organization.[110]

Specific Enforcers

Informal pressures exerted within a social system are its major enforcers of action and controllers of deviance. These stand strongest in stable systems of high organization [111] though groups of all sorts generally seek to enforce their lines of action by encouraging, protecting, and providing rationalizations for "proper" behavior—and by sending ridicule, antagonism, and threats of expulsion to deviants.[112]

Deviates thus get rejected while conformers become popular.[113] Popular teen-age girls are found to hold fast to their peer group's tastes in music.[114] Workers control one another's output when they are in direct contact.[115] If a person wants to remain part of the group, too, he generally lets himself be ruled by its enforcers.[116] Where he has outside sources of social approval he will be less likely to accept the group's control.[117]

Modal members are by definition more numerous and can generally exert greater pressure on deviants than vice versa.[118] Informal enforcement succeeds best, too, on matters of little personal import such as broad "social" issues rather than where the person is deeply involved.[119] When he has no personal vested interest in one judgment or another, the power of unanimous group opinion is a significant enforcer.[120]

Informal enforcement within a small group depends strongly upon the popularity of the enforcer. People tend to agree, for example, with the opinions of those they like.[121] In addition, one's friends appear to reward one's conformity; one's enemies punish deviance from group standards.[122] The more a person's conformity is rewarded by the group, the more likely it appears that he will attract some disapproval as well.[123]

The impact of peer group as norm setter and enforcer appears at several age levels in America. Where wealthy students are numerous in a high school, the college orientation of all students—rich and poor alike—is high.[124] But social ranks vary in their responsiveness to group pressures. The middle level has been described as more tightly squeezed by informal controls than the upper or lower levels.[125] In small, informal groups, too, the middle ranked are most likely to agree with the group's rules both publicly and privately.[126] The low ranked disagree privately but conform publicly. The top ranked most freely express disagreement with the rules both publicly and privately.

The greater freedom and tolerance attaching to high status appears in other contexts too. Lower echelons of power do *not* appear less strict than those above. Indeed, informal controls by America's rank and file are found to be significantly more rigid and intolerant than those of its community leaders. Of generally higher educational and socioeconomic level, community leaders appear more willing than do the rank and file to give nonconformists the right to speak—and to express their radical views on economic, political, and religious subjects.[127] The romantic-radical notion of the masses as a repository of political tolerance, liberalism, and virtue is simply not borne out by the data.

Conscience can be a powerful enforcer. Hall and Lindzey [128] state that the supergo is modeled by early images of father and mother as perfect and omnipotent. It internalizes the action of these external authority figures and exacts conformity to society. Parental warmth and the possibility of its withdrawal—rather than coldness—are major builders of a child's conscience.[129] Where parental teaching of "right" and "wrong" is confused, or inconsistent with parental behavior, the child's learning of conscience is impeded.[130] A deep learning of conscience marks middle-class rather than lower-class America.[131]

Conscience works as an enforcer by creating guilt. It is found that a person's capacity for guilt depends on his early training; it is carried diffusely to the systems in which he later operates. Throughout a broad range of societies, for example, the earlier the age at which the child is weaned, given modesty training, independence training, and training in heterosexual inhibition, the more distinct will be his tendency to feel guilt and blame himself when he gets sick for having gotten sick.[132]

Ideology as an enforcer depends for its strength on the system within which it operates. It may be quite strong in some—a Communist cell, for example, or a civil war with a cause deeply believed in. Dollard,[133] writing of the Spanish Civil War, states that ideological identification with a cause is like the joker in a deck of cards. It can substitute for another card as a functional equivalent. The man who has it will more strongly hold to duty despite inferior equipment, temporary defeat, weariness, or fear. But in World War II little personal, ideological commitment to the war occurred among American G.I.'s.[134] Exposure to combat, too, reduces rather than enhances the power of ideology as an enforcer.[135]

CHANGE

Several facets of change have been touched upon in earlier sections. Change will now be examined intensively.

There are limited alternatives by which change can occur in a social system: (1) it may develop within, (2) it may come about through a system's inflow or outflow, or (3) it may happen through a combination of these. In all of them change requires *contrast:* the new against a background of the old. A thoroughly constant item of energy/information, for instance, goes unperceived. In one experiment an unchanging image was projected upon a person's retina with no fluctuation whatsoever due to normal eye movements. Within a matter of seconds the image disappeared.[136]

Two items of change, when they involve a strong contrast between them, alert the gatekeepers of external attention with such force that exaggerated perception occurs. When two persons who are liked in unequal degrees are seen together, the amount of liking for each blends with the other so that the amount of liking is perceived as equal. But when two persons—one of whom is liked and the other disliked—are seen together, the liking for one and the dislike for the other are both exaggerated.[137]

The determinism fostered by normative background is well established. According to *Weber's Law,* the change perceived in adding a weight of one pound to a background of ten is identical to the change perceived when a weight of two pounds is added to twenty. A gain of one thousand dollars, similarly, means less of a change for a rich man than for a poor one.

This importance of contrast for awareness of change appears in many contexts. Events that occur in isolation from similar events are remembered better than those preceded or followed by similar ones.[138] Similarly, the beginning and end items of a series, for example, the first and last verses of a song, are learned more quickly than the middle.[139]

Where a system is highly organized and its power components wield great force, change or stability in these power units means comparable change or stability elsewhere. In communities that are highly dependent upon a single industry or plant, for example, tension within it rocks the whole community.[140] Similarly, harmonious relations there can hold the community together.[141]

Farming, when as a power component it dominates a system's tone as it does in many rural areas, produces far-reaching changes in other sectors of the community if a profound change reaches it. Broom and Selznick [142] note that the industrialization of farming breaks down unified and homogeneous rural communities. Land no longer is considered valuable as a place for living, for work, and for identity. It becomes a commodity to be bought and sold. Bendix and Lipset [143] too report far-reaching changes attendant upon industrialization. They observe that the materialism of industrial societies has destroyed many value systems. Social unity and solidarity have often crumbled under the onslaught of self-interest and individualism.

Certain parts of a social system appear to change in a quite orderly and systematic way. Vocabulary in a large society has in the past been one of these. Swadesh [144] reports that everyday words have changed at an even rate. In a broad range of cases—Classic Latin 50 B.C. to present-day Romanian, Old High German 850 A.D. to present-day German, Classic Chinese 950 A.D. to modern colloquial North Chinese, Old English 950 A.D. to present-day English, and others—about eighty percent of everyday vocabulary was retained over each span of a thousand years.

An item of change carries major impact when it is markedly different from the existent norm. Societies with an advanced technology can absorb, routinize, convert without strain a great amount of innovation of high-level technology. In less advanced economies the social consequences attendant on the introduction of complex technology are more often disruptive.[145]

Change, whether induced internally or from the outside, heightens communication within a social system. Studies of formal organizations reveal a rise of communication among members, both toward the task at hand and for mutual emotional support, when innovation strikes.[146]

Resistance to Change

Resistance to change or the ready acceptance of it, like many other features of a social system, rests with power structure. Leaders predominate as initiators of change. In small informal groups it is the high-ranked members who most freely express diagreement with the old ways.[147]

Significantly, there appears no general tendency for a social system either to resist change or to welcome it. Systems are intrinsically neither conservative nor radical. All kinds of changes do occur, many of them drastic in their impact. Others make a fleeting, tenuous appearance upon the scene and are overwhelmed.

Significantly, too, the actual functional-dysfunctional impact of a change appears of little consequence in its initial acceptance or rejection. Indeed, a strong case may be made that many deeply functional changes in an actual, empirical sense have found short shrift while others of truly dangerous mien have been received with open arms. What the change is means little for its success. The important arbiter and judge of a new item—and its executioner or welcoming committee to the extent that it can—is the power component of a social system. Its thumbs up or down appears crucial. What it sees as implementive to its present direction of system line is received warmly. What it eyes as threatening is opposed.

Power units utilize their various resources to this end. They alert their gatekeepers of inflow and outflow; they keep their internal enforcers on guard; they place labels of "deviance" and contra-action where they feel the hot breath of potential negative feedback; they salute happily the changes—a new missile, a walk in space—which they feel mean business as usual, or better than usual. Shouts of joy welcomed the invention that has come to be known as the public relations industry, for it made possible much tax deductible pleasure under the Puritan-ethic umbrella of work. Through it one has been able to serve God, Mammon, Bacchus, and Eros—and all at the same time.

Significantly, power units often seek to protect not themselves but their present line of action. Clearly visible signs of real danger, as an earlier chapter has shown, are ignored, repressed, and distorted in their meaning. Impending disaster may come unopposed if meeting its challenge demands drastic overhaul in current system action and direction. Even in terms of maintaining their on-going action, power components often err. Sometimes things are welcomed which soon grind the gears badly and twist the steering wheel crazily. Conversely, genuine aids in better mileage and power may be ignored forever. Chances are, however, that most new things that are welcomed do provide positive feedback initially at least, thus implementing the system's traditional way of life.[148] Indeed, they may be encouraged precisely because they are viewed as actually conservative of on-going action and combative of other change which threatens.[149]

Mead [150] and Nash [151] find change dependent on willingness and desire, pointing out that societies large and small possess tremendous capacity to resist the new and hang on to the old—or to remake themselves in a generation if they wish. Keesing [152] too finds willingness and definition crucial in change. He observes that changes defined as "progress" and "advances" are happily received in America.

Wide differences appear among social systems in their rapidity of change. Some—attitudinal patterns,[153] for example, and norms of sexual activity that hold from generation to generation [154]—are found to be marked by strong persistence and inertia. For others, change comes so often that its recurrence may itself be said to constitute a norm. In many social systems battles rage continually between the legions of change and the solid fortresses of stability. Millikan and Blackmer [155] observe that in developing nations of the world the impulses of modernization clash with powerful forces which retard and frustrate the transformation of the traditional society into full modernity.

What system factors, then, appear associated with change or resistant to it? Several distinguishing traits characterize the system slow to change: (1) *monolithic identity*—a specific norm directed by a specific power unit, guarded by specific internal watchdogs and enforcers and protected by specific gatekeepers of inflow and outflow, (2) *high organization*—strong mutual impact and visibility among components so that change may be quickly felt, and corrected, and (3) a *high frequency of contact along normative ways,* maintaining system momentum in its present course.

Systems of this sort appear not only well equipped to resist change but capable as well of converting it easily along lines of their basic action when it does occur.[156] For systems of *vague* identity, on the other hand, meaningful change usually means the development of specificity. Until then their resistance to change is really a resistance to systemization. System forces, whatever they may be, here maintain comparative entropy. The eternally vague system says "Tomorrow we'll get organized."

In systems containing subsystems (thus of multiple identity), change may come often. Here many, often competitive power units with their own gatekeepers and internal enforcers create a condition where much that is new can slip through or arise. Things helpful to one subsystem and its power structure are frequently anathema to another. Consistent judgments of the new as good or bad become difficult when judges disagree, battle, and subvert one another. In national heterogeneity, as in America, lies this *structural incapacity* to resist multiple, rampant change. For where power structure is vague or diversified, change generally meets lowered resistance. In Colombia, the Spanish *conquistadores* established no strong power unit in the valley of Antioquia.[157] According to Millikan and Blackmer,[158] it is the Antioqueños who today spearhead political and economic modernization throughout Colombia.

Stability, as noted, most thoroughly characterizes homogeneous, highly organized, monolithic systems of long identity.

Keesing [159] finds that they often bear the monolithic stamp of a single religion. Change comes readily where populations and ethnic traditions are mixed. For when these heterogeneous subsystems meet, the meeting is likely to foster change in both. Exposure to heterogeneity and a mutual interplay of sending and receiving with it alter all systems involved. To illustrate, discussion yields more change than a lecture produces.[160] Cities, teeming with mixtures of people, things, and ideas, are focal points of change as compared to the more slowly moving village.[161] The heterogeneously cross-pressured middle-of-the-roader, too, is easily swerved to either one of his identities [162] and back again.

Close-knit systems man strong ramparts against change. The opinion out of context carries little lasting power in contrast to the thoroughly systematized and integrated attitudinal cluster,[163] and the person out of contact with his group and its patterns of thought and action may be readily swerved to the new.[164]

Change foisted upon a social system by some outside, extraneous power unit normally beats upon ironsides of resistance.[165] Change clearly visible in its threat to present system line—as in the case of a new value whose potential conflict with the old stands out in bold relief—similarly meets bulwarks of opposition. It is for this reason that values predominate as monoliths of system identity. When they go it is likely that the winds of change have already crumbled the less easily protected fronts as well. The systemically pervasive power of values, their interweaving throughout the social fabric, and their thrust as prime movers may catalyze the collapse of a system when it comes. Keesing,[166] reviewing the work of several students of change, concluded that where values stand firm, changes in other realms of social structure are easily accommodated. But where values—the visible, basic foundations of identity—break down, total system collapse is imminent. The focal importance of values as a core of system identity, suggested by Parsons [167] and by Lipset,[168] appears strongly substantiated.

The young appear easily blown by the winds of change. Rigid lines of action, clear-cut directors, powerful self-enforcers, and gatekeepers have not yet grown. Long-term patterns are not yet established. In the Japanese village of Suye Mura which was studied in 1935-6 and again in 1952-3 after the immense changes of World War II, the United States occupation, unsettled economic conditions, and deliberate pressures toward change, the young people took on new ideas and styles of life while the old—with old and distinct ways—resisted change.[169]

Affect too presents a strong stone face to the winds of change. Both love and hate appear to be received and transmitted without transformation. Returning hostility with love seems reserved for saints.

Where change is frequent and identity is continually in flux, further change becomes easy. For no line of action lasts long enough to develop strong gatekeepers and enforcers. Herein lies a partial dynamic of the exponential or compound-interest growth of inventions whereby each new invention appears to increase the likelihood of further change.[170] It may explain too why one revolution, destroying long established identity and legitimacy, paves the way for another—and why revolutions are most likely to occur after change starts, after reforms begin, and after conditions improve and things are getting better. For with these changes the established order and its controls are by definition crumbling.

Power components—with most to lose—may resist change most tenaciously. Village leaders in Suye Mura[171] held out against the onslaughts of change in this Japanese village which were wrought by World War II and its aftermath. Privileged class strata, foci of antichange, vote conservatively throughout Western civilization.[172] Within each class too the top socioeconomic segment identifies most strongly with the political status quo.[173] Similarly, those in occupations of status and power strive to keep things as they are. Professionals, who are high in income and prestige, are found to be generally conservative in political preference.[174] And within the business milieu, big business is politically more conservative than small business; its subsystems are fewer, its identity more monolithic, its cross-pressures less, and its political line more constant.[175]

It is out-of-power units on their way up that appear to spearhead further change. Much of the modern business activity that flourishes in India has been initiated by several of the newly mobile minority groups, such as the Parsis, the Marwari, and others.[176] Intellectuals, often marginal to established power and open to a variety of ideas, have similarly furnished impetus to change. Frequently they have latched on to emergent, on-the-make revolutionary cadres and provided them with an ideology legitimizing their thrust for power and their disruption of the status quo.[177]

It is to be emphasized that the simple fact of being out of power is not in itself conducive to rapid change. Out-of-power social units whose identity and controls against change are long established—the lower class, for example—are slow to adopt new ways or mount an offensive for change.[178] Their intolerance of the new politically, religiously, and otherwise has been previously noted. New patterns in childrearing,[179] also, tend to reach them last.

Structure stands more rigid than content, pattern more change-resistant than the particular energy/information involved. Labor unions wishing to continue as organizational structures take on new goals and objectives as the old ones are achieved.[180] With the right to collective bargaining firmly established, the quest for workers' pensions came to the fore.[181]

Words, items of content rather than structure, are incorporated more readily than is grammar.[182] Functional equivalents in content which permit "business as usual"—vodka in lieu of gin, frozen foods in place of fresh—find easy acceptance.[183] New items of content perceived as conforming with present action and new items with the label POSITIVE FEEDBACK writ large upon them are welcomed warmly. Dubin [184] notes that only after the Industrial Revolution, which met great resistance, did additional items of industrial technology make easy entry. It is not so much material versus nonmaterial, artifacts versus ideas [185] that lies at the core of acceptability. It is the perceived relevance of any item—whatever it may be—for present system action and power structure.

Minor change with its normally lesser threat and easy adaptability occurs more readily than large. Hovland *et al.*[186] find new opinions that are close to the old ones a person holds meet least resistance. Change so vastly different, such as "culture leaps," that its threat to the old goes unperceived or uncombatted may similarly succeed.[187]

Significantly, when a threat to present action and direction screams, extensive change will often be tolerated[188] in the hope that it will provide salvation and permit the core of present action to go on. The crisis of Depression made easier the innovations of the New Deal. One is reminded of Aldous Huxley's *After Many a Summer Dies the Swan* in which the millionaire, terrified of death, chooses to accept existence as a "foetal" ape if life may thereby be continued.

Affect brings resistance to change. Where love or hate looms large as a system component, system tenacity is extreme.[189] Symbols, such as flags, which are frequent foci of affect, hold fast.[190] Emotional investment in an opinion or an attitude bolsters its internal consistency and its likelihood of retention.[191]

Moving into or out of a system, it has been earlier noted, leads to a learning of the new and an unlearning of the old. But the change that occurs is greater when moving upward than downward in status. Upwardly mobile people, long before they have fully entered the circle to which they aspire, partake of its political and sexual norms.[192] But where movement means a loss of power and status, of dignity and self-esteem, many traits of the old system are clung to tenaciously. Skid row vagrants born into the upper class may still think of themselves as Republicans.

Foci of Change

Foci of change, as noted, are two: (1) within the social system, and (2) in inflow and outflow with its environments. Scholars have argued the primacy of each, some claiming the major significance of internal forces while others have been more impressed with environmental conditioners of change. Foster writes along this line: "Contact between societies is the single greatest determinant of culture change."[193]

The question of which is more important is impossible of accurate measure. A systemic interplay of internal and external forces of change normally occurs. The rise of new subsystems within a larger milieu, for example, relates often to events of the environment. The openness of a system's gateways to the world can enhance its internal unfolding of the new.

Internal Change

Sudden change in a system's components—a substitution of negative affect for positive, for example, in a marriage or a friendship—may tear the system apart. The first new item appears more fully traumatic than later ones of its type. The first child rocks the family most intensely. He is more likely to be a problem for it —and it for him—than his brothers and sisters who come after.[194] Similarly, strikes produce less of a flurry now than when they first burst upon the economic scene. Today's economic system is generally equipped to handle them and they are settled faster than they used to be. Ross and Hartman [195] report a steady shortening of strikes in the twentieth century throughout the nations of Western civilization.

Agents of change within a social system are apt to be its independent, autonomous units rather than its highly organized components. Intellectuals, often of marginal attachment to social systems and their norms, stand in the forefront of change in developing nations of the world.[196] Similarly, it is the autonomous, self-directed college student, relatively "independent of his cultural past," who leads radical student movements on America's college campuses according to a recently released five-year study prepared for the American Psychological Association.

Subsystems

Outstanding in internal change is the rise of new subsystems within a larger milieu. As with other kinds of change, these do not necessarily run into opposition. Indeed, they are often built by a system's power units: the opening of a branch office, the creation of a new job specialty within a factory, the setting-up of a new rank of power by an army's leadership, the establishment of a new cabinet post or government agency. When subsytems are *self*-initiated, too, they arouse the ire of power structure only when they are perceived as actually or potentially contra-active: delinquent gangs, extremist political parties, and hallucinogenic drug circles. New subsystems defined as pro, for example, Little Leagues, Boys' Clubs, and Campfire Girls, are encouraged.

Subsystems either pro or contra may arise within any institutional realm. To illustrate, religious contrasystems are found especially likely to develop where a religion moves away from "sect" toward the bureaucracy of "church," where it broadens its base of membership, its ideas and its action, and where its leadership grows complacent or is thought to be.[197] As it becomes more "churchlike" the probability rises that dissenters within it will form new sects.[198] Both "church" and "sect," however, can help to routinize change elsewhere in the larger society. In the shift from agriculture to industry in a southern community in the United States, the churches helped to implement the switch by direct cooperation with the mill owners, the sects by sublimating antagonisms of the mill workers through redirecting their concerns from this world to the next.[199]

Growth in system size generally precipitates the emergence of subsystems. Chapin [200] in his examination of voluntary organizations finds that they divide into subgroups of smaller size as they grow. The size group containing five to seven members appears critical in small, informal groups. Beyond it, subgroups spring up rapidly.[201]

Small size permits high organization and a close, informal guarding of conformity. Change that emerges can be quickly detected and discouraged. The larger a system, however, the greater the variability and heterogeneity among its components. Religious differentiation characterizes large societies rather than small milieux.[202]

Heterogeneity heightens the probability of new subsystems arising, such as organizations and inventions, as it enlarges the universe of metaphor: it makes possible a greater number and variety of new combinations and permutations. Each new invention, too, provides material for others so that inventions build upon one another cumulatively.[203] At the same time, people of the same kind ethnically and otherwise in a large and heterogeneous society such as America create little subsystemic islands of homogeneity in which they can feel at home.[204]

Where a social system must be large—a political party, for example, needs members for majority success—it must accommodate and conjoin a variety of heterogeneous subsystems. The attempt by Alexander Hamilton and other right wing Federalist leaders to build a one-class party led to its demise.[205]

The *fact* of power generally means subsystems of *varying* power. A differentiated structure involving units of high and low manipulative action is a normal feature of social systems. It develops too among animals other than man: pecking orders arise among hens,[206] and a herd of cows will establish a status hierarchy and march in that order when returning from pasture.[207] Power units themselves divide into subunits as the total system goes on. To illustrate, in small, informal groups a split occurs into *instrumental* and *expressive* leadership. Slater [208] finds top positions in the "best ideas" and "best liked" categories to be held by the same person in fifty-six percent of cases at the first group session. The figure fell to twelve percent at the second meeting, and it was down to eight percent at the fourth.[209] Riecken and Homans [210] describe the split as role differentiation with one person assuming instrumental leadership while another arises as morale-leader. Splits within other power units similarly occur. A gatekeeper who has combined entry and exit activities, for example, may develop separate units for each.

Subsystems of high power appear most distinct—attitudinally, at least—from those of low power in coercive social systems such as the army; less so within economic organizations; least of all in religious and political organizations where a strong ideology prevails.[211] In the American Army, officers and enlisted men were found to agree on certain general issues of World War II but disagreed markedly as to what they considered proper relations between officers and enlisted men.[212]

Formal controls mount in organizations where differing perceptions of proper roles mark subsystems of high and low power.[213] Overt strife between leaders and led likewise begets a tightening of formal controls [214]—and often an amplification spiral of more conflict producing more controls and vice versa.

Extensive formal controls are thus most likely to be found in groups where power units stand separate and distinct from those below or where some other form of heterogeneity prevails.

A multiplicity of subsystems, in any case, means a multiplicity of norms. Informal enforcers, including conscience, work best where consensus for the whole system holds. Formal rules are likely to take the place of informal controls in strongly differentiated milieux.

New subsystems emerge when certain components miss out on positive feedback from the larger milieu. Rural Negroes in the South, when transplanted to the cold impersonality of Detroit, sometimes found emotional solace in subsystem affiliation as followers of Prophet Jones.[215] An internal dialectic is suggested, too, in that the rise of subsystems involving certain components of the larger milieu often creates dissatisfaction among other members of this larger milieu who cannot or will not join the emergent unit, or for some other reason oppose it. The rise of Big Business gave rise to Big Labor; the rise of one school board faction—members of the John Birch Society, for example—produced another to combat it; the emergence of labor unions within factories yielded impetus to the development of industrial relations departments.

Change vis-à-vis Environment

Change vis-à-vis environment relates directly to a system's gatekeeper action. The tighter a system's doormen are shut to its environment, the less change there is likely to be within it. With little movement into or out of a society, for example, its traditional pattern of class stratification remains firm.[216]

Environmental change creates more attention than an environment that remains as it has always been.[217] Environmental change that is complex and irregular gets more attention than one that is simple and regular.[218] Massive entrance of novelty from outside similarly induces more resistance than small, easily convertible change. It is reported that large numbers of new entrants to a social system awaken fears of inundation, or of separatism within.[219]

Environments of *heterogeneity* are most precipitous of change for the systems upon which these environments impinge. The greater the range of novelty to which a system is exposed, the greater the likelihood that it will adopt new forms.[220] Overwhelmed by inundative change from a plethora of economic and other environments that it is powerless to resist, a social system may put all its identity and gatekeepers into one highly visible basket and make its last stand there. Sections of the white South appear sometimes to lay all they have upon the barricade of resistance to Negro entry into previously segregated systems. Often, too, aspiring entrants to a social system may wrap their entire being around successful entry as a personal crusade.[221]

SYSTEM RESPONSES TO CHANGE: INTERNAL

A social system and its leadership, as noted, welcome change they regard as positive feedback. But change looked upon as destructive and contra-active finds short shrift if leadership can prevent it. Such preceivedly threatening change that arises within a system may be handled by *expulsion, confinement,* or *conversion*. When it threatens from outside it may occasion *withdrawal* from it, or a *tightening of gatekeepers. Conjunction* with an item of environment, similarly, can derive from a desire to reduce negative feedback or to enhance positive through the creation of a new system. If these devices for handling dangerous change should fail, if the change proves too much for a system's resources, collapse and *disintegration* will occur. But rarely is this forever. Components—some old, some new—tend to reform, regroup, and *resystematize*.

Parsons [222] has suggested that a social system at any one time contains a limited amount of energy/information. With gatekeepers closed, applying more energy/information at one point within it may require reducing the application of energy/information elsewhere. To illustrate, the extra police power needed to quell the Watts riots in Los Angeles during August, 1965, had to be drawn from other structures of America. In this case it was drawn largely from the economic structure by summoning the normally latent National Guard whose members are usually economic contributors. Parsons[223] suggests that beyond certain ranges such switches in the application of energy/information cannot be implemented, and system disintegration will occur.

Meeting disruptive change involves a cost for a social system. Expulsion, confinement and conversion, withdrawal, increased gatekeeper action, and conjunction all take a toll in energy/information, whether they occur singly or in combination. Even when a system falls apart and disintegrates there is a kind of price to be paid in loss of identity and a fading into entropy.

A question worthy of broad investigation is why particular changes are perceived as positive feedback and others as negative. Of those defined as dangerous, moreover, why are some expelled and others confined or converted? Why are some withdrawn from, some responded to with gatekeeper action, others met with conjunction on the principle that "if you can't beat 'em, join 'em"? And why are certain changes successfully disruptive, producing disintegration?

Expulsion

Expulsion drives the new item—whether it originates within or intrudes from outside—out of the system. Excommunication expels the heretic from a religious system, firing removes him from an economic organization, exile displaces him from a political unit, and disowning and disinheritance turn him out of a family.

Expulsion is sometimes temporary, as with suspension from school. In any case it constitutes a special kind of sending. Distinct from a system's normal sending which it receives at the same time that it sends because this sending generally yields positive feedback, items being expelled are sent out precisely because they do not yield positive feedback. They wear a mien that is perceived as abrasive, disturbing, and disruptive by a system's power structure. While they are being expelled, accordingly, they are often rendered ineffective as possible items of negative feedback. The executive on his way out may be first isolated, that is, confined, in a remote office, deprived of effective power, and pushed into autonomy and low impact. *Excommunication* is likely to be involved in all expulsion in that the expellee is generally removed in process of expulsion from communication—from sending and receiving—lest he insert negative feedback into on-going system action. The religious heretic, the employee being fired, and the politician going into exile are all potentially contaminative.

Expulsion, moreover, is cross-societally of ambiguous legitimacy. Indeed, it is an area of such great tension that little rigorous research appears concerning it. The expellee must generally be painted as bad so as to legitimize his expulsion. The amenities of friendly discourse with an in-process expellee that are required by some social systems in which expulsion is highly institutionalized and may last for a period of months—as with an employee's contract that is allowed to expire—are thus a role-strain for both the expelling system and the expellee. Confinement or self-isolation along the way make the process more bearable for both.

Systems develop norms of expulsion along with other norms of operation. Firing, for example, is likely to be structured as resignation the higher the status within the organization of the employee who is being expelled. The shipping clerk is fired; the executive resigns. Normative procedures of expulsion in some social systems, such as corporations, may include being "kicked upstairs" to such positions as titular Chairman of the Board for executives of former power and prestige.

Expulsion, as with other techniques of handling change, may involve other items of energy/information besides people. "Dangerous" ideas, artifacts, and habits may be purged from a system by its leadership. The relative status of (1) the system that is left and (2) the system that is entered provides a key to the question of whether expulsion or voluntary exit has occurred. Persons moving down as they move out, for example, are more likely to have been expelled than those moving up.

Where power within a social system is highly differentiated or weak, the expulsion of a component by a power unit often requires concerted, cooperative action by several forces of power who concur in the decision and join forces to implement it. Often, too, it may require the cooperation of a power unit from outside. To illustrate, expelling a professor from an academic department normally demands a cooperative power cluster within the department, and the aid of the university administration outside it.

Expulsion of the old is frequent after a change in power structure has been accomplished. In Russia, for example, the successfully revolutionary Bolsheviks drove out many elements of the former regime. New power units commonly "clean house."

Confinement

Confinement contains a perceivedly dangerous item of change—a person, a thing, an idea, an emotion—within a social system. It builds a screen around it, cutting it off from action. It especially insulates the item from sending or being sent, for here its contaminative impact is direct. Not only on its own, moreover, but in its influence upon other components to follow its ways is it apt to be regarded as dangerous. Thus prisons are believed by their advocates to protect potential criminals from contamination as well as protecting the social system and its power structure from the immediate onslaughts of the criminals confined within.

Confinement figures prominently throughout social systems. New items potentially disruptive to action are individually and collectively isolated. People repress much of the politically uncongenial propaganda they have learned.[224] Unpleasantness is rapidly insulated and "forgotten."[225]

Yet confinement, like expulsion, carries a cross-societal ambiguity as to its legitimacy. Genuine legitimization of it generally requires such devices as defining the confined thing as evil and thus deserving of rejection and confinement. Those favoring prisons, for instance, usually define criminals as evil folk. Sometimes confinement is legitimized by associating the confined thing with a negative reference group. Here may lie the essential mechanism behind certain forms of *projection*. To illustrate, girls strongly repressing their sexual urges are found to attribute (project) sexual licentiousness to certain ethnic minorities they despise.[226] For these girls it may help make sexual urges "evil," legitimize their confinement (repression) of them, and thus prevent guilt feelings which might otherwise result from the ambiguous legitimacy of confinement.

Sometimes confinement breaks down. Imprisoned criminals escape, segregated races crack the barriers of Jim Crow, repressed experiences sneak through the superego screen in disguise.[227] Such breakdown is likely to be at least temporarily traumatic. For example, race prejudice mounts where the previously segregated and confined begin to break out.[228] Patterns of confinement, moreover, themselves change. As new waves of immigrants reached America's shores they pushed earlier ones out of socioeconomic bondage.[229]

Conversion

Conversion gears new items into a social system. It springs into action where the change is regarded as only mildly abrasive—and both possible and desirable of conversion. Conversion is the normal mechanism of socialization: training in the norms of the system one has entered or will enter.

Typically, conversion changes the change. It bends it, twists it, hammers it into the shape of perceivedly positive feedback. Max Weber, in dealing with charisma and its conversion to ongoing action, called the process *routinization*. Anthropologists are often adopted into primitive societies and positioned in native families not so much because they are loved but because they are unmanageable, unrelatable, and productive of anxiety when they are not ordered into the society. The system can accommodate them most smoothly when they are fitted into normal roles within it. Much also that appears to destroy change is more properly, because of the essential indestructibility of energy/information, conversion of it to a nonabrasive form.

Power units take the lead in conversion as elsewhere. The way that influential members of the community feel about politics bends the political opinions of newcomers to the community.[230] Established religious hierarchies, similarly, often strive to accommodate new sects within the bosom of the mother church when they can.[231] The effective power of a system, however, need not necessarily vest in its human components. Whatever the force that keeps it going in the present direction, it is this force that carries the action of conversion. It is this that pushes the new item into line despite the apparent strength of the new. New leaders, introduced into groups with well-established lines of action, become converted to the group norm although they may still manage superficially to play the role of leader.[232]

By definition, the converting system dominates the item converted. While it may be itself somewhat changed in the process of converting another—and this normally occurs—it sends more change than it receives. If it does not, if it is itself converted by the item it has set out to convert, by definition it will have disintegrated and been resystematized in a new form. American Negroes have been largly converted by and to America rather than vice versa. According to Powdermaker [233] it is the Negro upper class that has been most fully converted, taking over both form and meaning; the middle class has adopted fewer white patterns, and more form than meaning; the lower class has been converted least—and generally only in the realm of form.

Change that is limited in scope appears more convertible than change that is large. Successful conversion of ethnic minorities into the total action of the American public school takes place most easily when the minority is relatively small, constituting at the very most not more than twenty-five percent of the school population.[234] Similarly, new items that are similar to a system's present components are most readily convertible. Communications only slightly out of line with a person's persuasions are judged favorably and generally welcomed while those strongly dissimilar are scoffed at as propaganda and denied entry.[235] Ethnic minorities, too, fit best into the American public school when they are of the same socioeconomic level as the current school population, when they are strongly Americanized through having been here for some time, and when they have come from a milieu comparably urban or rural as the receiving one may be.[236]

The easier convertibility of the new that is similar to the old appears also in the fact that word lists are learned better than lists of nonsense syllables, and nonsense syllables that most fully resemble words are learned better than others.[237]

A kind of *pseudo*-conversion at the boundary may sometimes occur. Persons whose attitude is close to that of the new tend to perceive it as being actually closer to their stand, and thus more fully welcomable as positive feedback than it really is.[238] A similar thing happens with uncongenial messages that enter forcibly or accidentally; it reduces their negative feedback potential as items of dissonance.[239]

Frequent contact between the converting system and the item it is converting hastens the process of conversion. In the United States, the Japanese immigrants on the West Coast picked up American culture faster than Mexicans did because their occupations brought them into constant touch with the larger society.[240]

Conversion is apt to proceed generally and diffusely rather than specifically. Economic acculturation and acculturation in other realms of living normally go together.[241]

SYSTEM RESPONSES TO CHANGE: WITH ENVIRONMENT

Withdrawal

Withdrawal carries a social system away from an environmental change that threatens. It builds a barrier of time/space between itself and the new phenomenon. An army in the field, unable to withstand an enemy attack, may seek to withdraw if it can.

Withdrawal constitutes a simple response to change. In many situations, however, it is blocked—sometimes by physical factors, sometimes by social barriers of various sorts. Merton [242] and Slater [243] noted the illegitimacy of several kinds of component withdrawal from the larger milieu: of the soldier deserting from the army, of the engaged or marital dyad from the community.

Suicide likewise is rarely legitimate withdrawal. Indeed, even death may sometimes arouse some resentment as inconsiderate "goofing off" ("How could he *do* such a thing to me!").

Where two items of threat—such as military death from remaining active in battle, or court-martial for refusing—challenge a person and barriers prevent withdrawal, the person may position himself between the two and oscillate there. Approach toward one horn of the dilemma increases the tendency to retreat toward the other since anxiety is least when distances from both are greatest.[244] Often when direct physical withdrawal is blocked or illegitimate, other lines of escape are utilized. An American pilot in Joseph Heller's *Catch 22* withdrew from World War II by arranging to crash-land and be interned in Sweden. Similarly, nonbattle casualties, accidents around camp and other accidents that permit a withdrawal from combat, are more frequent among soldiers lacking eagerness for combat.[245] Personal detachment from reality may provide a partial withdrawal from a dangerous military situation,[246] or from the brutality of concentration camp life.[247]

Alcohol furnishes a similar opportunity for withdrawal. Even laboratory animals (in one experiment, cats that were rendered neurotic) learned that they could find temporary relief from their neurotic symptoms by "getting high" on alcohol.[248] Psychosomatic ailments of various sorts provide other vehicles of withdrawal.[249] Spirals are common here. The introverted child withdrawing via myopia is often brought forcibly back to the environment he wishes to escape by eyeglasses which bring his vision up to normal. He has to achieve additional myopia to withdraw to the place he was—and this may again get frustrated by more "correction" in his lenses.

Withdrawal from certain environments is often implemented, or masked, by entry into another. Farber [250] suggests that much of the activity in social and athletic clubs, in veterans' and fraternal groups is generated by a desire to get away from a marriage or family situation. Spiral again is likely. The author notes that high participation in these organizations stemming "from a desire of the men to be away from home . . . aggravated difficulties in their marriage." [251]

Tightening of Gatekeepers

Gatekeeper action provides a significant resource of system stability when threatened by environmental change. Assaulted by change from outside, a social system may bolster its doormen of inflow against it. As noted, it may limit immigration selectively as did the United States inundated during the early twentieth century with hordes of immigrants from eastern and southern Europe. These immigrants awakened cries of alarm from various power units of America and precipitated the enactment of restrictive legislation against them. Immigrants from the countries of northern and western Europe, more closely resembling America's power units, found a warmer welcome.

Gatekeepers of outflow provide a source of protection when change threatens via loss of present components. Many nations of the world, for example, have imposed severe restrictions on emigration. Not always does a social system act to tighten its gatekeepers, however. While laments are heard today in Great Britain concerning the brain drain of scientists and other highly trained personnel to America, little has been done to combat it. It should be noted that strongly restrictive gatekeeper action —especially in regard to outflow yet relating in some degree to inflow as well—is of limited legitimacy as a resource of antichange in democratic social systems.

Conjunction

Conjunction meets change in the environment by joining with it to form a new and larger system. This need not necessarily be change perceived as threatening; indeed, most conjunction occurs with items of environment welcomed in their present impact. But it can provide a way of forestalling negative feedback by the environmental item through joining with it and creating a new system.

Conjunction is the basic process of system formation. Through it, the previously unjoined are brought together and systematized. Through it, too, new federations occur among those previously organized in other ways. It is a process found not only in social systems but in all systems. Isolation is resisted.[252]

Conjunction is illustrated in the joining together of American colonies into the United States, of individual nations to form the United Nations, of allies during a war, of corporations merging with one another, of combining religious bodies, of husband and wife in marital union, and of items of culture into a new pattern or invention. It is not to be confused with "joining" an on-going system—becoming a member of an established fraternity, for example—which is really entry into it. Similarly, it need not mean the establishment of a happy system involving positive affect as a component. Armies in the field may join battle. Nor need it depend upon the initiative of the joining components; it can draw its impetus from an outside source. Inventors, artists, scientists, and others bring together as creators and metaphor-makers a variety of items to form a new idea, a new product, a new melody, a new book.

This latter type of conjunction that is built by an external composite-maker appears more likely in certain kinds of social systems than in others. To illustrate, between 1947 and 1955 the ratio of brain to brawn personnel increased sharply in the United States in aircraft, electronics, chemicals, ordnance, and petroleum. Each of these industries spewed forth inventions (a prime form of conjunction) for their own use and for others. The proportion of brain to brawn personnel increased less rapidly in textiles, lumber, railroad, and utilities. These industries adopted for the most part innovations that were developed by others.[253]

The importance of an outside force in the making of new systems appears also in the impetus given to new conjunctions by an environment that threatens. The Soviet Union and the United States teamed up closely while Nazi Germany roared at both. Delinquent gangs form largely to protect their bewildered members from the onslaughts of a hostile world.[254] Girls frightened by the prospect of a supposedly painful experiment chose to wait for it together. Where little externally induced pain threatened, however, their affiliative, conjunctive behavior showed no increase.[255] When environmental threat is lifted, too, components who have conjoined because of it often break up. They may even become hostile—especially if this were the case previous to conjunction. A Cold War between the Soviet Union and America arose after their teamwork during World War II.

Systems appear to conjoin with others essentially to augment their present action. It is positive feedback they seek in the building of a "yes" group. Prime movers in the process of merging accordingly—and of staying together—are likely to be those who feel they have most to gain.

Systems conjoin most readily—even in forming new hostile systems—with those most like themselves. Here the prospect of positive feedback shines clearly. For a military system, for example, battle with another like itself—which permits it to use most fully its arms and men in normal ways—most fully constitutes positive feedback for it. Arms and armies are designed specifically to fight similar arms and armies. Rarely do spears challenge supersonic fighters.

Conjunction with those like oneself, in any case, is the basic form. It appears most helpful to each unit's on-going action and thus most likely to be maintained. Newcomb [256] writes along this line that the one way it is possible to satisfy individual-autistic needs and the demands of social living is to form subgroups with others of similar persuasion. Friendships grow most easily and last longest among persons already alike—in religion, social class, and ideals.[257] Marriage is found most likely to occur and to last where the mates share a variety of physical and social traits.[258] Political federations survive best when their members are alike. Politics may temporarily make strange bedfellows. But they are likely to stay together longest when they are least strange.

It is in regard to conjunction which involves the expectation of permanence, such as marriage and deep friendships, that insistence upon similarity appears strongest. The casual flirtation or hail-fellow-well-met acquaintanceship is likely to permit a wider range of difference between the units that are conjoined. It is possible that the observed shorter duration of intermarriage relates more often to a lesser expectation of permanence than to fierce conflict within.

Significant in conjunction is the factor of proximity. Units close in space are more apt to conjoin than those that are further apart. One is likely to love and to marry his neighbor.[259] Friendships too form most freely among those living close by. The greater the physical separation within a housing project, the fewer the friendships within it.[260]

Significant also in conjunction are the patterns established early in life. Where early affiliations—the child with his parents, for instance—have proved warm and satisfying, the person will conjoin eagerly throughout his life.[261] Chronic loners are likely to have been deprived of happy, early conjunctions.[262]

Conjunction involves an important structural source of tension. This inheres in the fact that conjoining systems rarely give up thoroughly their individual identities and resystematize without at least a backward glance. Hangovers of old identity remain. And often these move to secede or otherwise break asunder the new system. In many conjunctions, such as political federations, marriages, and business partnerships, some of the conjoining units simply do not wish a "more perfect union." They struggle against the death of individual identity involved in total togetherness. They strive to maintain "states' rights."

Certain conjunctions are thereby often quite unstable. The balance of centripetal and centrifugal forces within systemic conjunctions appears worthy of intensive scholarly investigation. In some cases outside forces are brought to bear to prevent their tearing asunder. Power structures with their interest in pro-unit stability often expend through their inadvertent agents—social workers and marriage clinics—significant amounts of energy/information to maintain family groups and discourage divorce and desertion.

Disintegration

Disintegration means systemic death. With it, components *de*systematize. It is a movement away from organization into entropy and randomness. Disintegration may occur as a by-product of conjunction with another system though rarely (as noted) is such loss of identity complete. It may occur through the conversion of the system into another, as Christianity engulfed earlier deities of Italy and fitted them into the new religion. Disintegration arrives as a result of inadequate defenses against change—or a willing acceptance of it.

A system may: (1) itself disintegrate, (2) produce the disintegration (destruction or conversion) of a subsystem within itself, or (3) produce the disintegration of a system in its environment. Generally, systems fight their collapse. Their power units seek to hold them together. They combat disorganization as negative feedback.

Systems do this, not groups. Certain ethnic minorities in America, for example, may actively seek disintegration so that forces which segregate and preserve their identity constitute negative feedback to their desire. Groups are not necessarily driven to last. At the same time it is often possible even here to find clusters of *detente*. While some persons in the Negro civil rights movement seek overall conversion and integration (more properly, *dis*integration) of the Negro population into the larger society, certain Negro subgroups, such as lawyers, undertakers, insurance companies, and certain Negro colleges, may subtly and sometimes overtly oppose their dissolution as ethnic strongholds. The situation is thus somewhat different from other ethnic minorities in America whose leadership has not been comparably cross-pressured. Here, those segments of the ethnic minority that have highest status within it have been the first to disintegrate ethnically and allow their conversion to America. High social status in Hungary, for example, has meant fast acculturation for this Hungarian immigrant in the United States.[263] Even when the entire ethnic group is predominantly of the lower class, as with Puerto Ricans in America, the middle class among them acculturates and thus disintegrates into the larger milieu more rapidly than does the lower class.[264]

Disintegration varies widely in its formality and institutionalization. In many social systems—those, for instance, that are casually and loosely integrated on a hail-fellow-well-met basis—disintegration follows comparably casual lines. But where extensive formalization is involved, as in marriage, techniques of proper dissolution—annulment and divorce—tend likewise to be highly structured. One may note that a process of disintegration, as in divorce, may itself constitute an elaborate social system.

The longer a social system lasts—friendships, marriages, business associations, and organizations—the more traumatic for its components is apt to be its dissolution. The more likely are such long-lasting systems, also, to resist disintegration. Expectedly temporary systems take a minor toll when they break. The intensive study of temporary social systems in this and other connections appears especially relevant as the numbers of these systems mount in all institutional realms with the increasingly mobile civilization of today.

Disintegration happens least often when the onslaughts of change are slow and thus easily convertible along the lines of a system's basic action. Where they come too fast and furiously for adequate defenses against them and accommodations of them, they will destroy. Many traditional ways in the emerging, developing nations of the Middle East, Southeast Asia, and Africa wither before the hand of massive change which reaches out from the modern, western, industrial milieu.[265]

Values hold on most tenaciously. They stand as focal points of system identity and heavily defended strongholds against change. A social structure may withstand, without disintegrating, extensive change in its other components—people and artifacts, for example—so long as its values hold firm.[266] When values go, when they are at last torn asunder, the total social edifice tends to crumble.

Resystematization

Old systems rarely die, or even fade away. Total disintegration and a movement of components out into entropy and randomness happens seldom. Rather do they regroup—with something old and something new, much that is borrowed, and many things blue, black, white, and tan. Historical data indicate that no society—regardless how dire the catastrophe that befalls it—ever simply abandons its traditional culture.[267] The old leaves significant marks upon the new.

Continuous change and adjustment,[268] a breaking down and

a building up, are common processes today. While only twenty percent of everyday vocabulary falls by the wayside and is replaced every thousand years,[269] other changes proceed rapidly so that a society may disintegrate and remake itself, that is, resystematize, in a generation if it wishes.[270]

Yet, resystematization may also come slowly sometimes. Under the onslaught of the new, disorganization can hold forth for quite a while before new patterns of order and system form.[271] It will probably be some time, for example, before the broken pattern of race relations in the American South moves out of disorganization and solidifies into a new and stable order. But chances are good that it will.

NOTES

Chapter 1

[1] The word *action* is generally substituted for the word *behavior* to avoid the biological connotations of the latter term. Ideas and rules are considered more properly to *act* than behave.

[2] Joseph H. Monane, "Indices of System Stability and Change." Unpublished paper read at meetings of the Eastern Sociological Society, 1965; Robert S. Gold, *A Jazz Lexicon* (New York, Knopf, 1964); D. W. Maurer, *Whiz Mob* (New Haven, Conn., College and University Press, 1964).

Chapter 2

[1] Robert C. Hanson, "The Systemic Linkage Hypothesis and Role Consensus Patterns in Hospital-Community Relations," *American Sociological Review,* 27 (June, 1962), pp. 304-313.

[2] Chester Barnard, *The Functions of the Executive* (Cambridge, Mass., Harvard University Press, 1950), p. 123.

[3] Edward A. Shils, "The Study of the Primary Group," in Daniel Lerner and Harold D. Lasswell, eds., *The Policy Sciences: Recent Developments in Scope and Method* (Stanford, Calif., Stanford University Press, 1951), p. 64.

[4] Leonard R. Sayles, *Behavior of Industrial Work Groups: Prediction and Control* (New York, Wiley, 1958), p. 153.

[5] Leslie A. White, "Ikhnaton: The Great Man *vs.* the Culture Process," *Journal of the American Oriental Society,* 68 (1948), pp. 101-102.

[6] *Ibid.*

[7] George P. Murdock, *Our Primitive Contemporaries* (New York, Macmillan, 1934), p. 348.

[8] Max Weber, *The Protestant Ethic and the Spirit of Capitalism,* trans. by Talcott Parsons (New York, Scribner, 1958), p. 177.

[9] *Ibid.*

[10] Robert K. Merton, "Puritanism, Pietism, and Science," in *Social Theory and Social Structure,* rev. ed. (New York, Free Press, 1957), pp. 574-575.

[11] *Ibid.,* p. 585.

[12] Harold H. Kelley, "Salience of Membership and Resistance to Change of Group-Anchored Attitudes," *Human Relations* 8 (1955) p. 275.

[13] Bernard Berelson and Gary A. Steiner, *Human Behavior: An Inventory of Scientific Findings* (New York, Harcourt, Brace & World, 1964), p. 430.

[14] *Ibid.,* p. 431.

[15] *Ibid.,* p. 412.

[16] *Ibid.,* p. 411.

[17] Morris Janowitz, "The Military Establishment: Organization and Disorganization," in Robert K. Merton and Robert A. Nisbet, eds., *Contemporary Social Problems* (New York, Harcourt, Brace & World, 1961), p. 522.

[18] Seymour M. Lipset and Juan J. Linz, "The Social Bases of Political Diversity in Western Democracies." Unpublished ms. (1956), p. 60.

[19] John W. Riley, Jr. and Matilda White Riley, "Mass Communication and the Social System," in Robert K. Merton *et al.,* eds., *Sociology Today: Problems and Prospects* (New York, Basic Books, 1959), p. 552.

[20] Berelson and Steiner, *op. cit.,* p. 301.

[21] Bernard Berelson, Paul F. Lazarsfeld, and William N. McPhee, *Voting: A Study of Opinion Formulation in a Presidential Campaign* (Chicago, University of Chicago Press, 1954), p. 99

[22] Edgar H. Schein, "Reaction Patterns to Severe, Chronic Stress

in American Army Prisoners of War of the Chinese," *Journal of Social Issues* 13 (1957), pp. 21-30.

[23] Berelson and Steiner, *op. cit.,* p. 329.

[24] Rose K. Goldsen, Morris Rosenberg, Robin M. Williams, Jr., and Edward A. Suchman, *What College Students Think* (Princeton, N.J., Van Nostrand, 1960), p. 101.

[25] Berelson and Steiner, *op cit.,* p. 330.

[26] *Ibid.,* p. 161.

[27] Personal communication from Professor Nicholas A. Beadles (Athens, Ga., University of Georgia).

[28] Leonard R. Sayles, *Behavior of Industrial Work Groups: Prediction and Control* (New York, Wiley, 1958), pp. 152-153.

[29] Gerhard Lenski, *The Religious Factor* (New York, Doubleday, 1961), p. 289.

[30] Berelson and Steiner, *op. cit.,* p. 570.

[31] Bernard Berelson, "Voting Behavior," *Encyclopaedia Britannica,* 23 (New York, Encyclopaedia Britannica, 1961), p. 259a; Angus Campbell and Homer C. Cooper, *Group Differences in Attitudes and Votes: A Study of the 1954 Congressional Election.* Survey Research Center (Ann Arbor, Mich., University of Michigan Press, 1956), p. 149; Rose K. Goldsen, Morris Rosenberg, Robin M. Williams, Jr., and Edward A. Suchman, *What College Students Think* (Princeton, N.J., Van Nostrand, 1960), pp. 164-168; Samuel A. Stouffer, *Communism, Conformity, and Civil Liberties: A Cross-Section of the Nation Speaks Its Mind* (New York, Doubleday, 1955), p. 90.

[32] Leonard Broom and Philip Selznick, *Sociology,* 3rd ed. (New York, Harper & Row, 1963), p. 279.

[33] Berelson and Steiner, *op. cit.,* p. 430.

[34] Joseph H. Monane, *A Profile of Human Factor Requirements in the Maritime Industry* (Washington, D.C., George Washington University, 1965); Clark Kerr and Abraham Siegel, "The Interindustry Propensity to Strike: An International Comparison," in Arthur Kornhauser, Robert Dubin, and Arthur M. Ross, eds., *Industrial Conflict* (New York, McGraw-Hill, 1954), pp. 190-195.

[35] Seymour M. Lipset and Juan J. Linz, "The Social Bases of Political Diversity in Western Democracies." Unpublished ms. (1956), pp. 58-59.

[36] Berelson and Steiner, *op. cit.,* p. 369.

[37] Leonard Broom, "Social Differentiation and Stratification," in Robert K. Merton *et al.,* eds., *Sociology Today: Problems and Prospects* (New York, Basic Books, 1959), p. 435.

[38] Robert E. Lane, *Political Life: Why People Get Involved in Politics* (New York, Free Press, 1959), p. 326.

[39] Samuel A. Stouffer, *Communism, Conformity, and Civil Liberties: A Cross-Section of the Nation Speaks Its Mind* (New York, Doubleday, 1955), p. 90.

[40] For example, it is found that women tend to be more attached to religious systems than are men, and to be more strongly influenced politically and otherwise by these religious ties. (Juan J. Linz, "The Social Bases of West German Politics." Unpublished Doct. Diss. [New York, Columbia University, 1959], p. 235.) In surveys of American students, too, men are found to be more strongly oriented toward systems of theoretical, economic, and political interest, women toward systems of aesthetic and religious concern. (William F. Dukes, "Psychological Studies of Values," *Psychological Bulletin,* 52 [1955], pp. 24-50.)

[41] Berelson and Steiner, *op. cit.,* p. 570.

[42] Shmuel N. Eisenstadt, *From Generation to Generation: Age Groups and Social Structure* (New York, Free Press, 1956), p. 22.

[43] Meyer Fortes, "Introduction," in Jack Goody, ed., *The Developmental Cycle in Domestic Groups,* Cambridge Papers in Social Anthropology, no. 1 (Cambridge University Press for the Dept. of Arch. and Anthro., 1958), p. 10.

[44] Berelson and Steiner, *op. cit.,* p. 79.

[45] David C. McClelland, John W. Atkinson, Russell A. Clark, and Edgar L. Lowell, *The Achievement Motive* (New York, Appleton-Century-Crofts, 1953), pp. 289-294.

[46] Berelson and Steiner, *op. cit.,* p. 401.

[47] *Ibid.,* p. 316.

[48] W. Lloyd Warner, "The Study of Social Stratification," in Joseph B. Gittler, ed., *Review of Sociology: Analysis of a Decade* (New York, Wiley, 1957), p. 243.

[49] Maurice Duverger, *Political Parties: Their Organization and Activity in the Modern State,* trans. by Barbara and Robert North, 2d English ed., rev. (London, Methuen, 1959), p. 113.

[50] Berelson and Steiner, *op. cit.*, p. 330.

[51] Morris Janowitz, *Sociology and the Military Establishment* (New York, Russell Sage Foundation, 1959), pp. 68-69, 74; Edward A. Shils and Morris Janowitz, "Cohesion and Disintegration in the *Wehrmacht* in World War II," *Public Opinion Quarterly,* 12 (1948), p. 281; Morris Janowitz, "The Military Establishment: Organization and Disorganization," in Robert K. Merton and Robert A. Nisbet, eds., *Contemporary Social Problems* (New York, Harcourt, Brace & World, 1961), p. 547.

[52] Samuel A. Stouffer *et al., The American Soldier,* Vol. I (Princeton, N.J., Princeton University Press, 1949), p. 449.

[53] Edward A. Shils and Morris Janowitz, "Cohesion and Disintegration in the *Wehrmacht* in World War II," *Public Opinion Quarterly,* 12 (1948), p. 281.

[54] Berelson and Steiner, *op. cit.*, p. 446.

[55] Terence K. Hopkins, "The Exercise of Influence in Small Groups." Unpublished Doct. Diss. (New York, Columbia University, 1959).

[56] Berelson and Steiner, *op. cit.*, p. 341.

[57] James F. Short, Jr. and Fred L. Strodtbeck, *Group Process and Gang Delinquency* (Chicago, University of Chicago Press, 1965).

[58] Berelson and Steiner, *op. cit.*, p. 466.

[59] Arnold M. Rose, "Race and Ethnic Relations," in Robert K. Merton and Robert A. Nisbet, eds., *Contemporary Social Problems* (New York, Harcourt, Brace & World, 1961), p. 365.

[60] Kingsley Davis, *Human Society* (New York, Macmillan, 1949), pp. 332-333.

[61] Berelson and Steiner, *op. cit.*, p. 368.

[62] *Ibid.*, p. 431.

[63] Edward A. Shils, "Class," *Encyclopaedia Britannica,* 5 (New York, Encyclopaedia Britannica, 1960), p. 767.

[64] Seymour M. Lipset and Reinhard Bendix, *Social Mobility in Industrial Society*. University of California, Institute of Industrial Relations (Berkeley, Calif., University of California Press, 1959), p. 275.

[65] See Seymour M. Lipset, "Political Sociology, 1945-55," in *Sociology in the United States* (New York, UNESCO, 1957), p. 6.

[66] F. Stuart Chapin, "Social Institutions and Voluntary Associations,"

in Joseph B. Gittler, ed., *Review of Sociology: Analysis of a Decade* (New York, Wiley, 1957), pp. 263-264.

[67] Berelson and Steiner, *op. cit.*, p. 358.

[68] *Ibid.*

[69] *Ibid.*

[70] Robert F. Bales, A. Paul Hare, and Edgar F. Borgatta, "Structure and Dynamics of Small Groups: A Review of Four Variables," in Joseph B. Gittler, ed., *Review of Sociology: Analysis of a Decade* (New York, Wiley, 1957), p. 394.

[71] Berelson and Steiner, *op. cit.*, p. 360.

[72] Theodore M. Mills, "Power Relations in Three-Person Groups," *American Sociological Review*, 18 (1953), p. 353.

[73] Berelson and Steiner, *op. cit.*, p. 360.

[74] *Ibid.*

[75] *Ibid.*

[76] Leonard Broom and Philip Selznick, *Sociology: A Text with Adapted Readings* (New York, Harper & Row, 1957), p. 382.

[77] Paul F. Lazarsfeld and Wagner Thielens, Jr., *The Academic Mind* (New York, Free Press, 1958), p. 147.

[78] Ozzie G. Simmons, *Social Status and Public Health*. Social Science Research Council, Pamphlet no. 13 (1958), pp. 17-18.

[79] *Ibid.*

[80] Hans H. Strupp, "Psychotherapy," *Annual Review of Psychology*, 13 (1962), pp. 445-478.

[81] *Ibid.*

[82] See Julius Seeman, "Psychotherapy," *Annual Review of Psychology*, 12 (1961), p. 179; Hans H. Strupp, "Psychotherapy," *Annual Review of Psychology*, 13 (1962), pp. 445-478.

[83] Judson T. Landis, "Marriages of Mixed and Non-Mixed Religious Faith," *American Sociological Review*, 14 (1949), p. 403.

[84] Seymour M. Lipset, "Political Sociology," in Robert K. Merton *et al.*, eds., *Sociology Today: Problems and Prospects* (New York, Basic Books, 1959), p. 102.

[85] Edward A. Suchman *et al.*, *Desegregation: Some Propositions and*

Research Suggestions, Anti-Defamation League of B'nai B'rith (1958), p. 50.

[86] Angus Campbell, Gerald Gurin, and Warren E. Miller, *The Voter Decides* (New York, Harper & Row, 1954), p. 99; Rose K. Goldsen, Morris Rosenberg, Robin M. Williams, Jr., and Edward A. Suchman, *What College Students Think* (Princeton, N.J., Van Nostrand, 1960), p. 101.

[87] Herbert H. Hyman, *Political Socialization: A Study in the Psychology of Political Behavior* (New York, Free Press, 1959), p. 35.

[88] Ronald Freedman, Amos H. Hawley, Werner S. Landecker, Gerhard E. Lenski, and Horace M. Miner, *Principles of Sociology,* rev. ed. (New York, Holt, Rinehart and Winston, 1956), p. 369.

[89] Bernard D. Nossiter, "U.S., Russia Spend Like Sums on Research," *The Washington Post,* December 15 (1965), p. A33.

[90] Berelson and Steiner, *op. cit.,* p. 327.

[91] Paul F. Lazarsfeld and Wagner Thielens, Jr., *The Academic Mind* (New York, Free Press, 1958), p. 147.

[92] George C. Homans, *The Human Group* (New York, Harcourt, Brace & World, 1950), p. 133.

[93] Josephine Klein, *The Study of Groups* (London, Routledge, 1956), p. 106.

[94] Muzafer Sherif, "The Formation of a Norm in a Group Situation," in Muzafer Sherif, *The Psychology of Social Norms* (New York, Harper & Row, 1936), pp. 102-103; Muzafer Sherif, "Group Influences upon the Formation of Norms and Attitudes," in G. E. Swanson *et al.,* eds., *Readings in Social Psychology,* rev. ed. (New York, Holt, Rinehart and Winston, 1952), p. 255.

[95] Berelson and Steiner, *op. cit.,* p. 336.

[96] *Ibid.,* p. 337.

[97] Harold H. Kelley and John W. Thibaut, "Experimental Studies of Group Problem Solving and Process," in Gardner Lindzey, ed., *Handbook of Social Psychology,* Vol. II (Cambridge, Mass., Addison-Wesley, 1954), p. 768.

[98] Bernard Berelson, Paul F. Lazarsfeld, and William N. McPhee, *Voting: A Study of Opinion Formulation in a Presidential Campaign* (Chicago, University of Chicago Press, 1954), p. 222.

[99] Leonard Broom and Philip Selznick, *Sociology: A Text with Adapted Readings* (New York, Harper & Row, 1957), p. 33.

[100] Theodore Caplow and Reece J. McGee, *The Academic Marketplace* (New York, Basic Books, 1958).

[101] *Ibid.*, p. 105. A project interesting of research would be to study the kinds of systems whose components underrate them as compared to the judgments of outside observers, and the kinds of components who underrate their systems.

[102] Joseph H. Monane, "Dynamics of Reactive Subculture." Unpublished paper read at meetings of the Amer. Anthrop. Assoc. (Chicago, 1962).

[103] Richard Christie, "Authoritarianism Re-examined," in Richard Christie and Marie Jahoda, eds., *Studies in the Scope and Method of the Authoritarian Personality* (New York, Free Press, 1954), p. 154.

[104] Harold H. Kelley and John W. Thibaut, "Experimental Studies of Group Problem Solving and Process," in Gardner Lindzey, ed., *Handbook of Social Psychology,* 2 (Cambridge, Mass., Addison-Wesley, 1954), p. 768.

[105] Noel P. Gist and L. A. Halbert, *Urban Society,* 4th ed. (New York, Crowell, 1956), pp. 119, 121.

[106] Daniel M. Wilner, Rosabelle P. Walkley, and Stuart W. Cook, "Residential Proximity and Intergroup Relations in Public Housing Projects," *Journal of Social Issues,* 8 (1952), pp. 68-69.

[107] Berelson and Steiner, *op. cit.,* p. 489.

[108] Bernard Berelson, Paul F. Lazarsfeld, and William N. McPhee, *Voting: A Study of Opinion Formulation in a Presidential Campaign* (Chicago, University of Chicago Press, 1954), p. 31.

[109] Leonard Pearlin and Melvin Kohn, *The Washington Post* (February 14, 1966), p. B1.

[110] Seymour M. Lipset, Martin A. Trow, and James S. Coleman, *Union Democracy* (New York, Free Press, 1956), p. 72.

[111] James G. March and Herbert A. Simon, with Harold Guetzkow, *Organizations* (New York, Wiley, 1958), pp. 72-73.

[112] Seymour M. Lipset, *Agrarian Socialism: The Cooperative Commonwealth Federation in Saskatchewan* (Berkeley, Calif., University of California Press, 1950), pp. 197-198.

[113] William Foote Whyte and Frank B. Miller, "Industrial Sociology," in Joseph B. Gittler, ed., *Review of Sociology: Analysis of a Decade* (New York, Wiley, 1957), pp. 289-345.

[114] Theodore V. Purcell, *The Worker Speaks His Mind on Company and Union* (Cambridge, Mass., Harvard University Press, 1953), pp. 263-264.

[115] Berelson and Steiner, *op. cit.,* p. 591.

[116] Richard Scudder and C. Arnold Anderson, "Migration and Vertical Occupational Mobility," *American Sociological Review,* 19 (1954), pp. 329-334.

[117] Berelson and Steiner, *op. cit.,* p. 310.

[118] Seymour M. Lipset and Juan J. Linz, "The Social Bases of Political Diversity in Western Democracies." Unpublished ms. (1956), pp. 17-18.

[119] Harold D. Lasswell and Abraham Kaplan, *Power and Society: A Framework for Political Inquiry* (New Haven, Conn., Yale University Press, 1950), p. 57.

[120] Robert A. Hall, Jr., *Linguistics and Your Language* (New York, Doubleday, 1960), pp. 146-147.

[121] *Ibid.*

[122] Berelson and Steiner, *op. cit.,* p. 310.

[123] Joseph H. Monane, "Vodu and Political Power in Haiti." Unpublished paper read at meetings of the Amer. Anthrop. Assoc. (Denver, 1965).

[124] Berelson and Steiner, *op. cit.,* p. 395.

[125] Liston Pope, "Religion and the Class Structure," *Annals of American Academy of Political and Social Science,* No. 256 (March, 1948), p. 86.

[126] Daniel Lerner, "Communication Systems and Social Systems: A Statistical Exploration in History and Policy," *Behavioral Science,* 2 (1957), p. 272.

[127] Robert K. Merton, "Puritanism, Pietism, and Science," in *Social Theory and Social Structure,* rev. ed. (New York, Free Press, 1957), pp. 574-606.

[128] Robert H. Knapp and H. B. Goodrich, *Origins of American Scientists* (Chicago, University of Chicago Press, 1952).

[129] David Wechsler, *The Wechsler Adult Intelligence Scale Manual,* Psych. Corp. (1955), p. 16.

[130] See Edward A. Shils, "The Study of the Primary Group," in Daniel

Lerner and Harold D. Lasswell, eds., *The Policy Sciences: Recent Developments in Scope and Method* (Stanford, Calif., Stanford University Press, 1951), p. 48.

[131] *Ibid.*, p. 64.

[132] Edward A. Shils and Morris Janowitz, "Cohesion and Disintegration in the *Wehrmacht* in World War II," *Public Opinion Quarterly*, 12 (1948), p. 284.

[133] Carl R. Rogers, "An Overview of the Research and Some Questions for the Future," in Carl R. Rogers and Rosalind F. Dymond, eds., *Psychotherapy and Personality Change* (Chicago, University of Chicago Press, 1954), pp. 416-417.

[134] Paul F. Lazarsfeld, Bernard Berelson, and Hazel Gaudet, *The People's Choice* (New York, Columbia University Press, 1948), p. 63.

[135] Ronald Freedman, Amos H. Hawley, Werner S. Landecker, Gerhard E. Lenski, and Horace M. Miner, *Principles of Sociology*, rev. ed. (New York, Holt, Rinehart and Winston, 1956), p. 178.

[136] Leon Festinger, *A Theory of Cognitive Dissonance* (New York, Harper & Row, 1957).

[137] Joseph T. Klapper, *The Effects of Mass Communication* (New York, Free Press, 1960), p. 96.

[138] *Ibid.*

[139] Paul L. Lazarsfeld, Bernard Berelson, and Hazel Gaudet, *The People's Choice* (New York, Columbia University Press, 1948), p. 68.

[140] Seymour M. Lipset, "Political Sociology," in Robert K. Merton *et al.*, eds., *Sociology Today: Problems and Prospects* (New York, Basic Books, 1959), pp. 94-95.

[141] *Ibid.*

[142] *Ibid.*

[143] Paul F. Lazarsfeld, Bernard Berelson, and Hazel Gaudet, *The People's Choice* (New York, Columbia University Press, 1948).

[144] F. J. Roethlisberger and W. J. Dickson, *Management and the Worker*, Part IV (Cambridge, Mass., Harvard University Press, 1939).

[145] Everett C. Hughes, "The Knitting of Racial Groups in Industry," *American Sociological Review*, 11 (1946), pp. 512-519.

[146] Michael Argyle, *The Scientific Study of Social Behavior* (London, Methuen, 1957), p. 159.

[147] Henry W. Riecken and George C. Homans, "Psychological Aspects of Social Structure," in Gardner Lindzey, ed., *Handbook of Social Psychology,* Vol. II (Cambridge, Mass., Addison-Wesley, 1954), p. 823.

[148] Robert F. Bales, "The Equilibrium Problem in Small Groups," in Talcott Parsons, Robert F. Bales, and Edward A. Shils, *Working Papers in the Theory of Action* (New York, Free Press, 1953), pp. 140-141.

[149] *Ibid.*

[150] *Ibid.*

[151] Henry L. Lennard and Arnold Bernstein, *The Anatomy of Psychotherapy: Systems of Communication and Expectation* (New York, Columbia University Press, 1960), p. 65.

[152] Neal E. Miller and Richard Bugelski, "Minor Studies of Aggression: II. The Influence of Frustrations Imposed by the In-Group on Attitudes Expressed Toward Out-Groups," *Journal of Psychology,* 25 (1948), pp. 440-441.

[153] Carl I. Hovland and Robert R. Sears, "Minor Studies of Aggression: VI. Correlations of Lynchings with Economic Indices," *Journal of Psychology,* 9 (1940), pp. 306-308.

[154] Norman R. F. Maier, *Frustration: A Study of Behavior Without a Goal* (New York, McGraw-Hill, 1949), p. 117, utilizing data of Goodwin Watson, "A Comparison of the Effects of Lax Versus Strict Home Training," *Journal of Social Psychology,* 5 (1934), pp. 102-105.

[155] *Ibid.*

[156] Berelson and Steiner, *op. cit.,* p. 348.

[157] Robert F. Bales, Fred L. Strodtbeck, Theodore M. Mills, and Mary E. Roseborough, "Channels of Communication in Small Groups," *American Sociological Review,* 16 (1951), p. 468.

[158] Edwin A. Fleishman, Edwin F. Harris, and Harold E. Burtt, *Leadership and Supervision in Industry: An Evaluation of a Supervisory Training Program* (Columbus, Ohio, Ohio State University, 1955).

[159] Samuel A. Stouffer *et al., The American Soldier: Adjustment During Army Life. Studies in Social Psychology in World War II,* Vol. I (Princeton, N.J., Princeton University Press, 1949), p. 408.

[160] Cecil A. Gibb, "Leadership," in Gardner Lindzey, ed., *Handbook of Social Psychology,* Vol. II. (Cambridge, Mass., Addison-Wesley, 1954), p. 894.

[161] Alexander H. Leighton, *The Governing of Men* (Princeton, N.J., Princeton University Press, 1945).

[162] Joseph H. Monane, "Vodu and Political Power in Haiti." Unpublished paper read at meetings of the Amer. Anthrop. Assoc. (Denver, 1965).

[163] Edward T. Hall, *The Silent Language* (New York, Doubleday, 1959), p. 16.

[164] James S. Coleman, "Community Disorganization," in Robert K. Merton and Robert A. Nisbet, eds., *Contemporary Social Problems* (New York, Harcourt, Brace & World, 1961), pp. 569, 604.

[165] Carle C. Zimmerman, *The Changing Community* (New York, Harper & Row, 1938).

[166] Everett C. Hughes, *French Canada in Transition* (London, Routledge, 1946).

[167] See Robert K. Merton, *Social Theory and Social Structure,* rev. and enlarged ed. (New York, Free Press, 1957), pp. 72 ff.

[168] Bernard Berelson, Paul F. Lazarsfeld, and William N. McPhee, *Voting: A Study of Opinion Formation in a Presidential Compaign* (Chicago, University of Chicago Press, 1954).

[169] Gunnar Myrdal, with the assistance of Richard Sterner and Arnold M. Rose, *An American Dilemma* (New York, Harper & Row, 1944).

[170] Elizabeth B. Hurlock, *Child Development,* 3rd ed. (New York, McGraw-Hill, 1956), pp. 411, 438, 406.

[171] Hugh Hartshorne and Mark A. May, *Studies in Deceit* (New York, Macmillan, 1928).

[172] M. D. Fite, "Aggressive Behavior in Young Children and Children's Attitudes Toward Aggression," *Genetic Psychology Monograph,* 22 (1940), pp. 151-319.

[173] E. R. Bartlett and D. B. Harris, "Personality Factors in Delinquency," *School and Society,* 43 (1935), pp. 653-656; G. E. Hill, "The Ethical Knowledge of Delinquent and Non-delinquent Boys," *Journal of Social Psychology,* 6 (1935), pp. 107-114; Sheldon Glueck and Eleanor Glueck, *Unraveling Juvenile Delinquency* (Cambridge, Mass., Harvard University Press for the Commonwealth Fund, 1950).

[174] Hugh Hartshorne and Mark A. May, *Studies in the Nature of Character* (New York, Macmillan, 1928); V. Jones, *Character and Citi-*

zenship Training in the Public School (Chicago, University of Chicago Press, 1936).

[175] E. L. Thorndike, "Mental Discipline in High School Studies," *Journal of Educational Psychology,* 15 (1924), pp. 94-95.

[176] Berelson and Steiner, *op. cit.,* p. 348.

[177] *Ibid.*

[178] *Ibid.*

[179] *Ibid.*

[180] *Ibid.*

[181] *Ibid.*

[182] Henry W. Riecken and George C. Homans, "Psychological Aspects of Social Structure," in Gardner Lindzey, ed., *Handbook of Social Psychology,* Vol. II. (Cambridge, Mass., Addison-Wesley, 1954) p. 798.

[183] "A Proper Patient," *Trans-action* 3 (January-February, 1966), p. 28, reporting on research by David Kantor and Victor Gelineau of Boston State Hospital.

[184] Lloyd Shearer, "Dictators Run Most of the World," *Parade* (March 13, 1966), pp. 4-5.

[185] Kingsley Davis, *Human Society* (New York, Macmillan, 1949), p. 366.

[186] Franklin Frazier, *The Negro in the United States,* rev. ed. (New York, Macmillan, 1957).

[187] W. Lloyd Warner, "The Study of Social Stratification," in Joseph B. Gittler, ed., *Review of Sociology: Analysis of a Decade* (New York, Wiley, 1957), p. 245.

[188] Morris Janowitz, *Sociology and the Military Establishment* (New York, Russell Sage Foundation, 1959), p. 83.

[189] Seymour M. Lipset and Juan J. Linz, "The Social Bases of Political Diversity in Western Democracies." Unpublished ms. (1956), p. 18.

[190] Berelson and Steiner, *op. cit.,* p. 344.

[191] *Ibid.,* p. 343.

[192] *Ibid.,* p. 344.

[193] *Ibid.,* p. 374.

[194] Stuart Adams, "Social Climate and Productivity in Small Military Groups," *American Sociological Review,* 19 (1954), pp. 421-425.

[195] Cecil A. Gibb, "Leadership," in Gardner Lindzey, ed., *Handbook of Social Psychology,* Vol. II (Cambridge, Mass., Addison-Wesley, 1954), p. 910.

[196] *Ibid.*

[197] Shmuel N. Eisenstadt, *From Generation to Generation: Age Groups and Social Structure* (New York, Free Press, 1956), p. 22.

[198] Theodore M. Newcomb, *Personality and Social Change: Attitude Formation in a Student Community* (New York, Holt, Rinehart and Winston, 1943).

[199] Berelson and Steiner, *op. cit.,* p. 376.

[200] Max Weber, *The Theory of Social and Economic Organization,* trans. by A. M. Henderson and Talcott Parsons (New York, Free Press, 1947).

[201] Philip Selznick, *Leadership in Administration* (New York, Harper & Row, 1957), pp. 108-109.

[202] Berelson and Steiner, *op. cit.,* p. 465.

[203] E. Digby Baltzell, *The Protestant Establishment* (New York, Random House, 1964).

[204] Leonard R. Sayles, *Behavior of Industrial Work Groups: Prediction and Control* (New York, Wiley, 1958), pp. 43-44.

[205] Berelson and Steiner, *op. cit.,* p. 344.

[206] Robert F. Bales, "Small Group Theory and Research" (referring to William Foote Whyte, *Street Corner Society* [Chicago, University of Chicago Press, 1943]) in Robert K. Merton *et al.,* eds., *Sociology Today: Problems and Prospects* (New York, Basic Books, 1959), p. 299.

[207] Berelson and Steiner, *op. cit.,* p. 344.

[208] Paul F. Lazarsfeld and Wagner Thielens, Jr., *The Academic Mind* (New York, Free Press, 1958), pp. 173-174.

[209] Terence K. Hopkins, "The Exercise of Influence in Small Groups." Unpublished Doct. Diss. (New York, Columbia University, 1959).

[210] Berelson and Steiner, *op. cit.,* p. 343.

[211] *Ibid.*

[212] Ferenc Merei, "Group Leadership and Institutionalization," in Eleanor E. Maccoby *et al.,* eds., *Readings in Social Psychology,* 3rd ed. (New York, Holt, Rinehart and Winston, 1958), pp. 522-532.

[213] Berelson and Steiner, *op. cit.,* p. 343.

[214] Seymour M. Lipset and Juan J. Linz, "The Social Bases of Political Diversity in Western Democracies." Unpublished ms. (1956), p. 18.

[215] Berelson and Steiner, *op. cit.,* p. 462.

[216] Edward A. Shils, "Class," in *Encyclopaedia Britannica,* 5 (New York, Encyclopaedia Britannica, 1960), p. 767.

[217] Samuel A. Stouffer *et al., The American Soldier: Adjustment During Army Life. Studies in Social Psychology in World War II,* Vol. I (Princeton, N.J., Princeton University Press, 1949), p. 408.

[218] Seymour M. Lipset and Juan J. Linz, "The Social Bases of Political Diversity in Western Democracies." Unpublished ms. (1956), pp. 17-18.

[219] Robert E. Lane, *Political Life: Why People Get Involved in Politics* (New York, Free Press, 1959), p. 216.

[220] *Ibid.*

[221] B. Schrieke, *Alien Americans: A Study of Race Relations* (New York, Viking, 1936), pp. 10-12.

[222] Alex Inkeles and Peter H. Rossi, "National Comparisons of Occupational Prestige," *American Journal of Sociology,* 61 (1956), p. 332.

[223] Berelson and Steiner, *op. cit.,* p. 466.

[224] Seymour M. Lipset and Reinhard Bendix, *Social Mobility in Industrial Society.* University of California, Institute of Industrial Relations (Berkeley, Calif., University of California Press, 1959), p. 13.

[225] George E. Simpson and J. Milton Yinger, *Racial and Cultural Minorities* (New York, Harper & Row, 1953), p. 362.

[226] Leonard R. Sayles, *Behavior of Industrial Work Groups: Prediction and Control* (New York, Wiley, 1958), p. 93.

[227] Berelson and Steiner, *op. cit.,* pp. 401-402.

[228] Raymond Firth, F. J. Fisher, and D. G. MacRae, "Social Implications of Technological Change as Regards Patterns and Models," in G. Balandier *et al., Social, Economic, and Technological Change: A Theoretical Approach.* International Bureau for Research in the Social Implications of Technical Progress (Paris, Presses Universitaires de France, 1959), p. 293.

[229] *Ibid.,* p. 270.

[230] David C. McClelland, *The Achieving Society* (Princeton, N.J., Van Nostrand, 1961).

[231] *Ibid.*

[232] *Ibid.*

[233] Robert E. Lane, *Political Life: Why People Get Involved in Politics* (New York, Free Press, 1959), p. 145.

[234] Milton J. Rosenberg, Carl I. Hovland, William J. McGuire, Robert P. Abelson, and Jack Brehm, *Attitude Organization and Change: An Analysis of Consistency Among Attitude Components,* Yale Studies in Attitude and Communication, ed. by Carl I. Hovland and Milton J. Rosenberg, Vol. III (New Haven, Conn., Yale University Press, 1960), p. 200.

[235] Eugene L. Horowitz, "The Development of Attitude Toward the Negro," *Archives of Psychology,* 28, no. 194 (1936).

[236] Samuel A. Stouffer *et al., The American Soldier: Adjustment During Army Life. Studies in Social Psychology in World War II,* Vol. I (Princeton, N.J., Princeton University Press, 1949), p. 594.

[237] Morton Deutsch and Mary E. Collins, *Interracial Housing: A Psychological Evaluation of a Social Experiment* (Minneapolis, Minn., University of Minnesota Press, 1951), p. 97.

[238] John F. Cuber and Peggy B. Harroff, *The Significant Americans* (New York, Appleton-Century-Crofts, 1965).

[239] Robert F. Bales, "The Equilibrium Problem in Small Groups," in Talcott Parsons, Robert F. Bales, and Edward A. Shils, *Working Papers in the Theory of Action* (New York, Free Press, 1953), p. 160.

[240] Berelson and Steiner, *op. cit.,* p. 343.

[241] Genevieve Knupfer, "Portrait of the Underdog," *Public Opinion Quarterly,* 11 (1947), pp. 103-114.

[242] Berelson and Steiner, *op. cit.,* p. 572.

[243] Seymour M. Lipset and Juan J. Linz, "The Social Bases of Political Diversity in Western Democracies." Unpublished ms. (1956), p. 30.

[244] Berelson and Steiner, *op. cit.,* p. 372.

[245] Kenneth Kenniston, *The Uncommitted: Alienated Youth in American Society* (New York, Harcourt, Brace & World, 1965).

[246] George Gallup, "KKK and Birchers Run Low in Public's Rating of Groups," *The Washington Post,* December 19 (1965), p. M2.

[247] *The Washington Post,* February 21 (1966), p. A2.

[248] Benjamin E. Lippincott, *Democracy's Dilemma: The Totalitarian Party in a Free Society* (New York, Ronald, 1965).

[249] Distinctions between "church" and "sect" have occupied the attention of many sociologists.

[250] James S. Coleman, *Community Conflict* (New York, Free Press, 1957), p. 21.

[251] Merton (Robert K. Merton, "Social Structure and Anomie," p. 139, and "Continuities in the Theory of Reference Groups and Social Structure," p. 296, in *Social Theory and Social Structure,* rev. and enlarged ed. [New York, Free Press, 1957],) has indicated the pressures against withdrawal from the American success-struggle, and the hostility of the terms "renegade," "turncoat," and "deserter" for defectors from a group. Slater (Philip E. Slater, "On Social Regression," *American Sociological Review,* 28 [1963], pp. 339-364) has surveyed the pressures resisting the withdrawal of the premarital and marital pair.

[252] Matilda White Riley and Richard Cohn, "Control Networks in Informal Groups," *Sociometry,* 21 (1958), pp. 30-49.

[253] Edward A. Shils, "The Study of the Primary Group," in Daniel Lerner and Harold D. Lasswell, eds., *The Policy Sciences: Recent Developments in Scope and Method* (Stanford, Calif., Stanford University Press, 1951), pp. 44-69; Elton Mayo, *The Human Problems of an Industrial Organization* (New York, Macmillan, 1933); Leonard R. Sayles, *Behavior of Industrial Work Groups: Prediction and Control* (New York, Wiley, 1958).

[254] Chester Barnard, *The Functions of the Executive* (Cambridge, Mass., Harvard University Press, 1950), p. 123.

[255] Berelson and Steiner, *op. cit.,* p. 371.

[256] Edward A. Shils, "The Study of the Primary Group," in Daniel Lerner and Harold D. Lasswell, eds., *The Policy Sciences: Recent Developments in Scope and Method* (Stanford, Calif., Stanford University Press., 1951), p. 64.

[257] F. J. Roethlisberger and W. J. Dickson, *Management and the Worker,* Part IV (Cambridge, Mass., Harvard University Press, 1939).

[258] Leonard R. Sayles, *Behavior of Industrial Work Groups: Prediction and Control* (New York, Wiley, 1958), pp. 152-153.

[259] Samuel A. Stouffer *et al., The American Soldier: Adjustment Dur-*

ing Army Life. Studies in Social Psychology in World War II, Vol. I (Princeton, N.J., Princeton University, 1949), p. 411.

[260] Flora Lewis, "N.Y. to Send Lobbyist Here," *The Washington Post* (December 19, 1965), p. M4.

[261] *The University Hatchet* (student newspaper of The George Washington University) (February 8, 1966), p. A13.

[262] Berelson and Steiner, *op. cit.,* p. 432.

[263] *Ibid.,* p. 316.

[264] *Ibid.,* pp. 634-635.

[265] Gresham M. Sykes, *Crime and Society* (New York, Random House, 1956), p. 74.

[266] Berelson and Steiner, *op. cit.,* p. 626.

[267] William J. Goode, "Family Disorganization," in Robert K. Merton and Robert A. Nisbet, eds., *Contemporary Social Problems* (New York, Harcourt, Brace & World, 1961), p. 455.

[268] Earl Raab and Gertrude J. Selznick, *Major Social Problems* (New York, Harper & Row, 1959), p. 62.

[269] Sidney Axelrad, "Negro and White Male Institutionalized Delinquents," *American Journal of Sociology,* 57 (1952), pp. 569-574.

[270] Nancy Morse and E. Reimer, "The Experimental Change of a Major Organizational Variable," *Journal of Abnormal and Social Psychology,* 52 (1956), pp. 120-129.

[271] David L. Sills, *The Volunteers: Means and Ends in a National Organization.* A report of the Bureau of Applied Social Research, Columbia University (New York, Free Press, 1957).

[272] Berelson and Steiner, *op. cit.,* p. 352.

[273] Henry W. Riecken and George C. Homans, "Psychological Aspects of Social Structure," in Gardner Lindzey, ed., *Handbook of Social Psychology,* Vol. II (Cambridge, Mass., Addison-Wesley, 1954), p. 810.

[274] Seymour M. Lipset and Juan J. Linz, "The Social Bases of Political Diversity in Western Democracies." Unpublished ms. (1956), pp. 1-2.

[275] Berelson and Steiner, *op. cit.,* p. 310.

[276] Theodore W. Adorno, Else Frenkel-Brunswik, Daniel J. Levinson, and R. Nevitt Sanford, *The Authoritarian Personality: Studies in Prejudice,* in Max Horkheimer and Samuel H. Flowerman, eds. (New York, Harper & Row, 1950).

[277] Robert Cooley Angell, "The Moral Integration of American Cities," *American Journal of Sociology,* 57, Part II (1951), p. 14.

[278] Harold D. Lasswell and Abraham Kaplan, *Power and Society: A Framework for Political Inquiry* (New Haven, Conn., Yale University Press, 1950), pp. 38-39.

[279] Berelson and Steiner, *op. cit.,* pp. 416-417.

[280] Seymour M. Lipset and Juan J. Linz, "The Social Bases of Political Diversity in Western Democracies." Unpublished ms. (1956), p. 13.

[281] Seymour M. Lipset, *Political Man: The Social Bases of Politics* (New York, Doubleday, 1960), pp. 39-40.

[282] Donald R. Taft, *Criminology* (New York, Macmillan, 1950).

[283] Leonard Broom and Philip Selznick, *Sociology: A Text with Adapted Readings* (New York, Harper & Row, 1957), p. 639.

[284] Donald R. Cressey, "Crime," in Robert K. Merton and Robert A. Nisbet, eds., *Contemporary Social Problems* (New York, Harcourt, Brace & World, 1961), p. 33.

[285] Leonard Broom and Philip Selznick, *Sociology: A Text with Adapted Readings* (New York, Harper & Row, 1957), p. 639.

[286] *Ibid.*

[287] Berelson and Steiner, *op. cit.,* p. 627.

[288] Sidney Axelrad, "Negro and White Male Institutionalized Delinquents," *American Journal of Sociology,* 57 (1952), pp. 569-574.

[289] Berelson and Steiner, *op. cit.,* p. 627.

[290] *Ibid.*

[291] Sidney Axelrad, "Negro and White Male Institutionalized Delinquents," *American Journal of Sociology,* 57 (1952), pp. 569-574.

[292] Cohen and Short (Albert K. Cohen and James F. Short, Jr., "Juvenile Delinquency," in Robert K. Merton and Robert A. Nisbet, eds., *Contemporary Social Problems* [New York, Harcourt, Brace & World, 1961], p. 86) note the exceptionally high delinquency rates in the United States of Negroes, Puerto Ricans, Mexicans, and American Indians.

[293] Leonard Broom and Philip Selznick, *Sociology: A Text with Adapted Readings* (New York, Harper & Row, 1957), p. 640.

[294] Michael Argyle, *Religious Behavior* (London, Routledge, 1958), p. 100.

[295] Noel P. Gist and L. A. Halbert, *Urban Society,* 4th ed. (New York, Crowell, 1956), p. 144.

[296] Berelson and Steiner, *op. cit.,* p. 628.

[297] Robert A. Nisbet, "The Study of Social Problems," in Robert K. Merton and Robert A. Nisbet, eds., *Contemporary Social Problems* (New York, Harcourt, Brace & World, 1961), p. 5.

[298] *Ibid.*

[299] Noel P. Gist and L. A. Halbert, *Urban Society,* 4th ed. (New York, Crowell, 1956), p. 144.

[300] Berelson and Steiner, *op. cit.,* p. 606.

[301] *Ibid.,* p. 358.

[302] D. W. Maurer, *Whiz Mob* (New Haven, Conn., College and University Press, 1964).

Chapter 3

[1] Otis Dudley Duncan, "Human Ecology and Population Studies," in Philip M. Hauser and Otis Dudley Duncan, eds., *The Study of Population: An Inventory and Appraisal* (Chicago, University of Chicago Press, 1959), p. 689.

[2] George P. Murdock, *Social Structure* (New York, Macmillan, 1949).

[3] Robert R. Sears, "Experimental Studies of Projection: I. Attribution of Traits," *Journal of Social Psychology* 7 (1936), p. 162.

[4] See Otis Dudley Duncan and Beverly Duncan, "Residential Distribution and Occupational Stratification," *American Journal of Sociology,* 60 (1955), p. 497.

[5] Seymour M. Lipset and Reinhard Bendix, *Social Mobility in Industrial Society*. University of California, Institute of Industrial Relations (Berkeley, Calif., University of California Press, 1959), p. 72.

[6] Bernard Berelson and Gary A. Steiner, *Human Behavior: An Inventory of Scientific Findings* (New York, Harcourt, Brace & World, 1964), p. 591.

[7] *Ibid.,* p. 407.

[8] Seymour M. Lipset, "Social Mobility and Urbanization," in Paul K. Hatt and Albert J. Reiss, Jr., eds., *Cities and Society: The Revised Reader in Urban Sociology* (New York, Free Press, 1957), pp. 458-466.

[9] Berelson and Steiner, *op. cit.*, p. 370.

[10] Peter M. Blau, *The Dynamics of Bureaucracy* (Chicago, University of Chicago Press, 1955).

[11] Genevieve Knupfer, "Portrait of the Underdog," *Public Opinion Quarterly*, 11 (1947), p. 114.

[12] Ralph Linton, "The Distinctive Aspects of Acculturation," in Ralph Linton, ed., *Acculturation in Seven American Indian Tribes* (New York, Appleton-Century-Crofts, 1940), p. 519.

[13] Bernard Berelson, Paul F. Lazarsfeld, and William N. McPhee, *Voting: A Study of Opinion Formation in a Presidential Campaign* (Chicago, University of Chicago Press, 1954), p. 183.

[14] Seymour M. Lipset and Juan J. Linz, "The Social Bases of Political Diversity in Western Democracies." Unpublished ms. (1956), pp. 58-59.

[15] *Ibid.*, p. 18.

[16] George P. Murdock, *Social Structure* (New York, Macmillan, 1949).

[17] Paul F. Lazarsfeld, Bernard Berelson, and Hazel Gaudet, *The People's Choice* (New York, Columbia University Press, 1948), p. 122.

[18] John W. Riley and Matilda White Riley, "Mass Communication and the Social System," in Robert K. Merton *et al.* eds., *Sociology Today: Problems and Prospects* (New York, Basic Books, 1959), p. 541.

[19] Berelson, Lazarsfeld, and McPhee, *op. cit.*, p. 111.

[20] Leon Festinger, "The Psychological Effects of Insufficient Rewards," *American Psychologist*, 16 (1961), p. 2.

[21] Elliot Aronson and Judson Mills, "The Effect of Severity of Initiation on Liking for a Group," *Journal of Abnormal and Social Psychology*, 59 (1959), pp. 177-181.

[22] Konrad Lorenz, in J. D. McCarthy and F. J. Ebling, *The Natural History of Aggression* (New York, Academic, 1965).

[23] Robert E. Lane, *Political Life: Why People Get Involved in Politics* (New York, Free Press, 1959), p. 264.

[24] Harold D. Lasswell and Abraham Kaplan, *Power and Society: A Framework for Political Inquiry* (New Haven, Conn., Yale University Press, 1950), pp. 38-39.

[25] Joseph T. Klapper, *The Effects of Mass Communication* (New York, Free Press, 1960), pp. 164-165.

[26] Berelson and Steiner, *op. cit.,* p. 529.

[27] Raymond A. Bauer and Alice H. Bauer, "America, Mass Society and Mass Media," *Journal of Social Issues,* 16 (1960), p. 29.

[28] William S. Robinson, "Radio Comes to the Farmer," in Paul F. Lazarsfeld and Frank N. Stanton, eds., *Radio Research 1941* (New York, Duell, Sloan & Pearce, 1941), pp. 224-294.

[29] Berelson and Steiner, *op. cit.,* p. 531.

[30] Matilda White Riley and John W. Riley, Jr., "A Sociological Approach to Communications Research," *Public Opinion Quarterly,* 15 (1951), p. 456.

[31] Gerald S. Blum, "An Experimental Reunion of Psychoanalytic Theory with Perceptual Vigilance and Defense," *Journal of Abnormal and Social Psychology,* 49 (1954), pp. 97-98.

[32] Gerald S. Blum, "Perceptual Defense Revisited," *Journal of Abnormal and Social Psychology,* 51 (1955), p. 28.

[33] Charles E. Fritz, "Disaster," in Robert K. Merton and Robert A. Nisbet, eds., *Contemporary Social Problems* (New York, Harcourt, Brace & World, 1961), p. 665.

[34] Eckhard H. Hess and James Polt, "Pupil Size as Related to Interest Value of Visual Stimuli," *Science,* 132 (1960), pp. 349-350.

[35] Personal communication with Eckhard H. Hess, 1963, reported in Berelson and Steiner, *op. cit.,* p. 104.

[36] Berelson and Steiner, *op. cit.,* p. 101.

[37] *Ibid.*

[38] *Ibid.,* pp. 145-146.

[39] Julius Seeman, "Psychotherapy," *Annual Review of Psychology,* 12 (1961), p. 179.

[40] Carl I. Hovland, Wallace Mandell, Enid H. Campbell *et al., The Order of Presentation in Persuasion,* Yale Studies in Attitude and Communication, Carl I. Hovland, ed. Vol. I (New Haven, Conn., Yale University Press, 1957), pp. 130-137.

[41] David C. McClelland and John W. Atkinson, "The Projective Expression of Needs: I. The Effect of Different Intensities of the Hunger Drive on Perception," *Journal of Psychology,* 25 (1948), p. 212.

[42] Else Frenkel-Brunswik, "Intolerance of Ambiguity as an Educational and Perceptual Personality Variable," *Journal of Personality,* 18 (1949), p. 128.

[43] Berelson and Steiner, *op. cit.,* p. 114.

[44] *Ibid.,* p. 119.

[45] Julian B. Rotter, "Psychotherapy," *Annual Review of Psychology,* 11 (1960), p. 403.

[46] E. A. Rubinstein and M. B. Parloff, "Research Problems in Psychotherapy," in *Research in Psychotherapy,* Amer. Psych. Assoc. (1959), p. 277.

[47] Berelson and Steiner, *op. cit.,* p. 11.

[48] *Ibid.*

[49] Seymour M. Lipset and Reinhard Bendix, *Social Mobility in Industrial Society.* University of California, Institute of Industrial Relations (Berkeley, Calif., University of California Press, 1959), pp. 127-128.

[50] Joseph A. Kahl, *The American Class Structure* (New York, Holt, Rinehart and Winston, 1957), p. 272.

[51] August B. Hollingshead, *Elmtown's Youth: The Impact of Social Class on Adolescents* (New York, Wiley, 1949), p. 286.

[52] Berelson and Steiner, *op. cit.,* p. 468.

[53] Carl I. Hovland, "Reconciling Conflicting Results Derived from Experimental and Survey Studies of Attitude Change," *American Psychologist,* 14 (1959), pp. 12-13.

[54] Harold H. Kelley and Edmund H. Volkart, "The Resistance to Change of Group-Anchored Attitudes," *American Sociological Review,* 17 (1952), pp. 453-465.

[55] Paul H. Lazarsfeld, Bernard Berelson and Hazel Gaudet, *The People's Choice* (New York, Columbia University Press, 1948), p. 90.

[56] Jerome M. Levine and Gardner Murphy, "The Learning and Forgetting of Controversial Material," *Journal of Abnormal and Social Psychology,* 38 (1943), pp. 512-513.

[57] Dorwin Cartwright, "Some Principles of Mass Persuasion: Selected Findings of Research on the Sale of United States War Bonds," *Human Relations,* 2 (1949), pp. 253-267.

[58] Shirley A. Star and Helen MacGill Hughes, "Report on an Edu-

cational Campaign: The Cincinnati Plan for the United Nations," *American Journal of Sociology,* 55 (1950), p. 397.

[59] Berelson and Steiner, *op. cit.,* p. 530.

[60] John W. Riley, Jr. and Matilda White Riley, "Mass Communication and the Social System," in Robert K. Merton *et al.,* eds., *Sociology Today: Problems and Prospects* (New York, Basic Books, 1959), p. 544.

[61] Carl I. Hovland, Irving L. Janis, and Harold H. Kelley, *Communication and Persuasion: Psychological Studies of Opinion Change* (New Haven, Conn., Yale University Press, 1953), p. 263.

[62] Edward A. Suchman *et al., Desegregation: Some Propositions and Research Suggestions.* Anti-Defamation League of B'nai B'rith (1958), p. 38.

[63] Carl I. Hovland, Wallace Mandell, Enid H. Campbell *et al., The Order of Presentation in Persuasion.* Yale Studies in Attitude and Communication, Vol. I, ed. by Carl I. Hovland (New Haven, Conn., Yale University Press, 1957), pp. 130-137.

[64] *Ibid.*

[65] *Ibid.*

[66] Marion Radke-Yarrow and Leon J. Yarrow, "Child Psychology," *Annual Review of Psychology,* 6 (1955), p. 11.

[67] Joseph T. Klapper, *The Effects of Mass Communication* (New York, Free Press, 1960), pp. 49-50, 58.

[68] Berelson and Steiner, *op. cit.,* p. 541.

[69] *Ibid.,* p. 529.

[70] E. Digby Baltzell, *The Protestant Establishment* (New York, Random House, 1964).

[71] Natalie Rogoff, *Recent Trends in Occupational Mobility* (New York, Free Press, 1953), p. 59.

[72] Leonard Broom and Philip Selznick, *Sociology: A Text with Adapted Readings* (New York, Harper & Row, 1957), pp. 437-438.

[73] Berelson and Steiner, *op. cit.,* p. 652.

[74] Harold D. Lasswell and Abraham Kaplan, *Power and Society: A Framework for Political Inquiry* (New Haven, Conn., Yale University Press, 1950), p. 35.

[75] Broom and Selznick, *op. cit.,* p. 487.

[76] Berelson and Steiner, *op. cit.,* p. 347.

[77] See in this regard Lasswell and Kaplan, *op. cit.,* p. 36.

[78] Alvin W. Gouldner, *Patterns of Industrial Bureaucracy* (New York, Free Press, 1954).

[79] Noel P. Gist and L. A. Halbert, *Urban Society,* 4th ed. (New York, Crowell, 1956), pp. 185-190, 195.

[80] Berelson and Steiner, *op. cit.,* p. 470.

[81] Raymond I. Haskell, "A Statistical Study of the Comparative Results Produced by Teaching Derivation in the Ninth Grade Latin Classes and in the Ninth Grade English Classes of Non-Latin Pupils in Four Philadelphia High Schools." Unpublished Doct. Diss. (Philadelphia, University of Pennsylvania, 1923).

[82] G. Hendrickson and W. H. Schroeder, "Transfer of Training in Learning to Hit a Submerged Target," *Journal of Educational Psychology,* 32 (1941), pp. 205-213.

[83] Berelson and Steiner, *op. cit.,* p. 84.

[84] *Ibid.,* p. 548.

[85] Hilde T. Himmelweit, A. N. Oppenheim, and Pamela Vince, *Television and the Child.* Published for the Nuffield Foundation (New York, Oxford University Press, 1958), pp. 29, 34.

[86] James S. Coleman, *The Adolescent Society: The Social Life of the Teenager and Its Impact on Education* (New York, Free Press, 1961), pp. 238-239.

[87] Carl I. Hovland, "Reconciling Conflicting Results Derived from Experimental and Survey Studies of Attitude Change," *American Psychologist,* 14 (1959), p. 12.

[88] Joseph T. Klapper, *The Effects of Mass Communication* (New York, Free Press, 1960), pp. 60-61.

[89] Carl I. Hovland, "Reconciling Conflicting Results Derived from Experimental and Survey Studies of Attitude Change," *American Psychologist,* 14 (1959), pp. 12-13.

[90] Harold H. Kelley and Christine L. Woodruff, "Members' Reaction to Apparent Group Approval of a Counternorm Communication," *Journal of Abnormal and Social Psychology,* 52 (1956), pp. 67-74.

[91] *Ibid.*

[92] *Ibid.*

[93] Bernard Berelson, Paul F. Lazarsfeld, and William N. McPhee, *Voting: A Study of Opinion Formation in a Presidential Campaign* (Chicago, University of Chicago Press, 1954), p. 111.

[94] Berelson and Steiner, *op. cit.,* p. 569.

[95] Shmuel N. Eisenstadt, *The Absorption of Immigrants* (New York, Free Press, 1955), p. 99.

[96] Berelson and Steiner, *op. cit.,* p. 531.

[97] Shmuel N. Eisenstadt, *The Absorption of Immigrants* (New York, Free Press, 1955), p. 99.

[98] Joseph T. Klapper, *The Effects of Mass Communication* (New York, Free Press, 1960), p. 96.

[99] Berelson and Steiner, *op. cit.,* p. 540.

[100] Woodburn Heron, "Cognitive and Physiological Effects of Perceptual Isolation," in Philip Solomon *et al.,* eds., *Sensory Deprivation,* a symposium at the Harvard Medical School (Cambridge, Mass., Harvard University Press, 1961), pp. 6-33.

[101] *Ibid.,* pp. 17-18.

[102] "Alone in Space," *Trans-action* 3 (March-April, 1966), p. 28, reported research by Soviet psychologists O. N. Kuznetsov and V. I. Lebedev.

[103] *Ibid.*

[104] See also Michael Wertheimer, "Principles of Perceptual Organization," in David C. Beardslee and Michael Wertheimer, eds., *Readings in Perception* (Princeton, N.J., Van Nostrand, 1958), pp. 115-135.

[105] Daniel Katz, "The Functional Approach to the Study of Attitudes," *Public Opinion Quarterly,* 24 (1960), p. 191.

[106] Jerome S. Bruner and Cecile C. Goodman, "Value and Need as Organizing Factors in Perception," *Journal of Abnormal and Social Psychology,* 42 (1947), pp. 33-44.

[107] W. W. Lambert, R. L. Solomon, and P. D. Watson, "Reinforcement and Extinction as Factors in Size Estimation," *Journal of Experimental Psychology,* 39 (1949), pp. 637-641.

[108] Berelson and Steiner, *op. cit.,* pp. 552-553.

[109] *Ibid.,* p. 72.

[110] Brinley Thomas, "International Migration" in Philip M. Hauser and Otis Dudley Duncan, eds., *The Study of Population: An Inventory and Appraisal* (Chicago, University of Chicago Press, 1959), pp. 510-543.

[111] Berelson and Steiner, *op. cit.,* p. 607.

[112] McClelland *et al.* (David C. McClelland, John W. Atkinson, Russell A. Clark, and Edgar L. Lowell, *The Achievement Motive* [New York, Appleton-Century-Crofts, 1953], p. 300) find that the earlier these parental demands occur, the stronger the subsequent drive for achievement.

[113] See Mary Ellen Goodman, *Race Awareness in Young Children* (Cambridge, Mass., Addison-Wesley, 1952); Marian Radke and Helen Trager, "Children's Perceptions of the Social Roles of Negroes and Whites," *Journal of Psychology,* 29 (1950), pp. 3-33; "The Effects of Segregation and the Consequences of Desegregation: A Social Science Statement," *Minnesota Law Review,* 37 (1953), pp. 427-439; Allison Davis, "Acculturation in Schools," in Milton L. Barron, ed., *American Minorities* (New York, Knopf, 1957), pp. 446-449.

[114] Berelson and Steiner, *op. cit.,* p. 75.

[115] See Harry F. Harlow and Margaret K. Harlow, "Social Deprivation in Monkeys," *Scientific American,* 207, no. 5 (1962), pp. 135-146; also Harry F. Harlow and Margaret K. Harlow, "The Effect of Rearing Conditions on Behavior," *Bulletin of the Menninger Clinic,* 26 (1962), pp. 213-224.

[116] Berelson and Steiner, *op. cit.,* p. 71.

[117] Charles E. Fritz, "Disaster," in Robert K. Merton and Robert A. Nisbet, eds., *Contemporary Social Problems* (New York, Harcourt, Brace & World, 1961), pp. 651-694.

[118] National Research Council, "A Brief Review of Salient Specific Findings on Morale and Human Behavior Under Disaster Conditions." Unpublished Memorandum (April 18, 1958).

[119] Berelson and Steiner, *op. cit.,* p. 624.

[120] Roger G. Barker, "An Experimental Study of the Resolution of Conflict by Children," in Quinn McNemar and Maud A. Merrill, eds., *Studies in Personality* (New York, McGraw-Hill, 1942), pp. 13-34.

[121] Berelson and Steiner, *op. cit.,* p. 275.

[122] *Ibid.,* p. 272.

[123] *Ibid.,* p. 274.

[124] John W. Atkinson and George W. Litwin, "Achievement Motive and Test Anxiety Conceived as Motive to Approach Success and Motive to Avoid Failure," *Journal of Abnormal and Social Psychology,* 60 (1960), pp. 52-63.

[125] Judson S. Brown, "Gradients of Approach and Avoidance Responses and Their Relation to Level of Motivation," *Journal of Comparative and Physiological Psychology,* 41 (1948), p. 457.

[126] Neal E. Miller, "Experimental Studies of Conflict," in J. McV. Hunt, ed., *Personality and the Behavior Disorders,* Vol. I (New York, Ronald, 1944), pp. 431-465.

[127] Berelson and Steiner, *op. cit.,* p. 276.

[128] Laurance F. Shaffer, "Fear and Courage in Aerial Combat," *Journal of Consulting Psychology,* 11 (1957), p. 139.

[129] Bruno Bettelheim, "Individual and Mass Behavior in Extreme Situations," in Eleanor E. Maccoby *et al.,* eds., *Readings in Social Psychology,* 3rd ed. (New York, Holt, Rinehart and Winston, 1958), p. 304.

[130] Joseph Wolpe, *Psychotherapy by Reciprocal Inhibition* (Stanford, Calif., Stanford University Press, 1958), p. 52.

[131] Berelson and Steiner, *op. cit.,* p. 277.

[132] *Ibid.,* p. 637.

[133] Robert A. Nisbet, "The Study of Social Problems," in Robert K. Merton and Robert A. Nisbet, eds., *Contemporary Social Problems* (New York, Harcourt, Brace & World, 1961), p. 5.

[134] *Ibid.*

[135] Edward A. Shils, "Primary Groups in the American Army," in Robert K. Merton and Paul F. Lazarsfeld, eds., *Continuities in Social Research* (New York, Free Press, 1950), p. 30.

[136] See, for example, W. I. Thomas and Florian Znaniecki, *The Polish Peasant in Europe and America* (New York, Knopf, 1927).

[137] Berelson and Steiner, *op. cit.,* p. 640.

[138] Joseph Greenblum and Leonard I. Pearlin, "Vertical Mobility and Prejudice: A Socio-Psychological Analysis," in Reinhard Bendix and Seymour M. Lipset, eds., *Class, Status, and Power: A Reader in Social Stratification* (New York, Free Press, 1953), pp. 480-491.

[139] Bruno Bettelheim and Morris Janowitz, *Dynamics of Prejudice:*

A Psychological and Sociological Study of Veterans (New York, Harper & Row, 1950), pp. 60-61.

[140] Theodore M. Newcomb, *Personality and Social Change: Attitude Formation in a Student Community* (New York, Holt, Rinehart and Winston, 1943).

[141] Berelson and Steiner, *op. cit.*, p. 582.

[142] Alfred C. Kinsey, Wardell B. Pomeroy, and Clyde E. Martin, *Sexual Behavior in the Human Male* (Philadelphia, Saunders, 1948), p. 419.

[143] Berelson and Steiner, *op. cit.*, pp. 145-146.

[144] Herbert C. Quay, "The Effect of Verbal Reinforcement on the Recall of Early Memories," *Journal of Abnormal and Social Psychology*, 59 (1959), pp. 254-257; Julius Seeman, "Psychotherapy," *Annual Review of Psychology*, 12 (1961), p. 179.

[145] Hollingshead and Redlich (August B. Hollingshead and Frederick C. Redlich, *Social Class and Mental Illness: A Community Study* [New York, Wiley, 1958], p. 267) find that the lower class neurotic is more likely to receive purely custodial care and organic therapy (shock, drugs, operations) than psychotherapy.

[146] See in this regard Theodore M. Newcomb, "The Study of Consensus," in Robert K. Merton *et al.*, eds., *Sociology Today: Problems and Prospects* (New York, Basic Books, 1959), pp. 277-292.

[147] Ronald Freedman, Amos H. Hawley, Werner S. Landecker, Gerhard E. Lenski and Horace M. Miner, *Principles of Sociology*, rev. ed. (New York, Holt, Rinehart and Winston, 1956), p. 452.

[148] Hilde T. Himmelweit, A. N. Oppenheim, and Pamela Vince, *Television and the Child*. Published for the Nuffield Foundation (New York, Oxford University Press, 1958); also James S. Coleman, *The Adolescent Society: The Social Life of the Teenager and Its Impact on Education* (New York, Free Press, 1961), pp. 238-239.

[149] Cecil A. Gibb, "Leadership," in Gardner Lindzey, ed., *Handbook of Social Psychology*, Vol. II (Cambridge, Mass., Addison-Wesley, 1954), p. 910.

[150] Wilbert E. Moore, *Man, Time and Society* (New York, Wiley, 1963), p. 113.

[151] *Ibid.*

[152] Michael Argyle, *The Scientific Study of Social Behavior* (London, Methuen, 1957), pp. 190-191.

[153] Raoul Naroll, "Does Military Deterrence Deter?", *Trans-action* 3 (Jan.-Feb., 1966), pp. 14-20.

[154] Berelson and Steiner, *op. cit.,* p. 630.

[155] Albert K. Cohen and James F. Short, Jr., "Juvenile Delinquency," in Robert K. Merton and Robert A. Nisbet, eds., *Contemporary Social Problems* (New York, Harcourt, Brace & World, 1961), pp. 77-126.

[156] Robert R. Sears, Eleanor E. Maccoby, and Harry Levin, *Patterns of Child Rearing* (New York, Harper & Row, 1957), p. 484.

[157] James F. Short, Jr. and Fred L. Strodtbeck, *Group Process and Gang Delinquency* (Chicago, University of Chicago Press, 1965).

[158] Thorsten Sellin, *The Death Penalty* (Philadelphia, American Law Institute, 1959), p. 63.

[159] *Ibid.*

[160] Berelson and Steiner, *op. cit.,* p. 377.

[161] "A Proper Patient," *Trans-action* 3 (Jan.-Feb. 1966), p. 28, reporting on the work of David Kantor and Victor Gelineau of Boston State Hospital.

[162] Berelson and Steiner, *op. cit.,* p. 76; see also Irvin L. Child, "Socialization," in Gardner Lindzey, ed., *Handbook of Social Psychology,* Vol. II (Cambridge, Mass., Addison-Wesley, 1954), p. 676.

[163] John W. M. Whiting and Irvin L. Child, *Child Training and Personality: A Cross-Cultural Study* (New Haven, Conn., Yale University Press, 1953), p. 256.

[164] Joseph Wolpe, *Psychotherapy by Reciprocal Inhibition* (Stanford, Calif., Stanford University Press, 1958), pp. 130-131.

[165] B. F. Skinner, "Pigeons in a Pelican," *American Psychologist,* 15 (1960), pp. 28-37.

[166] Ernest R. Hilgard, *Theories of Learning,* 2d ed. (New York, Appleton-Century-Crofts, 1956).

[167] Wayne Isaacs, James Thomas, and Israel Goldiamond, "Application of Operant Conditioning to Reinstate Verbal Behavior in Psychotics," *Journal of Speech and Hearing Disorders,* 25 (1960), pp. 8-12.

[168] Yasuko Filby, "Teaching Machines," *Nordisk Psykologi,* 13 (1961), pp. 209-256.

[169] James C. Holland, "Teaching Psychology by a Teaching Machine Program." Unpublished mimeographed report, Psychology Dept., (Cambridge, Mass., Harvard University, 1960).

[170] William O. Jenkins and Julian C. Stanley, Jr., "Partial Reinforcement: A Review and Critique," *Psychological Bulletin,* 47 (1950), pp. 193-234.

[171] Leonard Krasner, "Studies of the Conditioning of Verbal Behavior," *Psychological Bulletin,* 55 (1958), pp. 148-170; also William S. Verplanck, "The Control of the Content of Conversation: Reinforcement of Statements of Opinion," *Journal of Abnormal and Social Psychology,* 51 (1955), pp. 668-676.

[172] Irvin L. Child, "Socialization," in Gardner Lindzey, ed., *Handbook of Social Psychology,* Vol. II (Cambridge, Mass., Addison-Wesley, 1954), p. 676.

[173] Stanley Coopersmith, "Firm But Loving Parents Most Likely To Succeed, 7-Year Study Shows," *The Washington Post* (December 6, 1965), p. B5.

[174] Robert R. Sears, Eleanor E. Maccoby, and Harry Levin, *Patterns of Child Rearing* (New York, Harper & Row, 1957), p. 388.

[175] David C. McClelland, John W. Atkinson, Russell A. Clark, and Edgar L. Lowell, *The Achievement Motive* (New York, Appleton-Century-Crofts, 1953), p. 305.

[176] Jacob L. Gerwitz and Donald M. Baer, "Deprivation and Satiation of Social Reinforcers as Drive Conditions," *Journal of Abnormal and Social Psychology,* 57 (1958), pp. 165-172.

[177] Berelson and Steiner, *op. cit.,* p. 80.

[178] David C. McClelland, *The Achieving Society* (Princeton, N.J., Van Nostrand, 1961).

[179] David C. McClelland, John W. Atkinson, Russell A. Clark, and Edgar L. Lowell, *The Achievement Motive* (New York, Appleton-Century-Crofts, 1953), p. 294.

[180] William O. Jenkins and Julian C. Stanley, Jr., "Partial Reinforcement: A Review and Critique," *Psychological Bulletin,* 47 (1950), pp. 193-234.

[181] Berelson and Steiner, *op. cit.,* pp. 152-153.

[182] Leon Festinger, "The Psychological Effects of Insufficient Rewards," *American Psychologist,* 16 (1961), pp. 1-11.

[183] Elliot Aronson and Judson Mills, "The Effect of Severity of Initiation on Liking for a Group," *Journal of Abnormal and Social Psychology,* 59 (1959), pp. 177-181.

[184] Elliot Aronson, "Threat and Obedience," *Trans-action* 3 (March-April, 1966), pp. 25-27.

[185] E. G. Aiken, "The Effort Variable in the Acquisition, Extinction, and Spontaneous Recovery of an Instrumental Response," *Journal of Experimental Psychology,* 53 (1957), pp. 47-51.

[186] C. B. Ferster and B. F. Skinner, *Schedules of Reinforcement* (New York, Appleton-Century-Crofts, 1957).

[187] Ernest R. Hilgard, *Theories of Learning.* 2d ed. (New York, Appleton-Century-Crofts, 1956), p. 112.

[188] Berelson and Steiner, *op. cit.,* p. 75.

[189] John Bowlby, *Maternal Care and Mental Health.* Monograph Series, No. 2 (New York, World Health Organization, 1952), pp. 82-83.

[190] I. D. MacCrone, "Reaction to Domination in a Color-Caste Society: A Preliminary Study of the Race Attitudes of a Dominated Group," *Journal of Social Psychology,* 26 (1947), p. 86.

[191] Gunnar Myrdal, with the assistance of Richard Sterner and Arnold M. Rose, *An American Dilemma* (New York, Harper & Row, 1944), pp. 975-996.

[192] Berelson and Steiner, *op. cit.,* p. 82.

[193] *Ibid.*

[194] Harry F. Harlow and Margaret K. Harlow, "The Effect of Rearing Conditions on Behavior," *Bulletin of the Menninger Clinic,* 26 (1962), pp. 213-224.

[195] Berelson and Steiner, *op. cit.,* p. 376.

[196] Josephine R. Hilgard, "Sibling Rivalry and Social Heredity," *Psychiatry,* 14 (1951), p. 385.

[197] H. J. Eysenck and S. Crown, "National Stereotypes: An Experimental and Methodological Study," *International Journal of Opinion Attitude Research,* 2 (1948), p. 35.

[198] Gary A. Steiner, *The People Look at Television* (New York, Knopf, 1963).

[199] Richard Christie, "Authoritarianism Reexamined," in Richard

Christie and Marie Jahoda, eds., *Studies in the Scope and Method of the Authoritarian Personality* (New York, Free Press, 1954), p. 154; see also Donald T. Campbell and Boyd R. McCandless, "Ethnocentrism, Xenophobia, and Personality," *Human Relations,* 4 (1951), pp. 185-192.

[200] Carl I. Hovland, Wallace Mandell, Enid H. Campbell *et al., The Order of Presentation in Persuasion.* Yale Studies in Attitude and Communication, Vol. I, ed. by Carl I. Hovland (New Haven, Conn., Yale University Press, 1957), pp. 130-137.

[201] Irving L. Janis and Bert T. King, "The Influence of Role Playing on Opinion Change," *Journal of Abnormal and Social Psychology,* 49 (1954), pp. 211-218; Bert T. King and Irving L. Janis, "Comparison of the Effectiveness of Improvised Versus Non-improvised Role-Playing in Producing Opinion Changes," *Human Relations,* 9 (1956), pp. 177-186.

[202] Arthur I. Gates, "Recitation as a Function in Memorizing," *Archives of Psychology,* 6, no. 40 (1917); L. C. Seibert, *A Series of Experiments on the Learning of French Vocabulary.* Johns Hopkins University, Studies in Education, no. 18 (Baltimore, Md., Johns Hopkins University, 1932); G. Forlano, *School Learning with Various Methods of Practice and Rewards* (New York, Teachers College, Columbia University, 1936).

[203] Raymond A. Bauer, "The Communicator and the Audience," *Journal of Conflict Resolution,* 2 (1958), pp. 67-77.

[204] *Ibid.*

[205] Samuel A. Stouffer, "Intervening Opportunities: A Theory Relating Mobility and Distance," *American Sociological Review,* 5 (1940), pp. 845-867.

[206] Rose K. Goldsen, Morris Rosenberg, Robin M. Williams, Jr., and Edward A. Suchman. *What College Students Think* (Princeton, N.J., Van Nostrand, 1960), p. 101.

[207] Gordon W. Allport and Bernard M. Kramer, "Some Roots of Prejudice," *Journal of Psychology,* 22 (1946), pp. 9-39.

[208] Richard Christie, "Authoritarianism Reexamined," in Richard Christie and Marie Jahoda, eds., *Studies in the Scope and Method of the Authoritarian Personality* (New York, Free Press, 1954), p. 154.

[209] Johan Galtung, "A Framework for the Analysis of Social Conflict." Unpublished ms. (1958), p. 40.

[210] *Ibid.*

[211] Andrew F. Henry and James F. Short, *Suicide and Homicide: Some Economic, Sociological, and Psychological Aspects of Aggression* (New York, Free Press, 1954), pp. 101-102.

[212] Clyde Kluckhohn, "Culture and Behavior," in Gardner Lindzey, ed., *Handbook of Social Psychology,* Vol. II (Cambridge, Mass., Addison-Wesley, 1954), p. 947.

[213] *Ibid.*

[214] Kingsley Davis, "Prostitution," in Robert K. Merton and Robert A. Nisbet, eds., *Contemporary Social Problems* (New York, Harcourt, Brace & World, 1961), p. 283.

Chapter 4

[1] Judith Altman, "Psychologist Finds That Religious Jurors Are Prejudiced," *The Washington Post* (October 31, 1965), p. K11, reporting on research by Cody Wilson.

[2] Paul F. Lazarsfeld, Bernard Berelson, and Hazel Gaudet, *The People's Choice* (New York, Columbia University Press, 1948), p. 54.

[3] Samuel A. Stouffer, *Communism, Conformity, and Civil Liberties: A Cross-Section of the Nation Speaks Its Mind* (New York, Doubleday, 1955), p. 94.

[4] Bernard Berelson and Gary A. Steiner, *Human Behavior; An Inventory of Scientific Findings* (New York, Harcourt, Brace & World, 1964), p. 302.

[5] Daniel Bell, "The Disjunction of Culture and Social Structure." Unpublished paper read at American Academy of Arts and Sciences conference, "Toward a Redefinition of Culture" (May, 1963).

[6] Bernard Berelson, Paul F. Lazarsfeld, and William N. McPhee, *Voting: A Study of Opinion Formation in a Presidential Campaign* (Chicago, University of Chicago Press, 1954), p. 145.

[7] Berelson and Steiner, *op. cit.,* p. 234.

[8] Muzafer Sherif, "Group Influences upon the Formation of Norms and Attitudes," in G. E. Swanson *et al.,* eds., *Readings in Social Psychology,* rev. ed. (New York, Holt, Rinehart and Winston, 1952), p. 255.

[9] *Ibid.*

[10] John W. M. Whiting, "The Cross-Cultural Method," in Gardner Lindzey, ed., *Handbook of Social Psychology,* Vol. I (Cambridge, Mass., Addison-Wesley, 1954), p. 530.

[11] David C. McClelland, *The Achieving Society* (Princeton, N.J., Van Nostrand, 1961), pp. 100-105.

[12] *Ibid.*

[13] *Ibid.*

[14] Natalie Rogoff, "Local Social Structure and Educational Selection," in A. H. Halsey *et al.,* eds., *Education, Economy, and Society* (New York, Free Press, 1961), p. 4.

[15] Berelson and Steiner, *op. cit.,* p. 336.

[16] Stanley Coopersmith, "Firm But Loving Parents Most Likely To Succeed, 7-Year Study Shows," *The Washington Post* (December 6, 1965), p. B5.

[17] *Ibid.*

[18] *Ibid.*

[19] Jean Piaget, *The Moral Judgment of the Child* (London, Routledge, 1932).

[20] Elizabeth B. Hurlock, *Child Development,* 3rd ed. (New York, McGraw-Hill, 1956), p. 290.

[21] Earl Raab and Seymour M. Lipset, *Prejudice and Society*. Anti-Defamation League of B'nai B'rith (1959), pp. 32-33.

[22] Percy Black and Ruth Davidson Atkins, "Conformity Versus Prejudice as Exemplified in White-Negro Relations in the South: Some Methodological Considerations," *Journal of Psychology,* 30 (1950), p. 111.

[23] Verner M. Sims and James R. Patrick, "Attitude Toward the Negro of Northern and Southern College Students," *Journal of Social Psychology,* 7 (1936), p. 203.

[24] See in this regard Richard Christie, "An Experimental Study of Modification in Factors Influencing Recruits' Adjustment to the Army." Unpublished ms. Research Center for Human Relations (New York, New York University, 1953).

[25] Verner M. Sims and James R. Patrick, "Attitude Toward the Negro of Northern and Southern College Students," *Journal of Social Psychology,* 7 (1936), pp. 192-204.

[26] Samuel A. Stouffer *et al., The American Soldier: Adjustment During Army Life. Studies in Social Psychology in World War II,* Vol. I (Princeton, N.J., Princeton University Press, 1949).

[27] Charles E. Osgood, "The Nature and Measurement of Meaning," *Psychological Bulletin,* 49 (1952), pp. 197-237.

[28] *Ibid.*

[29] Bernard Berelson, Paul F. Lazarsfeld, and William N. McPhee, *Voting: A Study of Opinion Formation in a Presidential Compaign* (Chicago, University of Chicago Press, 1954), p. 185.

[30] Seymour M. Lipset, *The First New Nation* (New York, Basic Books, 1963).

[31] Robert R. Blake and Jane S. Mouton, "The Experimental Investigation of Interpersonal Influence," in Albert D. Biderman and Herbert Zimmer, eds., *The Manipulation of Human Behavior* (New York, Wiley, 1961), p. 231.

[32] See in this regard George C. Homans, *Social Behavior: Its Elementary Forms* (New York, Harcourt, Brace & World, 1961), p. 129.

[33] Ralph D. Minard, "Race Relationships in the Pocahontas Coal Field," *Journal of Social Issues,* 8 (1952), p. 31.

[34] Joseph D. Lohman and Dietrick C. Reitzes, "Note on Race Relations in Mass Society," *American Journal of Sociology,* 58 (1952), p. 244.

[35] Earl Raab and Seymour M. Lipset, *Prejudice and Society.* Anti-Defamation League of B'nai B'rith (1959), p. 22.

[36] Harold H. Kelley and John W. Thibaut, "Experimental Studies of Group Problem Solving and Process," in Gardner Lindzey, ed., *Handbook of Social Psychology,* Vol. II (Cambridge, Mass., Addison-Wesley, 1954), p. 768.

[37] Stanley Schachter, *Psychology of Affiliation: Experimental Studies of the Sources of Gregariousness* (Stanford, Calif., Stanford University Press, 1959), p. 46.

[38] Selwyn W. Baker and Jean Carroll, "Ordinal Position and Conformity," *Journal of Abnormal and Social Psychology,* 65 (1962), pp. 129-131.

[39] See in this regard Harold H. Kelley and John W. Thibaut, "Experimental Studies of Group Problem Solving and Process," in Gardner Lindzey, ed., *Handbook of Social Psychology,* Vol. II (Cambridge, Mass., Addison-Wesley, 1954), p. 764.

[40] *Ibid.*

[41] Samuel A. Stouffer *et al., The American Soldier: Combat and Its Aftermath. Studies in Social Psychology in World War II,* Vol. II. (Princeton, N.J., Princeton University Press, 1949).

[42] Samuel A. Stouffer *et al., The American Soldier: Adjustment During Army Life. Studies in Social Psychology in World War II,* Vol. I (Princeton, N.J., Princeton University Press, 1949), pp. 264-265.

[43] Terence K. Hopkins, "The Exercise of Influence in Small Groups." Unpublished Doct. Diss. (New York, Columbia University, 1959); see also Berelson and Steiner, *op. cit.,* p. 343.

[44] Ferenc Merei, "Group Leadership and Institutionalization," in Eleanor E. Maccoby *et al.,* eds., *Readings in Social Psychology,* 3rd ed. (New York, Holt, Rinehart and Winston, 1958), pp. 522-532.

[45] Berelson and Steiner, *op. cit.,* p. 343.

[46] H. Beloff, "Two Forms of Social Conformity: Acquiescence and Conventionality," *Journal of Abnormal and Social Psychology,* 56 (1958), pp. 99-104.

[47] Harold H. Kelley and Edmund H. Volkart, "The Resistance to Change of Group-Anchored Attitudes," *American Sociological Review,* 17 (1952), pp. 453-465.

[48] Berelson and Steiner, *op. cit.,* p. 338.

[49] *Ibid.*

[50] *Ibid.*

[51] Leon Festinger, Stanley Schachter, and Kurt Back, *Social Pressures in Informal Groups* (New York, Harper & Row, 1950), p. 91.

[52] Berelson and Steiner, *op. cit.,* p. 339.

[53] *Ibid.,* p. 338.

[54] *Ibid.,* p. 339.

[55] Terence K. Hopkins, "The Exercise of Influence in Small Groups." Unpublished Doct. Diss. (New York, Columbia University, 1959).

[56] Everett C. Hughes, "The Knitting of Racial Groups in Industry," *American Sociological Review,* 11 (1946), pp. 512-519.

[57] Berelson and Steiner, *op. cit.,* p. 339.

[58] Seymour M. Lipset and Juan J. Linz, "The Social Bases of Political Diversity in Western Democracies." Unpublished ms. (1956), p. 52.

[59] Wayne Dennis, "Variations in Productivity Among Creative Workers," *Scientific Monthly,* 80 (1955), pp. 277-278.

[60] Berelson and Steiner, *op. cit.,* p. 627.

[61] *Ibid.*

[62] Henry W. Riecken and George C. Homans, "Psychological Aspects of Social Structure," in Gardner Lindzey, ed., *Handbook of Social Psychology,* Vol. II (Cambridge, Mass., Addison-Wesley, 1954), p. 793.

[63] August B. Hollingshead and Frederick C. Redlich, *Social Class and Mental Illness: A Community Study* (New York, Wiley, 1958).

[64] *Ibid.*

[65] *Ibid.*

[66] *Ibid.*

[67] Berelson and Steiner, *op. cit.,* p. 640.

[68] *Ibid.*

[69] *Ibid.,* p. 316.

[70] S. E. Asch, "Effects of Group Pressure Upon the Modification and Distortion of Judgments," in Eleanor E. Maccoby *et al.,* eds., *Readings in Social Psychology,* 3rd ed. (New York, Holt, Rinehart and Winston, 1958), pp. 174-183.

[71] Ruth W. Berenda, *The Influence of the Group on the Judgments of Children* (New York, King's Crown, 1950).

[72] Morris Janowitz, "The Military Establishment: Organization and Disorganization," in Robert K. Merton and Robert A. Nisbet, eds., *Contemporary Social Problems* (New York, Harcourt, Brace & World, 1961), pp. 544-545.

[73] William Kornhauser, *The Politics of Mass Society* (New York, Free Press, 1959), p. 223.

[74] Clark Kerr and Abraham Siegel, "The Interindustry Propensity to Strike: An International Comparison," in Arthur Kornhauser, Robert Dubin, and Arthur M. Ross, eds., *Industrial Conflict* (New York, McGraw-Hill, 1954), pp. 189-212; see also Joseph H. Monane, *Human Factor Requirements in the Maritime Industry* (Washington D.C., George Washington University, 1965).

[75] William Kornhauser, *The Politics of Mass Society* (New York, Free Press, 1959), p. 223.

[76] Berelson and Steiner, *op. cit.*, pp. 226-235.

[77] Jacob W. Getzels and Philip W. Jackson, *Creativity and Intelligence: Explorations with Gifted Students* (New York, Wiley, 1962), pp. 57-58.

[78] Harold H. Kelley and John W. Thibaut, "Experimental Studies of Group Problem Solving and Process," in Gardner Lindzey, ed., *Handbook of Social Psychology,* Vol. II (Cambridge, Mass., Addison-Wesley, 1954), pp. 735-785.

[79] Morris I. Stein, "Social and Psychological Factors Affecting Creativity of Industrial Research Chemists." Unpublished ms., presented at Fall meeting of the Industrial Research Institute (Pittsburgh, Pa., October, 1957).

[80] The greater tendency toward norm conformity among those high in anxiety has been previously noted.

[81] Donald W. McKinnon, "Creativity in Architects," in Institute of Personality Assessment and Research, *The Creative Person* (Berkeley, Calif., University of California and University Extension, Liberal Arts Dept., 1961), pp. V–1–V–24.

[82] Frank Barron, "Creative Vision and Expression in Writing and Painting," in Institute of Personality Assessment and Research. *The Creative Person* (Berkeley, Calif., University of California and University Extension, Liberal Arts Dept., 1961), pp. II–1–II–19.

[83] *Ibid.,* p. II-6.

[84] Jacob W. Getzels and Philip W. Jackson, *Creativity and Intelligence: Explorations with Gifted Students* (New York, Wiley, 1962).

[85] Berelson and Steiner, *op. cit.,* p. 230.

[86] Jacob W. Getzels and Philip W. Jackson, *Creativity and Intelligence: Explorations with Gifted Students* (New York, Wiley, 1962), p. 42.

[87] Berelson and Steiner, *op. cit.,* p. 230.

[88] Frank Barron, Dorwin Cartwright, and Richard S. Crutchfield, *Creativity and Conformity*. Foundation for Research on Human Behavior (1958), p. 16.

[89] Berelson and Steiner, *op. cit.,* p. 234.

[90] See in this regard Gerald S. Blum, "An Experimental Reunion of

Psychoanalytic Theory with Perceptual Vigilance and Defense," *Journal of Abnormal and Social Psychology,* 49 (1954), pp. 94-98.

[91] Seymour M. Lipset and Juan J. Linz, "The Social Bases of Political Diversity in Western Democracies." Unpublished ms. (1956), p. 9.

[92] Berelson and Steiner, *op. cit.,* p. 431.

[93] See in this regard Amitai Etzioni, *A Comparative Analysis of Complex Organizations: On Power, Involvement, and Their Correlates* (New York, Free Press, 1961).

[94] *The Washington Post* (October 22, 1965), p. B3.

[95] *The University Hatchet* (student newspaper of The George Washington University), (November 9, 1965), p. 8.

[96] Kurt B. Mayer, *Class and Society* (New York, Doubleday, 1955), p. 39.

[97] August B. Hollingshead and Frederick C. Redlich, *Social Class and Mental Illness: A Community Study* (New York, Wiley, 1958).

[98] *Ibid.*

[99] Robert Dubin, *The World of Work: Industrial Society and Human Relations* (Englewood Cliffs, N.J., Prentice-Hall, 1958), p. 259.

[100] *Ibid.*

[101] Samuel A. Stouffer *et al., The American Soldier: Adjustment During Army Life. Studies in Social Psychology in World War II,* Vol. I (Princeton, N.J., Princeton University Press, 1949), pp. 411-412.

[102] *Ibid.*

[103] *Ibid.*

[104] See in this regard F. Stuart Chapin, "Social Institutions and Voluntary Associations," in Joseph B. Gittler, ed., *Review of Sociology: Analysis of a Decade* (New York, Wiley, 1957), p. 269.

[105] Nadel (S. F. Nadel, *The Foundations of Social Anthropology* [New York, Free Press, 1951],) and Kluckhohn (Clyde Kluckhohn, "Culture and Behavior," in Gardner Lindzey, ed., *Handbook of Social Psychology,* Vol. II [Cambridge, Mass., Addison-Wesley, 1954], p. 945) suggest that a culture offering few alternatives predisposes to suicide.

[106] As noted in connection with Chapter 2 (Footnote 251), Merton (Robert K. Merton, "Social Structure and Anomie," p. 139, and "Continuities in the Theory of Reference Groups and Social Structure," p.

296, in *Social Theory and Social Structure,* rev. and enlarged ed. [New York, Free Press, 1957],) has indicated the pressures against withdrawal from the American success-struggle and the hostility of the terms "renegade," "turncoat," and "deserter" for defectors from a group, and Slater (Philip E. Slater, "On Social Regression," *American Sociological Review,* 28 [1963], pp. 339-364) has surveyed the pressures resisting the withdrawal of the premarital and marital pair.

[107] Berelson and Steiner, *op. cit.,* p. 347.

[108] Leon Festinger and John Thibaut, "Interpersonal Communication in Small Groups," *Journal of Abnormal and Social Psychology,* 46 (1951), pp. 92-99.

[109] Berelson and Steiner, *op. cit.,* p. 337.

[110] *Ibid.,* p. 347.

[111] Festinger *et al.* (Leon Festinger, Stanley Schachter, and Kurt Back, *Social Pressures in Informal Groups* [New York, Harper & Row, 1950],) found that people having close personal attachments within their housing units were least deviant from group standards.

[112] Berelson and Steiner, *op. cit.,* p. 337.

[113] Michael Argyle, *The Scientific Study of Social Behavior* (London, Methuen, 1957), p. 155.

[114] John Johnstone and Elihu Katz, "Youth and Popular Music: A Study in the Sociology of Taste," *American Journal of Sociology,* 62 (1957), pp. 563-568.

[115] Everett C. Hughes, "The Knitting of Racial Groups in Industry," *American Sociological Review,* 11 (1946), pp. 512-519.

[116] Leon Festinger, Stanley Schachter, and Kurt Back, *Social Pressures in Informal Groups* (New York, Harper & Row, 1950), p. 91.

[117] George C. Homans, *Social Behavior: Its Elementary Forms* (New York, Harcourt, Brace & World, 1961), p. 129.

[118] Berelson and Steiner, *op. cit.,* p. 332.

[119] Robert R. Blake and Jane S. Mouton, "The Experimental Investigation of Interpersonal Influence," in Albert D. Biderman and Herbert Zimmer, eds., *The Manipulation of Human Behavior* (New York, Wiley, 1961), p. 231.

[120] S. E. Asch, "Effects of Group Pressure Upon the Modification and Distortion of Judgments," in Eleanor E. Maccoby *et al.,* eds., *Read-*

ings in Social Psychology, 3rd ed. (New York, Holt, Rinehart and Winston, 1958), pp. 174-183.

[121] Berelson and Steiner, *op. cit.,* p. 30.

[122] *Ibid.,* p. 337.

[123] Matilda White Riley and Richard Cohn, "Control Networks in Informal Groups," *Sociometry,* 21 (1958), pp. 30-49.

[124] Natalie Rogoff, "Local Social Structure and Educational Selection," in A. H. Halsey *et al.,* eds., *Education, Economy, and Society* (New York, Free Press, 1961), pp. 241-251.

[125] George C. Homans, *Social Behavior: Its Elementary Forms* (New York, Harcourt, Brace & World, 1961).

[126] Berelson and Steiner, *op. cit.,* p. 341.

[127] Samuel A. Stouffer, *Communism, Conformity, and Civil Liberties: A Cross-Section of the Nation Speaks Its Mind* (New York, Doubleday, 1955).

[128] Calvin S. Hall and Gardner Lindzey, "Psychoanalytic Theory and Its Applications in the Social Sciences," in Gardner Lindzey, ed., *Handbook of Social Psychology,* Vol. I (Cambridge, Mass., Addison-Wesley, 1954), pp. 143-180.

[129] Robert R. Sears, Eleanor E. Maccoby, and Harry Levin, *Patterns of Child Rearing* (New York, Harper & Row, 1957), p. 388.

[130] Berelson and Steiner, *op. cit.,* p. 78.

[131] *Ibid.,* p. 480.

[132] John W. M. Whiting and Irvin L. Child, *Child Training and Personality: A Cross-Cultural Study* (New Haven, Conn., Yale University Press, 1953).

[133] John Dollard, with the assistance of Donald Horton, *Fear in Battle.* Institute of Human Relations (New Haven, Conn., Yale University, 1943), p. 56.

[134] Samuel A. Stouffer *et al., The American Soldier: Adjustment During Army Life. Studies in Social Psychology in World War II,* Vol. I (Princeton, N.J., Princeton University Press, 1949), p. 449.

[135] Berelson and Steiner, *op. cit.,* p. 448.

[136] R. W. Ditchburn, D. H. Fender, and Stella Mayne, "Vision with Controlled Movements of the Retinal Image," *Journal of Physiology,* 145 (1959), pp. 98-107.

[137] Helen Peak, "Psychological Structure and Psychological Activity," *Psychological Review,* 65 (1958), pp. 325-347.

[138] Berelson and Steiner, *op. cit.,* p. 183.

[139] Leo J. Postman and Lucy Rau, "Retention as a Function of the Method of Measurement," *University of California Publications in Psychology,* 8, no. 3 (Berkeley, Calif., University of California, 1957).

[140] See W. Lloyd Warner and J. O. Low, *The Social System of the Modern Factory.* Yankee City Series, Vol. IV (New Haven, Conn., Yale University Press, 1947); also Charles R. Walker, *Steeltown: An Industrial Case History of the Conflict Between Progress and Security.* Yale Labor and Management Center Series (New York, Harper & Row, 1950).

[141] Frederick H. Harbison and Robert Dubin, *Patterns of Union-Management Relations* (Chicago, Science Research Associates, 1947).

[142] Leonard Broom and Philip Selznick, *Sociology: A Text with Adapted Readings* (New York, Harper & Row, 1957), p. 427.

[143] Reinhard Bendix and Seymour M. Lipset, "Political Sociology: An Essay and Bibliography," *Current Sociology,* 6 (1957), pp. 79-169.

[144] Morris Swadesh, "Lexico-statistic Dating of Prehistoric Ethnic Contacts," *Proceedings of the American Philosophical Society,* 96 (1952), pp. 452-463.

[145] Raymond Firth, F. J. Fisher, and D. G. MacRae, "Social Implications of Technological Change as Regards Patterns and Models," in G. Balandier *et al., Social, Economic and Technological Change: A Theoretical Approach.* International Bureau for Research in the Social Implications of Technical Progress (Paris, Presses Universitaires de France, 1959), p. 270.

[146] Berelson and Steiner, *op. cit.,* p. 370.

[147] *Ibid.,* p. 341.

[148] Charles D. Hockett, "The Origin of Speech," *Scientific American,* 203, no. 3 (1960), p. 96.

[149] *Ibid.*

[150] Margaret Mead, *New Lives for Old* (New York, Morrow, 1956).

[151] Manning Nash, "Applied and Action Anthropology in the Understanding of Man," *Anthropological Quarterly,* 32 (1959), pp. 67-81.

[152] Felix M. Keesing, *Culture Change: An Analysis and Bibliography*

of Anthropological Sources to 1952 (Stanford, Calif., Stanford University Press, 1953), p. 83.

[153] Bernard Berelson, Paul F. Lazarsfeld, and William N. McPhee, *Voting: A Study of Opinion Formation in a Presidential Campaign* (Chicago, University of Chicago Press, 1954).

[154] Alfred C. Kinsey, Wardell B. Pomeroy, and Clyde E. Martin, *Sexual Behavior in the Human Male* (Philadelphia, Saunders, 1948), p. 397.

[155] Max F. Millikan and Donald L. M. Blackmer, eds., *The Emerging Nations: Their Growth and United States Policy.* Massachusetts Institute of Technology, Center for International Studies (Boston, Little, Brown, 1961), p. 19.

[156] Berelson and Steiner, *op. cit.,* p. 615.

[157] See in this regard Max F. Millikan and Donald L. M. Blackmer, eds., *The Emerging Nations: Their Growth and United States Policy.* Massachusetts Institute of Technology, Center for International Studies (Boston, Little, Brown, 1961), pp. 9 ff.

[158] *Ibid.*

[159] Felix M. Keesing, *Culture Change: An Analysis and Bibliography of Anthropological Sources to 1952* (Stanford, Calif., Stanford University Press, 1953), p. 83.

[160] David C. Dietrick, "Review of Research," Appendix A, in Richard J. Hill, *A Comparative Study of Lecture and Discussion Methods.* Fund for Adult Education (1960), pp. 90-118; Kurt Lewin, "Studies in Group Decision," in Dorwin Cartwright and Alvin Zander, eds., *Group Dynamics: Research and Theory* (New York, Harper & Row, 1953), p. 289.

[161] George M. Foster, *Traditional Cultures, and the Impact of Technological Change* (New York, Harper & Row, 1952), p. 29.

[162] Carl I. Hovland, "Reconciling Conflicting Results Derived from Experimental and Survey Studies of Attitude Change," *American Psychologist,* 14 (1959), p. 12.

[163] Berelson and Steiner, *op. cit.,* p. 580.

[164] Henry W. Riecken and George C. Homans, "Psychological Aspects of Social Structure," in Gardner Lindzey, ed., *Handbook of Social Psychology,* Vol. II (Cambridge, Mass., Addison-Wesley, 1954), p. 827.

[165] Berelson and Steiner, *op. cit.,* p. 614.

[166] Felix M. Keesing, *Culture Change: An Analysis and Bibliography of Anthropological Sources to 1952* (Stanford, Calif., Stanford University Press, 1953).

[167] Talcott Parsons, *The Social System* (New York, Free Press, 1951).

[168] Seymour M. Lipset, *The First New Nation* (New York, Basic Books, 1963).

[169] I. Roger Yoshino, "A Re-study of Suye Mura: An Investigation of Social Change," *Proceedings of the Pacific Sociological Society* (1956).

[170] Ronald Freedman, Amos. H. Hawley, Werner S. Landecker, Gerhard E. Lenski, and Horace M. Miner, *Principles of Sociology,* rev. ed. (New York, Holt, Rinehart and Winston, 1956), p. 330.

[171] I. Roger Yoshino, "A Re-study of Suye Mura: An Investigation of Social Change," *Proceedings of the Pacific Sociological Society* (1956).

[172] Reinhard Bendix and Seymour M. Lipset, "Political Sociology: An Essay and Bibliography," *Current Sociology,* 6 (1957), p. 91.

[173] See in this regard Seymour M. Lipset and Juan M. Linz, "The Social Bases of Political Diversity in Western Democracies." Unpublished ms. (1956), p. 6.

[174] *Ibid.,* p. 9.

[175] Berelson and Steiner, *op. cit.,* p. 431.

[176] See Max F. Millikan and Donald L. M. Blackmer, eds., *The Emerging Nations: Their Growth and United States Policy.* Massachusetts Institute of Technology, Center for International Studies (Boston, Little, Brown, 1961), pp. 9 ff.

[177] *Ibid.,* p. 36.

[178] Seymour M. Lipset and Juan M. Linz, "The Social Bases of Political Diversity in Western Democracies." Unpublished ms. (1956), p. 28.

[179] Urie Bronfenbrenner, "Socialization and Social Class Through Time and Space," in Eleanor E. Maccoby *et al.,* eds., *Readings in Social Psychology,* 3rd ed. (New York, Holt, Rinehart and Winston, 1958), pp. 400-425.

[180] Peter M. Blau, *Bureaucracy in Modern Society* (New York, Random House, 1956), p. 95.

[181] *Ibid.*

[182] Alfred L. Kroeber, *Anthropology,* rev. ed. (New York, Harcourt, Brace & World, 1948), p. 241.

[183] Berelson and Steiner, *op. cit.,* p. 616.

[184] Robert Dubin, *The World of Work: Industrial Society and Human Relations* (Englewood Cliffs, N.J., Prentice-Hall, 1958), p. 117.

[185] See in this regard William F. Ogburn, *Social Change* (New York, Viking, 1927).

[186] Carl I. Hovland, O. J. Harvey, and Muzafer Sherif, "Assimilation and Contrast Effects in Reactions to Communication and Attitude Change," *Journal of Abnormal and Social Psychology,* 55 (1957), p. 251.

[187] The inability of a "backward" society's power structure to cope with a change of vast magnitude may serve partly to explain "culture leaps" out of "backwardness."

[188] Berelson and Steiner, *op. cit.,* p. 616.

[189] *Ibid.,* p. 615. The authors find change occurring more readily in the less emotionally charged items of a culture.

[190] *Ibid.,* p. 616.

[191] Lane (Robert E. Lane, *Political Life: Why People Get Involved in Politics* [New York, Free Press, 1959], p. 145) reports that the more concerned a person is about the outcome of an election, the more his political attitudes "hang together" in a consistent bundle.

[192] See in this regard Eleanor E. Maccoby, Richard E. Matthews, and Anton S. Morton, "Youth and Political Change," *Public Opinion Quarterly,* 18 (1954), pp. 23-39.

[193] George M. Foster, *Traditional Cultures, and the Impact of Technological Change* (New York, Harper & Row, 1962), p. 25.

[194] Berelson and Steiner, *op. cit.,* p. 73.

[195] Arthur M. Ross and Paul T. Hartman, *Changing Patterns of Industrial Conflict* (New York, Wiley, 1960), pp. 24-25.

[196] Max F. Millikan and Donald L. M. Blackmer, eds., *The Emerging Nations: Their Growth and United States Policy.* Massachusetts Institute of Technology, Center for International Studies (Boston, Little, Brown, 1961), p. 36.

[197] Berelson and Steiner, *op. cit.,* p. 390.

[198] Charles Y. Glock, "The Sociology of Religion," in Robert K. Merton *et al.*, eds., *Sociology Today: Problems and Prospects* (New York, Basic Books, 1959), p. 158.

[199] See in this regard Liston Pope, *Millhands and Preachers* (New Haven, Conn., Yale University Press, 1942).

[200] F. Stuart Chapin, "Social Institutions and Voluntary Associations," in Joseph B. Gittler, ed., *Review of Sociology: Analysis of a Decade* (New York, Wiley, 1957), pp. 263-264.

[201] Berelson and Steiner, *op. cit.*, p. 358.

[202] *Ibid.*, p. 388.

[203] Ronald Freedman, Amos H. Hawley, Werner S. Landecker, Gerhard E. Lenski, and Horace M. Miner, *Principles of Sociology,* rev. ed. (New York, Holt, Rinehart and Winston, 1956), p. 330.

[204] David L. Sills, "A Sociologist Looks at Motivation," in Nathan E. Cohen, ed., *The Citizen Volunteer* (New York, Harper & Row, 1960), p. 75.

[205] Seymour M. Lipset, "Political Sociology, 1945-55," in *Sociology in the United States* (New York, UNESCO, 1957), p. 6.

[206] T. Schjelderup-Ebbe, "Social Behavior of Birds," in Carl Murchison, ed., *Handbook of Social Psychology* (Worcester, Mass., Clark University Press, 1935), pp. 947-972.

[207] Berelson and Steiner, *op. cit.*, p. 253.

[208] Philip E. Slater, "Role Differentiation in Small Groups," in A. Paul Hare *et al.*, eds., *Small Groups: Studies in Social Interaction* (New York, Knopf, 1955), p. 504.

[209] *Ibid.*

[210] Henry R. Riecken and George C. Homans, "Psychological Aspects of Social Structure," in Gardner Lindzey, ed., *Handbook of Social Psychology,* Vol. II (Cambridge, Mass., Addison-Wesley, 1954), pp. 823-824.

[211] See Amitai Etzioni, *A Comparative Analysis of Complex Organization: On Power, Involvement, and Their Correlates* (New York, Free Press, 1961).

[212] Hans Speier, "The American Soldier and the Sociology of Military Organization," in Robert K. Merton and Paul E. Lazarsfeld, eds., *Continuities in Social Research* (New York, Free Press, 1950), pp. 106-132.

[213] See in this regard Alvin W. Gouldner, *Patterns of Industrial Bureaucracy* (New York, Free Press, 1954).

[214] Berelson and Steiner, *op. cit.,* p. 377.

[215] Thomas Ford Hoult, *The Sociology of Religion* (New York, Holt, Rinehart and Winston, 1958), pp. 122-123. The rise of the Black Muslims is a comparable case.

[216] Berelson and Steiner, *op. cit.,* p. 467.

[217] *Ibid.,* p. 245.

[218] Daniel E. Berlyne, "The Influence of Complexity and Novelty in Visual Figures on Orienting Responses," *Journal of Experimental Psychology,* 55 (1958), pp. 289-296; Daniel E. Berlyne, "The Influence of the Albedo and Complexity of Stimuli on Visual Fixation in the Human Infant," *British Journal of Psychology,* 49 (1958), pp. 315-318.

[219] Berelson and Steiner, *op. cit.,* p. 330.

[220] George M. Foster, *Traditional Cultures, and the Impact of Technological Change* (New York, Harper & Row, 1962), p. 25.

[221] See James Meredith, *Three Years in Mississippi* (Terre Haute, Ind., Indiana University Press, 1966).

[222] Talcott Parsons, *The Social System* (New York, Free Press, 1951), pp. 28-29.

[223] *Ibid.*

[224] Jerome M. Levine and Gardner Murphy, "The Learning and Forgetting of Controversial Material," *Journal of Abnormal and Social Psychology,* 38 (1943), pp. 507-517.

[225] Ernest R. Hilgard, "Experimental Approaches to Psychoanalysis," in E. Pumpian-Mindlin, ed., *Psychoanalysis as Science* (Stanford, Calif., Stanford University Press, 1952), pp. 7-8.

[226] Else Frenkel-Brunswik and R. Nevitt Sanford, "Some Personality Factors in Anti-Semitism," *Journal of Psychology,* 20 (1945), pp. 280-281.

[227] Lawrence S. Kubie, "Problems and Techniques of Psychoanalytic Validation and Progress," in E. Pumpian-Mindlin, ed., *Psychoanalysis as Science* (Stanford, Calif., Stanford University Press, 1952), p. 92.

[228] D. Pierson, "Race Prejudice as Revealed in the Study of Racial Situations," *International Social Science Bulletin,* 2 (1950), p. 473.

[229] Berelson and Steiner, *op. cit.,* p. 467.

[230] Theodore M. Newcomb, *Personality and Social Change: Attitude Formation in a Student Community* (New York, Holt, Rinehart and Winston, 1943).

[231] Berelson and Steiner, *op. cit.*, p. 390.

[232] Ferenc Merei, "Group Leadership and Institutionalization," in Eleanor E. Maccoby *et al.*, eds., *Readings in Social Psychology*, 3rd ed. (New York, Holt, Rinehart and Winston, 1958), pp. 522-532.

[233] Hortense Powdermaker, *After Freedom: A Cultural Study in the Deep South* (New York, Viking, 1939), p. 61.

[234] Allison Davis, "Acculturation in Schools," in Milton L. Barron, ed., *American Minorities* (New York, Knopf, 1957), p. 446.

[235] Carl I. Hovland, O. J. Harvey, and Muzafer Sherif, "Assimilation and Contrast Effects in Reactions to Communication and Attitude Change," *Journal of Abnormal and Social Psychology*, 55 (1957), p. 251.

[236] Allison Davis, "Acculturation in Schools," in Milton L. Barron, ed., *American Minorities* (New York, Knopf, 1957), p. 446.

[237] John A. McGeoch, "The Influence of Associative Value upon the Difficulty of Nonsense-Syllable Lists," *Journal of Genetic Psychology*, 37 (1930), pp. 421-426.

[238] Carl I. Hovland, O. J. Harvey, and Muzafer Sherif, "Assimilation and Contrast Effects in Reactions to Communication and Attitude Change," *Journal of Abnormal and Social Psychology*, 55 (1957), p. 251.

[239] Leon Festinger, *A Theory of Cognitive Dissonance* (New York, Harper & Row, 1957), p. 265.

[240] Leonard Broom and Philip Selznick, *Sociology: A Text with Adapted Readings* (New York, Harper & Row, 1957), p. 470.

[241] Ronald Freedman, Amos H. Hawley, Werner S. Landecker, Gerhard E. Lenski, and Horace M. Miner, *Principles of Sociology*, rev. ed. (New York, Holt, Rinehart and Winston, 1956), pp. 404-405.

[242] Robert K. Merton, "Continuities in the Theory of Reference Groups and Social Structure," *Social Theory and Social Structure*, rev. and enlarged ed. (New York, Free Press, 1957), p. 296.

[243] Philip E. Slater, "On Social Regression," *American Sociological Review*, 28 (1963), pp. 339-364.

[244] Berelson and Steiner, *op. cit.*, p. 276.

[245] *Ibid.*, p. 448.

[246] Laurance F. Shaffer, "Fear and Courage in Aerial Combat," *Journal of Consulting Psychology,* 11 (1957), p. 139.

[247] Bruno Bettelheim, "Individual and Mass Behavior in Extreme Situations," in Eleanor E. Maccoby *et al.,* eds., *Readings in Social Psychology,* 3rd ed. (New York, Holt, Rinehart and Winston, 1958), p. 304.

[248] Jules H. Masserman and K. S. Yum, "An Analysis of the Influence of Alcohol on Experimental Neuroses in Cats," *Psychosomatic Medicine,* 8 (1946), p. 36.

[249] Berelson and Steiner, *op. cit.,* p. 278.

[250] Bernard Farber, "Effects of a Severely Mentally Retarded Child on Family Integration," *Monographs of the Society for Research in Child Development,* 24, no. 2 (1959), p. 80.

[251] *Ibid.*

[252] Stanley Schachter, *Psychology of Affiliation: Experimental Studies of the Sources of Gregariousness* (Stanford, Calif., Stanford University Press, 1959), pp. 6-8.

[253] Samuel E. Hill and Frederick Harbison, *Manpower and Innovation in American Industry.* Industrial Relations section, Dept. of Economics and Sociology (Princeton, N.J., Princeton University, 1959), pp. 54-55.

[254] James F. Short, Jr. and Fred L. Strodtbeck, *Group Process and Gang Delinquency* (Chicago, University of Chicago Press, 1965).

[255] Stanley Schachter, *Psychology of Affiliation: Experimental Studies of the Sources of Gregariousness* (Stanford, Calif., Stanford University Press, 1959).

[256] Theodore M. Newcomb, "The Study of Consensus," in Robert K. Merton *et al.,* eds., *Sociology Today: Problems and Prospects* (New York, Basic Books, 1959), p. 288.

[257] Charles P. Loomis and J. Allan Beegle, *Rural Sociology: The Strategy of Change* (Englewood Cliffs, N.J., Prentice-Hall, 1957), pp. 110-111; Josephine Klein, *The Study of Groups* (London, Routledge, 1956), p. 106.

[258] Milton L. Barron, *People Who Intermarry* (Syracuse, N.Y., Syracuse University Press, 1946); August B. Hollingshead, "Cultural Factors in the Selection of Marriage Mates," *American Sociological Review,* 15 (1950), pp. 619-627; Robert F. Winch, "Marriage and the Family," in Joseph B. Gittler, ed., *Review of Sociology: Analysis of a Decade* (New

York, Wiley, 1957), pp. 346-390; Judson T. Landis, "Marriages of Mixed and Non-Mixed Religious Faith," *American Sociological Review,* 14 (1949), pp. 401-407; and William J. Goode, "Family Disorganization," in Robert K. Merton and Robert A. Nisbet, eds., *Contemporary Social Problems* (New York, Harcourt, Brace & World, 1961), pp. 390-458.

[259] Ronald Freedman, Amos H. Hawley, Werner S. Landecker, Gerhard E. Lenski, and Horace M. Miner, *Principles of Sociology,* rev. ed. (New York, Holt, Rinehart and Winston, 1956), p. 81.

[260] Leon Festinger, Stanley Schachter, and Kurt Back, *Social Pressures in Informal Groups* (New York, Harper & Row, 1950).

[261] Irvin L. Child, "Socialization," in Gardner Lindzey, ed., *Handbook of Social Psychology,* Vol. II (Cambridge, Mass., Addison-Wesley, 1954), p. 676.

[262] *Ibid.*

[263] Berelson and Steiner, *op. cit.,* p. 656.

[264] *Ibid.*

[265] *Ibid.,* p. 615.

[266] Felix M. Keesing, *Culture Change: An Analysis and Bibliography of Anthropological Sources to 1952* (Stanford, Calif., Stanford University Press, 1953).

[267] Max F. Millikan and Donald L. M. Blackmer, eds., *The Emerging Nations: Their Growth and United States Policy.* Massachusetts Institute of Technology, Center for International Studies (Boston, Little, Brown, 1961), p. 19.

[268] See in this regard Felix M. Keesing, *Culture Change: An Analysis and Bibliography of Anthropological Sources to 1952* (Stanford, Calif., Stanford University Press, 1953), p. 83.

[269] Morris Swadesh, "Lexico-Statistic Dating of Prehistoric Ethnic Contacts," *Proceedings of the American Philosophical Society,* 96 (1952), pp. 452-463.

[270] Margaret Mead, *New Lives for Old* (New York, Morrow, 1956).

[271] Ronald Freedman, Amos H. Hawley, Werner S. Landecker, Gerhard E. Lenski, and Horace M. Miner, *Principles of Sociology,* rev. ed. (New York, Holt, Rinehart and Winston, 1956), p. 448.

INDEX